Praise for *Schuyler's Monster*

"A gripping explication, shot through with equal parts horror and hope, of how parenthood can turn ordinary people into passionate advocates."
—Neal Pollack, author of *Alternadad*

"Robert Rummel-Hudson is brave enough to reveal the damage the discovery of his child's condition did to his marriage and to his own sense of self. He manages to repair some of the damage through close involvement with Schuyler and vigorous campaigning on her behalf. His memoir is honest, often painful, and deeply personal."
—Charlotte Moore, author of *George & Sam*

"The book is engaging and honest—I'm sure it will help many parents who are struggling to find the most loving way to help their children who have 'issues.'"
—Dana Buchman, designer, author of *A Special Education: One Family's Journey Through the Maze of Learning Disabilities*

"Rummel-Hudson's memoir offers a moving account of his and wife Julie's unrelenting efforts to give their buoyant little girl a way to communicate."
—*People* magazine

"Relating the battle for his exceptional daughter with nimble wit, ardor, and considerable descriptive ability, Rummel-Hudson has evolved from blogger to author."
—*Kirkus Reviews*

"A study not only in Schuyler's vivacious and resilient personality, but also in the redeeming power of understanding."
—*Publishers Weekly*

"This memoir, full of fear and rage and disappointment and acceptance and advocacy and ferocious love, offers plenty of touchstones

for parents who have dealt with diagnoses that are infuriatingly wrong or frighteningly right."   —Terri Mauro, author of
The Everything Parent's Guide to Sensory Integration Disorder

"Rummel-Hudson chronicles, with disarming frankness, the experience of parenting a child no one knows how to help."
—*Brain, Child* magazine

"This story will both compel and inspire readers on their own self-journey."   —*Texas Family* magazine

"We all play the hand that we are dealt in life. Knowing that there are many people like Robert, Julie, and Schuyler who play their difficult hand with grit, tenacity, and love makes this world a much better place in which to live."   —*The Citizen* (Auburn, New York)

Schuyler's
Monster

Schuyler's Monster

A Father's Journey with His Wordless Daughter

ROBERT RUMMEL-HUDSON

St. Martin's Griffin ❧ New York

Although this is a memoir, some events have been compressed and a few of the characters are composites. The names and identifying details of some of the people appearing in these pages have been changed to protect their privacy.

www.stmartins.com

Illustration by Ben Rollman

The Library of Congress has catalogued the hardcover edition as follows:

Rummel-Hudson, Robert.
  Schuyler's Monster : a father's journey with his wordless daughter / Robert Rummel-Hudson.
    p. cm.
  ISBN-13: 978-0-312-37242-2
  ISBN-10: 0-312-37242-6
  1. Hudson, Schuyler Noelle—Mental health. 2. Developmentally disabled children—United States—Biography. 3. Brain—Abnormalities—Patients—United States—Biography. 4. Language disorders in children—Patients—United States—Biography. 5. Fathers—United States—Biography. I. Title.

RJ506.D47.H83 2008
618.92—dc22   2007040915

ISBN-13: 978-0-312-53880-4
ISBN-10: 0-312-53880-4

First St. Martin's Griffin Edition: February 2009

10   9   8   7   6   5   4   3   2   1

For Schuyler,
my weird and wondrous monster-slayer

CONTENTS

We are accustomed to look upon the shackled form of a conquered monster, but there—there you could look at a thing monstrous and free.

— Joseph Conrad, Heart of Darkness

Prologue

The first time we met Schuyler's monster, it lay waiting to pounce, not from behind a rock or from the mouth of a cave, but peeking out from between the lab coats of two nervous and sad-faced doctors.

When we stepped into Dr. Simon's office, we only expected to see Schuyler's pediatrician. Instead, we found her waiting with Dr. Ment from the Yale University Medical School's Department of Neurology. When we saw the sheet of MRI photos already in place on the light board, our world stopped. The doctors looked at us as if they wanted to be anywhere but in that office, and Julie and I looked back at them with the slow realization that we were about to get kicked in the teeth. We all stood there for a moment, none of us sure what to do.

No one except Schuyler, of course.

She'd been to doctors' offices before. She was only three years old, looking for all the world like a perfectly normal, pretty little girl. Friends and strangers alike often pointed out that she was a dead ringer for a young Drew Barrymore. Schuyler wasn't like most little girls, however. She couldn't articulate a single word.

Without being told, Schuyler had enough experience walking

into doctors' offices to tell with a glance what kind of visit it was going to be. Six months earlier, she'd been given a vague autism spectrum diagnosis that didn't seem to fit, aside from her persistent, maddening silence. The gut feeling that the diagnosis was wrong had led to the MRI, and ultimately this meeting.

A quick assessment of the room told Schuyler what she needed to know. There would be no exam this time; this was going to be nothing but grown-ups talking. As we slowly entered the room and took our seats in front of the doctors like reluctant students, Schuyler set out to find amusement. She explored the room quietly as Julie and I sat and listened to Dr. Ment explain what they'd found in the MRI.

After two years of questions and tests and at least one unsatisfactory diagnosis, two years of trying to unlock the secret of Schuyler's silence, there was an answer. Not just an answer, but a diagnosis. Thanks to the MRI, we could see it.

At the time, when friends would attempt to comfort us by saying that at least we had an answer, at least we knew what the problem was now, I explained how it felt. Imagine walking through the woods at night, all alone. In the darkness behind you, something is following, stalking you. You can hear it disturbing the leaves as it moves, and while it never goes away, it remains hidden from view. In your mind, you wonder. *What is it? A feral dog? A coyote? Or even a mountain lion?* Your imagination kicks into high gear and your mind conjures up the most likely explanations. Suddenly you stumble into an open area bathed in moonlight. You step to the center and turn to see what is following you.

The bushes part, and out steps a *Tyrannosaurus rex.*

That's how it felt, this answer to Schuyler's mystery.

The meeting didn't take long. Dr. Ment gave us the diagnosis and explained how rare this disorder was. It had taken them three weeks to figure out what Schuyler had, she said, and even then only with the help of a geneticist in Chicago who was the leading researcher in this field. She explained how there were only a very few diagnosed cases of it, fewer than a hundred in the entire world.

Then she named it. The monster in Schuyler's head had a name.

We sat and we listened. As she explained what it all meant, I felt a hard thing in my stomach, almost as if I'd eaten bread dough, but harder. I felt all those secret hopes for my daughter's future slipping away from me, all the ambitions parents pretend not to have for their kids. Julie's face said the same; she was starting to cry.

Schuyler looked up at us, not understanding. I picked her up and played with her quietly, my face set in a smile for her. I listened to them and I played with her.

"I know when you get home, the first thing you're going to do is go online and look this up," Dr. Ment said. "I just want you to be ready. It's going to be pretty rough."

And it was.

We left the office and stepped out into the late summer afternoon. Julie cried, and I walked ahead a short distance with Schuyler. She spun and danced and laughed, pulling me along, frustrated at my slow pace and totally unaware that the world was a different place than it had been an hour before.

Nothing had changed. Everything had changed.

Part One

A Monster Hiding

1

Kalamazoo

Julie's pregnancy wasn't a huge surprise to us. I suppose it shouldn't have been a surprise at all. We'd been married a few months, and we'd been discussing the future, one with fabulous new jobs in some exotic new location that was in no way Kalamazoo, and that future had kids in it, too. Julie was young, in her early twenties, and I was starting over after a childless first marriage had sucked the life and the better part of a decade out of me. I'd left Texas after twenty-nine years to be with Julie, and I was still adjusting to the upper Midwest. So many changes were afoot, why not a baby, too? How hard could it be? With a merry chuckle and a total lack of any sort of intelligent consideration for the future, we began "trying." It didn't take long.

Kalamazoo, Michigan, is our setting, a town located in the strangest place I'd ever experienced, the narrow strip of land running up the western side of the state about thirty miles inland from Lake Michigan. Here's the Mister Science explanation. During the winter, which in Michigan lasts roughly six months, big fat clouds suck up moisture from Lake Michigan and then move to the east over the landmass of the state. About thirty miles in, the moisture starts to freeze and dumps snow on the poor exposed earth below.

This is called "lake effect" snow, and it is extreme. The first time I experienced it, I woke up one morning to discover that thirty-two inches of snow had fallen in the hours I had been sleeping, warm and ignorant, in my bed. Thirty-two inches. I took pictures.

My point about this little factoid is not *"Wow, it sure snows a lot in western Michigan,"* but rather that it tells you something about the people who lived there. Long ago, when fur trappers and Indians were the only humans who were trudging through this thirty-two inches of lake effect frostiness, settlers arrived, saw this meteorological weirdness and said, "Jebediah, by golly, we've found our home." It wasn't just Kalamazoo, either. Grand Rapids, which is neither grand nor possessing rapids, falls under the lake's crazy spell, too. Michigan is a state founded by masochists, and probably not the fun kind, either.

When I look back on our days in Kalamazoo, I find myself missing it more than I ever would have thought possible at the time. I'd had a rough start a few years before, the first time I tried to move to Michigan. The computer sales job I'd secured a few weeks before vanished before my eyes, followed shortly by an impacted tooth in my now uninsured mouth. My boss back in Dallas graciously offered to give me my old job back, but my failure sent me and my swollen mouth limping back to Texas through an actual, honest to goodness blizzard within about a week. I never quite got over the idea that Kalamazoo was trying to kill me just a little.

Truthfully, however, the winters were bad in a way that still thrilled me; when I called my best friend, Joe, who still lived in Dallas, and confessed that having my ass handed to me by such extreme winter conditions was still rather cool, he referred to it as "the pleasurable irritation of the new." The Kalamazoo summers were pleasant enough, with Lake Michigan so close. The city was home to Western Michigan University and had a funky little college town feel to it, which was a refreshing change from the rustic "Michigan Militia" ambience enjoyed by much of the rest of the state. The town's most visually striking landmark was a century-old, sinister-looking water tower on the grounds of the state mental hospital, and the park at the center of town was surrounded by tall, grim-faced churches and featured a fountain full of what appeared to be petrified children. Perhaps most impressive, the Burger King near the campus was the site of the very first sighting of Elvis after his death. Or his "death," if you prefer.

Kalamazoo was a peculiar little town. Even when it was trying to kill me, it charmed me a little.

"Do you want to know?"

"I don't know," I said. "I mean, of course, I want to know." Pause. "Don't you want to know?"

"I want to know," Julie replied quietly. "I think I already know the answer. I think I knew it when I ordered the surf and turf at dinner."

"Yeah?"

"Yeah. So. You want to know?"

"Yeah," I said. "Let's find out."

And so it happened that on Mother's Day 1999, Julie peed on a stick and changed our lives forever.

The story behind Schuyler's name isn't nearly as interesting as you might think. I actually considered making something up; judging from the questions we received when she was born, you might think we just chose some random term right off the table of periodic elements. It's not all that unusual; pronounced SKY-ler and often Americanized as Skyler or even Skylar, it's a Dutch name meaning "scholar." I'd like to say we chose it because we wanted to predetermine our child's great mind (or inexplicable Dutchness?), but the truth is even less impressive.

About a month after we were married, before that fateful, peeful Mother's Day, Julie and I went to dinner at a fancy restaurant called

the Great Lakes Shipping Company. Well, it was fancy for Kalamazoo. None of the vehicles in the parking lot had snowplows attached
to the front bumper, and Elvis hadn't been sighted there just yet.
We'd been given a gift certificate for a free dinner for two by Julie's
parents as a *"we can't stop this or have the groom killed so we might as well give
them some food"* wedding gift. It was the holiday season, we were in
love, and we were hungry.

As we sat at our table, trying not to look like goobers, our waitress walked up and introduced herself. Her name was Schuyler, and
she was friendly and pretty and funny. Mostly, though, she had a
cool name.

"Schuyler," said Julie as we drove home, repeating it softly.
"Schuyler. I really like that name."

And there it was.

Later, during the pregnancy, Julie decided that when the day
came for us to have the sonogram and The Answer, she didn't want
to know. I, on the other hand, wanted to learn every single fact I
could. I didn't want surprises; I was scared enough as it was. On the
day of the sonogram, we saw the baby but had no idea what we were
looking for. I found myself squinting and thinking, *"Is that a penis? Oh,
surely THAT'S not a penis. . . ."* After we explained that I wanted to
know and Julie didn't, the lab technician led me out into the hallway
and whispered conspiratorially in my ear, as if Julie might hear from
the other room.

"It's a girl," she said. "Congratulations."

"Are you sure?" I asked.

"Oh, I'm pretty sure. She gave us a pretty clear shot of the
goods."

The goods. I was shocked that our baby even had goods already.

When we started talking about names, I found myself in a strange
predicament. I had to consider boy names with as much seriousness
as I did the girl names or I'd give away the big secret. The problem
was, we both realized almost immediately that if we had a girl, we

wanted to name her after a waitress. A girl was going to be Schuyler; we knew that all along.

Boy names, however, were a matter of contention, and I had to be something of a jerk about fighting the ones I didn't like in order to protect Schuyler's secret.

So Schuyler, if you're reading this one day, know that your mother loved you very, very much, but if you'd been a boy, you might have been named Jasper.

The day after Julie took the test, we visited our local Planned Parenthood to take another one. We'd always been told this was a good thing to do, although really, I suspect they were using the same test we bought at the grocery store, so I suppose we could have just gone and done it again ourselves. However, there was something about having someone in doctory-looking clothes make an official proclamation (*"Thou art preggers!"*) that sealed the deal for us. We left the clinic through a crowd of protesters shoving horrific, bloody posters in our faces.

"We're keeping it! Go away!" Julie shouted as we made our way to the car, waving free pamphlets at them as we passed.

The booklets were an unexpected bonus for us, containing little cartoons of our baby as she developed. I halfway expected it to have a cute name like "Cletus the Fetus," but sadly it wasn't the case. Still, we got some basic information, which was good since we had to wait another week and a half for Julie's first doctor's appointment. Ten days felt like an eternity to wait before talking to a health care professional. How did they know we weren't going to go out and celebrate with a big bowl of crack or some thalidomide milk shakes?

I feel as if it should go without saying, assuming most men react the same way to imminent fatherhood, but I was a mess. I cried when Julie told me, and I cried the next day when I was driving to work. At one point, Julie asked me if I needed to take a pregnancy test, too. Part of the emotional overflow was the joy of impending parenthood and the miracle of new life, I'm sure, but mostly, it was pure, unblinking, soul-freezing, *"boy, I sure am glad I wore my brown pants"* terror. I'd seen that episode of *ER*, where Dr. Green tries to deliver the baby and everything goes to hell. If you saw the episode, you remember it, too.

Julie was calm and unconcerned. Like all pregnant women, she was transforming into a magical being. She'd also never seen that episode of *ER*.

We bought a pregnancy diary. Julie wanted to have a place to record events from the experience (*"Today I puked!"*), but I was completely sold on the journal because for every day of the pregnancy, it had a little blurb telling you how your child was developing, along with little artistic renderings of the happy fetus. This book told me, for example, that a week later, our child (whom we were calling the Grub, because we were filled with love) was now approximately the size and general appearance of a Gummy Bear. It had a tiny little brain nubbin and could respond to stimuli, presumably by wriggling like bait. I figured it was boring in there, so I gave Julie's belly a poke every so often, just to give the Grub something to do.

The Grub also had tiny little nubs that would eventually turn into arms and legs, and tiny little ankles and knees were beginning to form, as well as toes. Who knew we get toes before we get feet? Best of all, she had nipples. I had no idea nipples occurred so soon, inasmuch as I'd considered the matter at all. I guess I assumed they would be one of the last things to form, sort of a biological "Inspected by Number 12" stamp bestowed on her before she tumbled into a waiting world.

Even as we prepared to see a doctor for the first time, we knew Kalamazoo wasn't going to work out. We'd ended up there because Julie was a music major at Western Michigan University; I'd moved from Texas because I hated long-distance relationships and didn't care much for Texas at that point, either. I'd worked in computers in Texas, but honestly, I wasn't very good at it and didn't love my work.

When I got to Kalamazoo, I got some work teaching trombone lessons, and I got a job as the classical music guy at the local Barnes & Noble, in the music department. Shortly after I started working at B&N, Julie also got a job there. She started off in the café, but being the overachiever she was, she quickly moved up and became a bookseller. By the time we got married and found out we were having a baby, we were both primed to move into management positions. Advancement wasn't likely to happen in Kalamazoo, but in the Detroit area, there were jobs aplenty. Not only that, Julie's family lived in the area, and what better place to have a child than in the loving embrace of your family?

Detroit is our setting, or more accurately, the suburbs of Detroit. It was only a few weeks later that we arrived at our new place in Fraser, Michigan. If Eminem lived a life of trouble and heartbreak on Eight Mile Road (and did he, really? Our dentist's office was on Eight Mile; it never struck me as particularly ghetto, although admittedly I was usually doped up on Novocain and nitrous oxide when I was there), our lives on Thirteen Mile Road were something less than film worthy. We did see a prostitute walking up to the drive-through window at Taco Bell once, but she wasn't turning tricks. Even hookers need a bean burrito now and again. In retrospect, it probably wasn't the best environment in which to bring a new baby, but we knew almost from the beginning we weren't destined to stay there long.

We'd been hired as managers at the two Barnes & Noble stores in Bloomfield Hills, Julie as a community relations manager in one and me as the music manager in the other. I was nervous about my first manager position, and the situation at the store didn't help. My new store manager informed me that one of my predecessors had been marched out of the store in handcuffs. While this might have lowered the bar as far as expectations for my job performance were concerned, it nevertheless made for an uncomfortable transition. Still, it wasn't the Mars mission. I sold CDs to rich suburbanites and hired teenagers and retirees to do the same. I built up a large and impressive selection of classical music, which no one ever bought. Once I even lectured a famous jazz musician about another famous jazz musician because I didn't recognize him. (I probably shouldn't say who it was, but his initials were Earl Klugh.) In a particularly brilliant move, I chased a shoplifter out of the store and down the block, treating the clientele of the Big Boy restaurant next door to a show. *"Look, honey! That fat man is chasing a young, fit teenager!"* And I waited for our baby.

According to the pregnancy journal, the Grub was now entering a phase where she resembled an exercise in Mister Potatoheadedness. It was a time for lots of add-ons. Nostrils and a tiny little nose, eyelids, the beginnings of elbows and a tongue were all popping up. Her eyes and ears were also appearing, but not where I might have expected. The ears started off near the bottom of her head, and the eyes weren't peering forward but were located on the sides of her head. ("Much like a rabbit," said the journal cheerfully, as if the idea of having Rabbit Head Baby didn't make Daddy want to drive straight to one of Detroit's many drive-through liquor stores.)

In the midst of all this change, our baby's brain would very soon begin to form in earnest, with the tiny ridges that would make it look, well, brainy. It would be then, in these early days of development, before we'd even heard her heartbeat, that Schuyler's monster would be born.

Detroit was problematic. I can't be the first person who ever wrote those words.

It wasn't really the city as such. Growing up in Texas, I'd always imagined Detroit as a sort of urban demilitarized zone. I half expected to see burning tires on the street corners when I pulled into town, but honestly, it was just another big, nondescript midwestern city. I never really got a sense of what Detroit was trying to be, but to us, it was a large, somewhat dirty and grumpy but otherwise nonthreatening place we inexplicably found ourselves occupying af- ter three years in hip, weird little Kalamazoo. I wish I could give a better description of Detroit, but honestly, all I really remember about the city itself is bad traffic and dirty snow.

The people, on the other hand, left an impression. I remember our fellow downstairs neighbors in our little apartment building, a surly clan with vaguely Old World accents who stared unblinkingly at us every time we left the apartment or came home. They never became accustomed to us; they watched us from the moment we stepped out of our cars to the instant we shut the apartment door. They argued loudly and incomprehensibly, and their improbably gigantic television was elevated just high enough in their bedroom overlooking the parking lot that we could see what they were watching as we walked past the window at night. It was like living next to a drive-in movie theater. One night, they were watching porn. We snickered like teenagers as we walked underneath a giant blow job.

One day we came home to find a pair of baby mittens hanging on the door, with a note saying simply "Congratulations." They noticed us, and I guess they wanted to contribute something to our lives. Something besides free porn.

Our jobs were fine. Really. We kept telling ourselves this. There was obviously going to be a period of transition in any situation, but the people we served at our bookstores were so different from what we were accustomed to back in Kalamazoo. For all its quirks, Kala- mazoo had a very savvy music clientele. In Bloomfield Hills, I had a customer complain because a full-price CD he was looking at only had four songs on it. It was Beethoven's Ninth Symphony.

One hot night in late August, I was driving home from work when I found myself caught up in a police chase. One minute I was toodling along; the next, I was surrounded by screaming sirens and flashing lights. Even in my little Volkswagen, I felt huge and lum- bery, like the one adult in a room full of playing children. Minutes after the whole crime show parade was gone, I was still a little shaken. I was no small town yokel, but I wasn't dealing well with Detroit.

A few months later, I drove past an accident on the freeway on my way to work, and there in the road was a dead body under a sheet, its sad shoeless feet sticking out.

Through it all, our baby grew.

The Grub was now beginning to grow thicker, less transparent skin, so she didn't look quite so much like a guppy now. With this new viewer-friendly skin also came lanugo, a strange white fur grown by developing fetuses, which they shed during development. No one really seems to know what it does, other than give you a little albino Wookiee for a few months.

We heard the heartbeat, a fast-paced "bwow, bwow, bwow" that sounded more like the pulse of a gerbil than a human child. It was another moment mixed with tender tears and mortal terror. The Theoretical Grub had become real. This was all happening so fast.

In our panic to prepare for this most unpreparable of events, we went out and spent an obscene amount of money on a crib. If you've not gone into your local baby superultramegastore recently, you really should go treat yourself. The furniture section will blow your mind. A little box of grass might have done the job for the Baby Jesus, but for the modern American parent-to-be, there's a lot of stuff to buy. Need a place to change your baby's diaper? Well, of course you do, and here's a fancy little changing table for just that purpose, complete with little rails to keep your dear wee one from rolling off into the annals of tragedy. Despite the fact that all her clothes are teeny tiny and she will outgrow them all in mere weeks, you will need a dresser in which to store them all. If you're a savvy shopper, perhaps you'll get the dresser with a changing station on top. As for the crib, it's a beast, and not a cheap one, but there's good news. The fancier ones will change into other items as your child grows, like a

Transformer. *"Zow! It's a crib! Zam! It's a daybed! Ping! It's a toddler bed! Boom! It's a giant killer robot!"*

Our baby was the size of a hamster. We weren't buying a crib because we needed one yet and God knows we didn't need to assemble it six months before the baby's arrival. We did it because we wanted to feel like parents, and we needed to trick ourselves into thinking we were near the end of this journey.

Silly fools. I miss being those people.

Summer turned to fall, which in Michigan happens in late August, and Schuyler grew. I had already learned we were having a girl, and we saw, through the magic of sonogram, the tiny face of our child. In 1999, before 3-D imaging became all the rage, the ultrasound would react very strangely to different types of tissue in the baby's body, so the amount of bone showing up in the image really depended upon the perspective. When viewed from the side, Schuyler looked like a tiny, ethereal being, a creature of light and magic. From the front, she looked like a bug-eyed alien.

I found myself thinking a great deal about my own father during this time. After all, I was about to become one myself, a concept that did not play very easily in the little movie of my life I was filming in my head. My own models for fatherhood weren't very promising, either, not unless I tried to supplant the ones in my real life with fathers from television. My father's behavior was bad enough to make me think I hated him (I didn't, I later figured out, when it was much too late), and also just enough to generate a rebellious streak that has never quite subsided. If my father taught me one thing, it was that I did not like to be told what to do.

My dad, as bad as he was, nevertheless had to be considered a vast improvement over his own father. Herman Hudson was a rough, ignorant oil field worker who treated his own sons badly in ways I can only imagine; my father never talked about it, and only hinted to me when he was being unusually cruel that I should consider myself fortunate he was so much kinder than his own father. Herman was pure Texas; his sons were named Tommy Wayne and Bobby Ray, and that's how their names appeared on their birth certificates. Herman had no time to waste with Thomases or Roberts; I was no junior, being named instead after a distant relative on my mother's side.

Almost two decades after his death, I can see now how hard my father tried. Bobby Hudson was a junior high school coach and apparently a good one, and I think he tried to apply his "make men out of boys" philosophy on my brother and me, with decidedly mixed results. It haunted my father, the knowledge that while he honestly wasn't a very intelligent person, certainly not compared to my mother or even to my brother, my sister, or myself, he was nevertheless smart enough to recognize his deficiency. I think he resented my mother the most, which I suspect is one reason he cheated on her for so many years before finally leaving her at a very dark time in her life. As for his kids, I think he just didn't understand us, and for the last few years of his life he didn't try, remarrying and largely turning his back on us all. When he died, we discovered he had attempted to write us out of his will. (Not being a brilliant man, he failed to do so, fouling up the witnessing of signatures in such a way that in the end, the will was thrown out and we all three ended up with a small inheritance that we all spent foolishly. I used part of mine to get out of jail during a brief but impressive drinking episode during college.)

I don't hate my father, and I don't hold any ill feelings toward his second wife. It's taken me awhile to reach this point, and I don't think my brother or my sister are quite there yet. The sad truth is, all the players in the drama of my family did the best they could with the limited tools they were given and within their own personal limitations. In 1999, just shy of a decade after my father's sudden death and with my own child on the way, it was more important than ever for me to figure out what his legacy to me would be.

Fortunately, I always had a pretty realistic view of my father and his actions, even when I was a child, and I never labored under the misconception that what he was doing was right or justified, or that one day I would raise my own child the same way I was raised.

The bad news was, at the age of thirty-two, with my own child mere months away from being a squirming reality, I only knew how *not* to be a father.

Autumn in Michigan is a time of unspeakable beauty, with an explosion of colors taking place in early October that transforms the landscape seemingly overnight, but inherent in that beauty is a whiff of menace. You see the colors and you hear the honking of the geese flying over your apartment in the morning, and if you're a yokel from Texas, you think, *"Garsh, that's sort of cool."* You might even go buy a sweater.

But if you've lived in the upper Midwest for a while, you get the message. The trees are telling you something. *"You'd better get out of here,"* they say. *"This winter's going to be bad. If you stay, you're going to die."* The geese don't have to be told twice.

The ominous shifts in the weather paralleled Julie's own feelings of transformation as she entered her third trimester. Her body was changing in ways much less magical than they'd seemed in theory only weeks before. As her belly grew (and here's a tip, future fathers: use that word "belly" sparingly), Julie found that people wanted to reach out and touch it. I understood why it bothered her; it was actually pretty creepy to me, too, and it wasn't even my belly that was being groped. Julie's temper grew shorter; at one point, after being blown off for an appointment with her doctor, she angrily told the receptionist, "How can you be so casual about this? This isn't a potato, it's a baby!" I'll leave it to you to decide what that means.

It was during this time I started providing music for the Grub. Sometimes it was in the form of my own singing, in which I would make up such timeless lyrics as *"It's a boy! It's a girl! It's a bug! It's a tarantula!"* (Judge me if you must.) At other times, and thank God I had a camera, I would put my big puffy headphones on Julie's belly and begin the indoctrination early, with Shostakovich symphonies and "My Heart Belongs to Daddy."

If it seems as if we were hurtling along toward our baby's impending birth with very little information and seemed to be making it up as we went along, well, that's probably about right. We weren't too worried, though, because soon, so very soon, all would be revealed. We had signed up for Lamaze classes; we were finally going to learn how exactly one goes about having a baby.

I was a little surprised at both the brevity of the class and its late placement in the whole baby-having process. The sum total was four classes, about two hours each, taking place once a week. It took me longer to get my driver's license than it was going to take to learn how to have a baby. Or help someone have a baby, really, because if there's one thing you don't want to say in front of someone who is weeks away from giving birth, it is how you, the father, are going to have a baby. *"Gosh, this pregnancy thing isn't so bad. . . . What? What did I say?"*

If the months leading up to Lamaze were all about the pastel-washed dream of parenthood, with the cute tiny clothes and the idea of a clean, perfect, cooing little baby, the reality came home in the first several minutes of class, when the teacher showed us the monitoring sensor that *screws* into the baby's head during childbirth. She passed it around.

Well, I thought, holding the tiny, curled wire in my hand as if it was the most natural thing in the world. *I didn't see that coming.*

The baby head screw wasn't the only implement the teacher showed us, either. For example, I did not actually know that in the waning days of the twentieth century, if a woman went into labor and her water didn't break, the solution involved a big plastic hook. They broke her water with a plastic hook so you could have your baby with a screw in its head.

I didn't love the teacher, mostly because she insisted on referring to the men in the room as "support persons." This was after we went around the room and all introduced ourselves as the fathers, so this bit of sensitive political correctness was unnecessary. Mothers got to be mothers; I kept waiting for her to refer to them as "host organisms." I was so irritated that I counted the number of times she said it. In the course of one class, she said "it" thirteen times and only stopped and switched over to "father" after she saw me making marks in my notes. The whole thing was making me punchy and sarcastic.

"So the first thing the nurse will do is hand the new baby to you, mommies, so you can count their little fingers and toes. . . ."

"And heads!" I offered helpfully.

When she discussed the possibility of fathers actually cutting the umbilical cord, I decided pretty early on that I wasn't interested. Part of my decision was a reaction to my feeling that this was just a cheap way to make fathers feel more involved in the process. To be honest, however, the primary reason I didn't go for the idea was simple. I didn't think I could resist the urge to pretend I was the mayor of Baby Town, with a big tall hat, a red sash and oversized scissors, ceremonially opening a new mall. I know without a shred of doubt that I would have been the only one in the room laughing as I posed for my imaginary press corps.

Very much like driver's education class, the thing everyone talks about in Lamaze is the movie portion of the evening. We'd been dreading the C-section film ever since we read a graphic description of the procedure while flipping through pregnancy books at Target. We were so queasy, we both ended up sitting down in the aisle, green-faced and suddenly not feeling the magic so much as before. But the C-section movie wasn't too bad. They showed a little bit of cutting, but mostly they fixed upon the mom's blissful face as she grinned stupidly through the haze of drugs. It didn't look so bad if you didn't think about what was going on below the sheets. (Or, you know, if you were a man.) With apologies to the whole natural childbirth crowd, it was becoming clear that drugs were the answer to doing this thing right. I was sort of hoping for an epidural myself.

More disturbing were the natural childbirth videos, which went back and forth between shots of the mother screaming and bugging out her eyes and the actual birth itself. I don't mean to demean the beauty of the moment. As I sat there watching, I knew that when it was my time to watch this event and witness the birth of my own beautiful daughter, I would be moved to tears, even if she had a screw in her head. But my overwhelming thought as I watched the childbirth video was a resounding *"yuck."*

When the big day came, it arrived quickly and with much drama. Julie suffered a fall at work, and a bad one, serious enough to warrant rushing her to the hospital. We spent an evening worrying while the doctors ran tests and checked her out, and the baby was eventually deemed to be fine. We went home, secure in the knowledge that everything was going according to plan after all.

The next day, two weeks before her due date, Julie's water broke. Twenty-six hours later, Schuyler Noelle Hudson was born.

Schuyler, and the monster she carried inside her head.

We had no idea.

2

When I Grow Up

I never said to myself that I wanted to manage a music store. I can't say it was something I ever gave any thought to at all, not until I saw the film version of Nick Hornby's book *High Fidelity*. It starred John Cusack as Rob Gordon, the neurotic and unambitious owner of an old school vinyl record store in Chicago and an unrepentant music snob. In retrospect, his lifestyle must have appealed to me on some level because once I became the manager of a music store, it was usually this movie driving my management style. It didn't always work; running a tiny independent store like the one in the movie was a far cry from managing part of a giant corporate entity, and my days were often more *Office Space* than *High Fidelity*. Still, the job mostly suited me, even if it was never one of my youthful dreams.

Like almost every male in America, I wanted to be a fireman. Unusual for me, however, was the timing. The impulse didn't hit until college, and only after I was so sick of school and so disillusioned with my life that I wanted to walk away from it all and just watch things burn up. In retrospect, it's probably a good thing I didn't pursue that line of thinking.

My childhood ambitions were safer but also slightly weird. I

wanted to be a zookeeper. I realize now, I was probably a little confused. I think what I actually wanted was to grow up to be a guy with
a lot of pets, which is exactly what I eventually did, so I suppose in
that sense, I realized my childhood ambitions splendidly. As a child,
I thought of the zookeeper as the guy who had all the animals. I
didn't think too much beyond that.

I was an unmotivated child, I can see that now. I went to school
and didn't do too badly but certainly didn't excel. (Math was a particular issue for me; when I took the SAT in high school, I received a
perfect verbal score and a near remedial math score.) I walked home
to a blissfully empty house every day. I was in college the first time I
heard the term "latchkey child," and I remember thinking, *Hey, that
was me!* It never occurred to me that there was a term for what I was.
I just assumed every kid in my school was going home to an empty
house, having a bowl of Cocoa Puffs and enjoying a few hours of
parent-free time in front of the television. I never thought I was dis-
advantaged. To me, it sounded like the American Dream.

In fourth grade, my school librarian looked at me and saw, I don't
know, something. A kid with a mostly unused brain and nothing
much to do, I suppose. In her mind, I was clay. Before I disappear in
a haze of remembrance, I should confess that I didn't actually care
for this librarian much. Her husband was a friend of my father's,
never a good place to start, and I found her to be fussy and self-
absorbed. The fact that I had a crush on her older and cooler daughter for years improved her standing in my eyes, but not much.

One summer, she and her family went on vacation, and it was
left up to me to ride to their house on my bike every day and take
care of their place. I don't recall now what sort of princely sum I was
paid for this service. The list of instructions she left included four pages
of watering instructions for her houseplants. Four typewritten pages.
One plant required a quarter of an inch of standing water, while another needed a fine mist (with the settings for the water bottle clearly
indicated). You can only imagine how well I did as a scatterbrained

nine-year-old with instructions like those. Indeed, I can't imagine doing a very good job of it now. She came home from vacation to find a house full of autumnal plants, yellow and sad.

Either she found it in her heart to forgive my sorry horticultural skills, or she saw more than ever my need for salvation. Whatever the reason, she began to give me books. There's one thing I value the most about her now, the reason that thirty years later, I do feel genuinely bad for killing her plants. Quite simply, she didn't give me children's books. She gave me books that challenged me and made me look up words and turn difficult phrases over and over in my head until I figured them out. She gave me a copy of *Watership Down* and ignited something in me. I fell in love with that book and with the written word. For that, she'll always have a special place in my heart.

It wasn't until junior high that I thought I might want to grow up to be a writer. As was often the case with my confused young psyche, it was just as often a result of the little crushes I developed on my English teachers as their teaching prowess that got me fired up, but the end result was the same. I should have figured out that writing held the key to my future when I was a junior in high school and wrote a short story for a friend of mine who was in a panic over the assignment. All of our stories were reviewed and judged, and the story I turned in under my own name won third place. The story I wrote for my friend won second.

I should have realized it then, but I had another dream to distract me for another decade or so. It wouldn't be until the early days of the Web that I rediscovered my love of words.

Before words, there was music.

I should stop here and tell you about my hometown. Odessa is our setting, the grubby West Texas oil town in which I grew up. I don't know what it would have been like to spend a childhood in the 1970s in Normal America, but in Odessa (aka Slowdeatha, Odessalation,

and my personal favorite, Jimbobwe), radical change wasn't remold-
ing society. Even now, when I go back to see my family and drive
Odessa's dusty streets, I feel as if I've hit an air pocket in time, where
people might still be voting for Eisenhower and running duck and
cover drills in school. Odessa was a rough town with a past rooted in
the unforgiving world of oil production (my father left the oil business after watching a co-worker burn to death in an industrial accident), but it was also filled with churchgoing citizens and wholesome
Ronald Reagan values and gritty West Texas characters. I, on the
other hand, was a snotty teenager whose idea of country and western music was "I Wanna Be a Cowboy" by Boys Don't Cry and the
Dead Kennedys' cover of *Rawhide*.

Naturally, I couldn't wait to get out.

After he left the oil field, my father became a junior high school
coach, hardly a surprising career move since he had been the quar-
terback at his tiny West Texas high school. When the time came for
me to decide what extracurricular activities I was going to sign up
for in junior high, it seemed like an obvious choice. At the age of
twelve, I was already almost six feet tall and wearing size eleven
shoes. Not knowing I was only two inches away from my adult
height, I thought I was going to end up as some *Guinness World Records*
freak. It terrified me, the idea that one day I could be ten feet tall,
misshapen and stooped, my poor heart struggling to keep me alive. I
was also afraid of spontaneous human combustion and snakes in the
toilet, although I can't even begin to tell you why.

What my father and all his coaching buddies saw was a kid who
was destined to play football. In Odessa during the 1980s, this was no
small thing. Better writers than myself have documented the phe-
nomenon of West Texas high school football, so I'll simply say that
the more I heard about my future as a star on the football field, the
more I wanted to do anything else with my life.

In fifth grade, the Anything Else introduced itself to me in grand
style. We were all bussed to the high school auditorium for a free

concert by the local symphony, the idea being that we would all get stars in our eyes and sign up for orchestra class the next year. To seal the deal, the orchestra devoted most of its program to music from *Star Wars*. It was a sly bit of programming, and it worked, at least for me. You can probably imagine that the Midland Odessa Symphony Orchestra was not going to find itself listed among the titans of the music world any time soon, but truthfully, they weren't half bad at all. To my young ears, they sounded like gods. Gods playing *Star Wars*.

(Years later, when I was performing semiprofessionally, I found myself subbing for my bass trombone teacher in the orchestra. The gig? The fifth grade *Star Wars* concert, which by this time had morphed into a John Williams medley, including music from *E.T.* and *Raiders of the Lost Ark*. Ah, the Spielbergian 80s.)

At the age of twelve, I joined my junior high school band and became what I still secretly identify myself as when someone asks me what I do. I became a trombonist. I'll just come out and say it, I was a good trombonist. By the time I graduated from high school, I was actually a very good trombonist, having won a bunch of solo medals (it feels silly to look at them now), attended the National Music Camp (now the Interlochen Arts Camp), in Michigan, and eventually sat second chair in the Texas All-State Symphony Orchestra. I wasn't a great trombonist, certainly not as good as I thought I was, but I was good. I'm not half bad now, although I'm not half good, either. I don't play my dusty trombone very often, for the same reason aging beauty pageant contestants don't go up to the attic and try on their sash and swimsuit in front of the mirror. Time is cruel.

I was a competitive player in high school; truthfully, I was a bit of an ass about it. When I went to college, things changed somewhat, partly due to the calming influence of my new trombone teacher but also as a result of big changes in my life.

At eighteen, I'd married my high school sweetheart, a decision that proved to be an error almost immediately. At twenty-two, without any warning, my complicated relationship with my father was frozen in time when, as he stood in his yard talking to a neighbor, he collapsed mid-sentence from an aneurism; he was dead before he hit the ground. My world was growing more and more complicated. It suddenly didn't matter so much if I was a better player than the guy sitting next to me. Without the testosterone-fueled competition of my high school days, I was left with the music, and I belatedly began to understand the soul of the sound world in which I'd been living as a tourist for so many years. I grew up just a little, just enough to finally get it.

I suppose it's one of the great ironies of my life. I had to become a good musician in order to understand that I wasn't going to ever become a great musician. As I opened up to the power and the possibilities of music, I discovered the composers whose work would come to change my life. I found the Austrian composer Gustav Mahler, from whose manic depressive, troubled mind sprang huge orchestral sounds and structures seemingly born not from the mind of a man but rather fully formed in nature, like mountains, discovered rather than created. I immersed myself in the work of the composer who would become my favorite, the Soviet Union's Dmitri Shostakovich, who served in the great Russian tradition of the *yurodivy*, or "holy fool," like King Lear's faithful servant who was allowed to speak the truth about the king and remain unharmed, serving as he did a higher purpose. It was in the living room of my trombone teacher, after trying to discuss my confused feelings about war and violence, that I first heard Benjamin Britten's *War Requiem* and read his setting to music of the poetry of World War I poet soldier Wilfred Owen, understanding at last what it meant to be a pacifist.

In college, as I came to know the power of music, I also realized I had neither the raw talent nor the work ethic to become much more than a competent musician myself. I could play in local orchestras and Sunday church gigs, I could teach young trombone students, but after years of practice and moderately hard work, I wasn't going to be the great musician I'd dreamed of becoming.

It's hard, letting go of a dream like that, if for no other reason than having to finally turn around and listen to the world say *"Okay, smart guy. Now what?"*

While I'd enjoyed writing in high school, I never set out to become a writer when I grew up. I certainly never thought about the possibility of establishing myself as some sort of populist writer on the Internet, which of course only existed as a playground for the military and university-based super nerds in those days.

I'd been wandering since leaving the music world. I worked as a recording engineer at my college music department and did some teaching and freelance performing, but it was more out of familiarity than commitment. I spent a summer working as a long distance telephone operator. One night, a young woman tried to leave her boyfriend, only to have him walk out onto their balcony with a gun and start shooting at her. Cowering behind a pay phone on the street as bullets pinged around her, she picked up the phone in a panic and hit the "0" button, praying for an experienced telecommunications professional who could help her. She got me instead. To my credit, I was able to lead the police to her and successfully extract her from the situation. It was, however, the very last telephone call I assisted as a professional long distance telephone operator. I went to a bar after my shift ended and never returned to work.

By the time a handful of mostly academic sites began appearing on what we goofily referred to as the World Wide Web (*"Because, you know, it's all about being connected, like a web! A web across the WHOLE WORLD!"*), I had stumbled into a job at my university's academic computing service. It started with a summer job working for my brother in the computer repair shop, building PCs out of a pile of cases and motherboards and wires and screws. It was total monkey work; he would walk me through assembling one computer and then leave it sitting as a model, with the instructions "Okay, do that seventeen more times." After working my way up to running network cable in academic offices, I became a Macintosh software consultant. In that capacity, almost as an afterthought, I was pointed to the still infant Web and told to "figure it out," just in case it amounted to something.

Being uninspired to learn these skills by making nothing but boring university computing center Web sites, I experimented with creating personal sites of great importance, such as the very first Web page dedicated to my hometown of Odessa. The page was objectively subtitled The Armpit of Texas. Some time later I found out that discussion of my site had actually become an agenda item for an Odessa Chamber of Commerce meeting, so I like to think I had an impact.

I also created a page of personal reflections on the world around me called Robservations, a title which probably could have benefited from another few minutes of consideration. This site, begun in January 1996, would eventually grow through several incarnations into the online journal that eventually came to chronicle the strange and sad and wonderful story of Schuyler. It became the Greek chorus watching over all our shoulders and expanding the circle of people who cared for Schuyler beyond our wildest dreams or most dramatic expectations.

That was years away, however. For the moment, I was quietly finding my voice as a writer. That voice, as it turned out, could best be described as "Everyman Dumb Guy." I was surprisingly okay with that.

I can clearly remember the first time I met Julie. I was sitting on the steps of a friend's boathouse, looking out over Green Lake in northern Michigan. The sounds of my friend's party were going on in the house behind me, but I was having a few quiet moments alone. That sounds melodramatic, I know, but it was that kind of a summer. I had plenty to think about. I was working for my fifth summer at the Interlochen Arts Camp, the once mighty music institution I had attended in high school. Interlochen had gone a long way toward convincing me that I was going to one day be a professional musician. I was employed as an administrator, after spending a few years working with the kids, and that summer, I was there alone. The soon-to-be-former Mrs. Rob remained in Texas for the summer.

My ten-year marriage was in its final death spasms, having finally succumbed to our increasing apathy and hostility. The hostility had actually become the fun part, in some ways. Like most married couples, we had nicknames for each other. She called me "The Man-child"; my name for her was "The Enemy of Fun." We were charming company, I'm sure. We'd married at eighteen, after all, and had some growing up to do. When we did so, we discovered a surprising truth. We weren't actually all that fond of each other. I think the realization hit when we were about twenty-two, shortly after my father's death. We soldiered on for another few years, I think because we were both afraid to be alone, until the day came that we figured out that being alone was exactly what we wanted. We had no kids and a minimum of property, and when the divorce came, it was fairly bloodless. My dog was actually named on the divorce decree, which should give you an idea of how very little we had to divide between us. Just like that, it was over. That summer, I was feeling a little like Rip van Winkle. *"I've been asleep for how long?"*

Sitting on those steps and looking out over the lake, I was alone and thinking, but not melancholy. When Julie sat down beside me with a bottle of wine, I was immediately charmed. She was young, seven years younger than me, in fact, but she was also calm and had an easy sense of humor. She was pretty and curvy and had these impossibly big eyes, and I was transfixed. All these years later, the thing I remember most about that night with Julie was laughing with her.

The next year was rocky for us both. We knew pretty quickly that we were falling in love, and we also knew this wasn't exactly the greatest idea for either of us. At the end of the summer, I returned to Texas without even having kissed Julie. She waited for my divorce to become final, and shortly after, we started dating. Well, we dated as much as two people can when one of them lives in Dallas and the other lives in Kalamazoo, Michigan. (I know, I know. *"I've got a gal in Kalamazoo. . . ."*) We ran up huge phone bills, we sent letters, and we did what we could to develop a bond. I flew up to see her and meet her parents, who were immediately unimpressed by the fact that I was seven years older than Julie, hadn't actually finished my degree (although that certainly wasn't for a lack of time spent trying), was an agnostic, and had been divorced. Very recently divorced. Also, they detected early on that I might just be a gigantic smart-ass. It wasn't a strong beginning by any standard.

Through it all, we stuck it out.

Which is how I ended up in Kalamazoo, and later in Detroit, and finally in New Haven, Connecticut, interviewing for a job providing computer support in the patient ward of a mental hospital.

I'm getting ahead of myself, however. I first had to become the very last thing I ever thought I'd be when I grew up.

A father.

3

A Joyful Kind of Chaos

I knew the phone was there. I'd even used it several times over the past twenty-four hours. I never expected it to ring right there on the bedside table in Julie's room as she was giving birth. It never even occurred to me that such a thing might happen. I stood there beside the bed as Julie struggled to bring a human life into the world, and I considered the protocol. When your wife is having your baby and a telephone rings, who answers it? You? A nurse? Shouldn't there be someone there to handle weird things like that when they come up?

Judging from the look I received from every health care professional busy at work in that room, it was apparently my job to answer the phone. Feeling as if I was trapped in a Monty Python sketch, I picked up the receiver.

"Hello?"

"Robert, this is Sandy." It was Julie's mother. Well, of course it was. "Can I speak to Julie?"

I looked over at my wife, who was breathing quickly between contractions and looking over at me in disbelief.

"Um, she's sort of busy having a baby right now. Are you guys coming up here?"

"We're about to leave. Ask Julie what she wants to get her brother for Christmas."

"Who is that?" Julie asked.

"It's your mom," I said.

"What? Where is she? What does she want?"

I hesitated, long enough to see the look on Julie's face change as another contraction approached. "She wants to know what you want to get Garth for Christmas."

"What?" She closed her eyes and put her head back as the contraction hit. "Just hang up!"

"Did you hear that?" I asked her mother.

"I heard it," she answered, and I swear I could actually hear her lips tighten. "Tell her we're on our way."

Julie was completely stoned on lovely, enchanting drugs; in all fairness, she doesn't remember this episode at all. In the interest of full disclosure, I have a confession to make. That little story doesn't really have a relevant point. I just like telling it.

Throughout the course of my life, I have had very little use for guilt. Perhaps that says more about myself than I really want to share, I don't know. It's quite possible that my rejection of guilt is a defensive mechanism, a way to avoid dealing with all that nasty guilt that I should be feeling. Bad person? Gutless narcissist? You be the judge.

There are a few things in my life that I do feel legitimately guilty about. When I was a kid, I accidentally left my hamster, Pooh, out in the garage during a cold, cold night, and when I found him motionless the next day, I tearfully buried him out in the alley behind our house. It was years later that I learned how hamsters sometimes react to cold by hibernating; poor Pooh was probably buried alive. In high school, I stood up a girl on a date, not because there was anything wrong with her, but because I thought she was beautiful and that scared the crap out of me. In college, I once ran over a cat and was so horrified, I didn't go back to see how he was doing. (From the sound he made under my car, I'm going to go out on a limb and say he wasn't doing well at all.)

But the thing I feel the most guilty about is the one which makes the least amount of sense. It kills me that when Schuyler was a new-born baby and I was holding her, first in the Detroit hospital where she was born on a snowy afternoon a few days before Christmas, and countless times after, I looked into her eyes and I saw nothing, absolutely nothing at all that made me suspect there was something wrong. I know that's ridiculous and stupid and wrong, but it bothered me then and it still bothers me today.

I looked into those tiny eyes and her monster looked back out at me. And I didn't suspect a thing.

Schuyler was born four days before Christmas 1999, two weeks before she was due. This was a big deal to me, for some reason. On one hand, if Julie went into labor on New Year's Eve, we would be at the mercy of Y2K. It seems silly to think of it now, but at the time, no one knew what would happen. Would the power grid go down? Would there be unrest in the streets? Riots? Jesus? Zombies? No one knew. Add to that the fact that we were living in Detroit, a city that suffered regular outages already, thanks primarily to (and this is absolutely true) rodents chewing the wires. If squirrels could black out the city, bad computer programming sounded to me like Godzilla approaching the power station, hungry for juice. Having our baby while the apocalypse raged outside wasn't a terribly comforting scenario.

On the other hand, I liked the idea of Schuyler being a Millennium Baby, albeit only to people like myself who were careless with their math. I had secret dreams of her being born right at the stroke of midnight and being the First Baby of 2000, with all the free stuff and news crews with their cameras, assuming they weren't too busy filming the end of the world outside.

As it turned out, Schuyler decided not to wait, and so we jettisoned the middle name we'd halfheartedly chosen (so halfheartedly, I can't actually remember for sure what it was now) and settled on the seasonal Noelle instead. The details of the actual birth are a blur. I remember at one point, Schuyler sat on the umbilical cord in the womb and cut off her own oxygen, causing a few moments of panic before she fidgeted and moved off it again. At one point, the nurses couldn't find the heartbeat, but the scary moment soon passed, right into another, the scariest of all, really.

I remember watching her little scalp appear and seeing that, yes, she had the screw in her head. I remember that the whole business was a lot messier than I had anticipated, which was surprising because in my head, it was going to be pretty bad. But the reality? No one tells you how extremely . . . *extreme* the birth is going to be, and afterward, you don't talk about it because you've got a clean, happy little baby to play with, and besides, who wants to remind the love of their life that such a thing happened? But it did, and man oh man. I'm just saying.

Okay, moving on now.

There are a few things I remember from the first moments I saw Schuyler. I saw she had Julie's chin, and I saw she was blue. That changed soon enough, as she turned pink and then later, when she cried, tomato red. I saw she had hair, and a lot of it. She was never going to be one of those little bald babies, although my fears of having a little werewolf cub turned out to be unfounded, as she shed her fur a few months later. (She had hair on the tips of her ears. Schuyler is a beautiful little girl, and one day she'll be a lovely young woman, perhaps reading this in embarrassed horror. But I'm not kidding when I say she had hair on the tips of her ears when she was born.) I could see she had cheeks that I would find it very hard not to bite on a daily basis.

It was one thing to have a baby that was blue or red, but shortly before we left the hospital, we were suddenly facing another surprise on the color spectrum. Our child was turning yellow. The hospital said jaundice was fairly common in newborns, and we should bring her back the next day to have her bilirubin tested. I had no idea what that meant; "bilirubin" sounded like a baseball player's name to me. Not surprisingly, it's not (or at least no one playing in the majors); it's a pigment produced by the liver and is normally broken down automatically. Sometimes, however, little newborn babies have immature, slacker livers that aren't up to the job, and that's when they turn yellow and scare the crap out of everyone.

We returned to the hospital the next day with our yellow baby, only to discover that the lab had closed early for Christmas Eve. We ended up at the emergency room on Christmas morning having a lab tech (who clearly drew the short straw on the whole holiday shift thing) extract blood from our crying, miserable baby. This, after a conversation with a nosy old man in the waiting room who wanted to know if Julie was going to breastfeed the baby, and if not, why not? She took it in stride. ("I didn't say anything because he's going to be dead soon anyway," she said miserably when he left.) None of this was the way we wanted to spend the day, but we soldiered on and got out in time to go to Julie's parents' house for Schuyler's first Christmas. During the opening of the presents, we got a call from the hospital.

Schuyler's bilirubin levels were high. Dangerously high.

We gave our address to the lab tech on the phone, and by the time we got back to our apartment, a nurse was waiting for us with a strange electric blanket that emitted ultraviolet light in a cool crisscross pattern. The plan was to wrap Schuyler in the glowing Jedi blanket and let the light bring down her bilirubin levels. I thought it sounded suspect, but the alternatives were a return to the hospital and possibly a blood transfusion, so I was all for the glow treatment.

We spent Christmas evening 1999 watching our yellow baby sleep while wrapped in her strange glowing blanket. If you're thinking this perhaps isn't how we thought we'd be spending that night, either, why, you'd be absolutely correct.

Schuyler's bilirubin problem didn't go away immediately, but it slowly improved with the glowing blanket. We took her to see a doctor a few days later. Recommended by the hospital, he was a brusque Yugoslav whose comments on meeting Schuyler for the first time were "Is cute," and "Is boy?" and, most charmingly, "Is yellow like Chinese man!" He examined her and pronounced her in good health, and had nothing but sour words for the hospital for sending her home in the first place. I heard it's a fairly standard practice for the hospital to send home sick babies in order to keep costs down, but it seemed like a foolish policy in the long run. What did I know, though? I was just some guy with a yellow baby.

As Schuyler continued to improve and turn a more natural shade of baby color, we received gifts from people out in the world whom we had never even met and probably never would. Ever since we'd found out we were having a baby and I'd started writing about the whole experience, the number of people dropping by my Web site had increased dramatically. Apparently I had discovered my niche market: readers who either liked babies or wanted to see how badly I would screw one up.

Shortly before Schuyler was born, one of the people who had written me became more real when I went and read her Web site and discovered we had a very similar sense of humor. We became friends immediately. Her name was Dana, and she lived and worked in New Haven, Connecticut. To a hick from Odessa, New England sounded like a magical place accessible only by twisty roads winding through postcard-worthy trees, past picturesque farms with lazy cows (the black and white ones, of course) looking over a white wooden fence, and perhaps an apple cider stand parked out front. Some guy with a straw hat and a pipe would wave as you drove past, and Martha Stewart would greet you with a fruit basket when you arrived at your ultimate destination. If it seemed a million miles from the West Texas desert, it was at least half a million miles from scary, dirty Detroit. Dana suggested if we hated Michigan so much then we could certainly do much worse than Connecticut, and invited me to come stay with her and her husband for a few days while I looked for a job. Julie and I discussed it for maybe an hour before she made her decision. It wasn't a tough one; a few days before, a little girl had been shot to death in a Detroit elementary school by a fellow student. Both were six years old.

"Go out there," she said. "Get a job. I hate it here."

Which is why, six weeks before Schuyler's birth, I flew to New Haven and got a job working as a computer technician at a mental hospital, and why, six weeks *after* Schuyler's birth, we loaded up our furniture and our belongings and our furry-eared little baby and moved to New England. Just like that.

New Haven, Connecticut, is our setting. We landed in an apartment which had been carved out of a beautiful old house on Whitney Avenue (named for Eli Whitney, whose house, farm, and inventing barn are forever preserved right down the street, in case you have any cotton that needs, you know, ginning). It was a tiny place, and cold enough in the winter that Julie would sleep wearing her silliest winter hat, but it had a huge bay window and hardwood floors, and the neighborhood was charming in an old university sort of way. Whitney Avenue ran right through Yale's old campus, and the houses seemed to be split between Old Money (which in Connecticut is very old indeed) and graduate students. The house on Whitney was filled with the latter, and was blissfully quiet, especially on days when the earth was blanketed in snow. It was the silence of academic anxiety, perhaps, but with a new baby, we'd take it.

New Haven was a fascinating town. Yale University, my new employer, was preparing to celebrate its 300th anniversary, a mind-blowing number to me. Just walking around the campus, Julie and I encountered history at every turn. The famous dead resided in Grove Street Cemetery (with its giant carved stone archway stating THE DEAD SHALL BE RAISED, which I interpreted as a threat to unleash zombies on the town), and across the street were the famed secret societies, their buildings looming ominously (and windowless) behind iron gates.

Julie was mesmerized by the secret societies. "These places creep me out," she said one day as we pushed Schuyler's stroller past what I believed was the Cloisters. "I'll bet it's filled with a bunch of guys doing weird rituals, rolling around naked in chicken blood."

My job is probably worth describing, if only for the gawking factor. It was a pretty boring job on the surface. I provided computer support for the Abraham Ribicoff Research Facilities, which were housed at the Connecticut Mental Health Center on the Yale Med School campus. All the computers were Macs, so I didn't even have all that challenging of a support position. Essentially, I was showing some of the most advanced thinkers in the world of clinical neuroscience how to double-click a mouse. (Hint: you do it twice.) It was a cushy job that didn't pay very well but also didn't exactly overheat my brain. Best of all, I had a supervisor who not only had no interest in micromanaging me, but seemed to genuinely want to be left to his own devices as much as possible. Jim was a gregarious, generous man with whom I became good friends, but where work was concerned, he kept a low profile. I always got the sense Jim was up to something, but since he left me free to do my own thing, I had no problem with the arrangement.

The medical aspect of my work was likewise not of great interest, although it must be said, this was largely because every single bit of it went right over my head. One afternoon at a staff meeting, one of the doctors was discussing some of the medications being used in a particular study. (Don't try Googling these medications, by the way. I'm making them up.)

"So let's take a hypothetical pharmacy situation here," he said to the group. "Let's say we have a patient who's in the study, and I've got him taking Traxadone." (Made-up drug, remember.) "Now, at the end of the study period, we're going to want to change him over to . . ." He paused, waiting for someone to answer.

One of the nurses snickered and said, "Fraxadone?"

Immediately, the entire room erupted into laughter. I'm talking about guffaws, too. Full-blown belly laughs. Believe me when I say that every single person in the room got the joke and found it to be the height of hilarity. Everyone but me.

No, the interesting part of the job was the location. In order to get to my little office, I entered the building through a security checkpoint, took an elevator up to the third floor, and opened a big heavy door with a key. On the other side of this door was a secure mental ward. With patients wandering around, being, well, mental. I walked past the nurses station (where sadly, no one ever said "Medication time. . . ." while Montovani played softly in the background) and down the ward, past patient examination rooms and what looked like dorm rooms (if your college had safety glass and doors that locked from the outside in its dorms, which it very well might have had). From time to time, spoken bulletins came over the ceiling speakers that announced either a Code Three or a Code Four in progress, followed by a location. A Code Three meant all the medical personnel were expected to run to that location and help regain control of an upset patient; a Code Four meant screw that, we need cops. (The hospital had its own police officers.) I often worked on the computer used by the patients in their main congregating area; once, an upset patient threw it against a huge but unbreakable window, cutting his hand and bleeding all over it in the process. I fixed that thing, I am proud to report, and did so wearing surgical gloves.

If working on a secure ward in a mental hospital gave me a certain amount of *"oo, wow"* credit when sitting at a bar with strangers describing where we worked, it also taught me to look beyond the things that make us different so I could see the common core of humanity we all share. I don't want to make it sound like I was a nasty person before, but I think working at a job every day while surrounded by broken people changed me. Most of them suffered from addictions, and often I got the sense they were barely hanging on. I came to see them as people not so very unlike myself, and when they would occasionally wander into my office looking for their doctor, I simply pointed them in the right direction.

Some of the patients were funny, appreciating their situation enough to laugh about it. One day as I was leaving, a patient called out to me as I unlocked and opened the security door. "Hold the door!" he said. Then, with an impish smile, he said "Just kidding." Another time, I was treated to an impromptu piano recital in the main patient area by a genuinely talented musician whose mind seemed to float like a blimp broken free of its moorings, out of touch with the world around him but not unhappily so.

Most of the patients struggled, however, and as I worked among them, I began to lose my detachment and also that unspoken sense of something akin to superiority we all feel when we watch the unfortunate make their way through the same world in which we live. I watched a man who suffered from intermittent catatonia walk from one end of the ward to the other, maybe a hundred yards, each step the result of a force of will that must have simply said "Keep moving, whatever you do." I could see the wall at my end of the ward, and when he reached it and slapped it hard in wordless triumph, I found myself saying "Shit yeah!" softly to myself.

I was learning how these broken people faced their monsters, never dreaming that I had one to face in the coming years. Had I known, I might have paid closer attention.

Biology is a funny thing. Before Schuyler was born, I always took statements about how someone's baby had their mother's nose or their father's chin with a grain of salt. I understood the desire to see a piece of yourself in the face of your offspring, but honestly, when people said it, I always thought that in truth, babies look pretty much the same. As the conventional wisdom says, they all look like Winston Churchill.

But then biology comes into play, because when I looked at baby Schuyler, I could see Julie, clear as day. I could see her big, round, vaguely sleepy eyes and her pinchable, chewable cheeks. Most of all, I could see Julie's smile. The more I think about it, though, the less convinced I become that biology allows us to recognize these traits in our babies. When Julie looked at Schuyler, she saw me. I never have been able to see that, and perhaps it's just as well. Walking around with my mug is not something I'd wish on any little girl in the world. It's tough enough, making this face work for me.

Schuyler had a rough first few months on this earth. Born early and tiny, she turned yellow with jaundice and then rough with eczema during her first few weeks. She was a little on the fuzzy side, although I was relieved to see her thick dark hair quickly transforming into a sort of dirty blond, and not on the tips of her ears, either. But the space age light blanket solved her bilirubin problem in short order, and her eczema cleared up as soon as we moved to New Haven and its salty sea air. By the time we settled into a routine in Connecticut, Schuyler had found her little baby groove, or so it would seem.

The thing about babies that seems like a no-brainer until you have one is this: they cry. It's the only way they have to let you know what their needs are, and they don't mess around with subtlety. They cry when they are hungry, they cry when they are sleepy, they cry when they are sitting in a load. They need something? They cry. *Easy enough,* I thought. I wasn't Superdad, but crying I could deal with. Just run down the list, try everything until something works.

The thing no one tells you as a new parent is that sometimes babies cry just because they are pissed off. It's hard to know why. Maybe they are outraged at being short. I know that would get to me after a while. For the first few months in New Haven, I worked during the day and Julie worked in the evenings, and during those evenings, for whatever the reason, Schuyler cried. It was hard not to take it personally. I know how silly that is, but there were so many evenings when there was nothing in the world wrong, nothing she needed, and yet Schuyler cried as if there were scorpions in her diaper. Her wails sounded like accusations, as if she were telling me she could see right through my façade and knew, with infant clarity, that I was a sham of a father.

And yet, sometimes it wasn't so. Most nights we played a variation on the game "I Cry Unless You Are Holding Me the Whole Time, and Maybe Even Then," the rules to which I was unsuccessfully trying to renegotiate, but there were moments.

One night, as we sat across from each other, Schuyler began producing that sound, the one indicating that soon, so very soon, the crying will begin. I sighed and looked at her helplessly.

"Good lord, Schuyler, please. Please don't cry? Please? I'll give you anything you want, I'll give you money if you won't cry. Please?"

As I said "please," I raised my eyebrows. She stopped her little pre-wail gurgle and looked back at me, suddenly wide-eyed. And then she raised her eyebrows.

I lowered mine and she did the same. I raised my eyebrows again and she followed. I opened my mouth in mock surprise, and her lips made a little "O." I blew a raspberry, and she tried to do the same. This cracked me up, and when I laughed, she laughed with me.

At three months of age, she was imitating me. It was the very beginning of something, a sort of acceptance from her, a grudging acknowledgment that I wasn't going away and that every so often, I might be sort of amusing. When I read to her, she would sit silently, blinking her sleepy little Julie-eyes, struggling to keep them open as she watched my mouth with interest. Schuyler loved to hear us read, and we loved to read to her. At such an early age, she was missing the good stuff, of course. One night, Julie was reading a story that mentioned birch trees.

"When I was a little girl, I used to get in trouble for picking the bark off our neighbor's birch tree," she said thoughtfully to Schuyler. "It's like I didn't think anyone would notice."

"You're telling her stories about your juvenile delinquency," I said. "That's so cool."

"You do the same thing when you read *Curious George*," Julie said.

"Yeah, I know. Well, he smokes and sniffs ether. That's the appeal of Curious George. I *get* him."

Julie turned back to her book. "You're both bad little monkeys," she muttered.

As the months passed, things got better. Dana would come over and take us to the mall or out to dinner, and I realized something about Schuyler that was key to her happiness, then and now. She became bored with routine. When we were out and about, she was absorbing the big movie that was the world around her. And since I was usually her guide and companion on these outings, being an easily bored person myself, I became her go-to guy for exploration. It was a pattern that established itself and endured. Schuyler had very different expectations for Julie and me, and we learned to play to our strengths. Julie was home, security, familiar surroundings, and comfort. I was exploration, new sights and sounds, someone to "oo" and "ah" with. I suppose most families are like that at the beginning.

As Schuyler grew older, my relationship with her changed. By the time she was six months old, whatever it was she had once found so cry-worthy about me was gone, and all my frustrations with her seemed to evaporate. I didn't notice it until one afternoon in September, when we spent a day together just hanging out on the lawn of the house on Whitney Avenue. Dana had enrolled in an AIDS charity bicycle marathon from Boston to New York, and by some crazy coincidence, the path through New Haven took the riders right down Whitney. We camped out on a blanket, enjoying the afternoon sun, waving to the cyclers as they rode past and waiting for Dana. Julie came out and stayed with us for part of the time, and it was, I think, one of the happiest days I've ever spent, although nothing earthmoving took place. What happened was quite simply this: Schuyler looked up into my eyes that day and, for reasons known only to her, decided she loved me, and not just a little, and not conditionally, but totally and with all her little heart. It's funny to think back on it and how it seemed to ignite all at once, but she fell in love with me that day, and I with her. A day hasn't passed since then where we didn't still feel it. Corny and clichéd, I know. But absolutely true.

It was our summer of love, Schuyler and me. She and Julie had a very close relationship all along, one based on warmth and security and "gimme some food." My bond with Schuyler was more complicated, and seemed to revolve around exploring her world and figuring out how things work. She watched the world slip by with intense scrutiny, and I endeavored to put as much of that world as possible in front of her eyes. Yet the closer I became with Schuyler, the more anxiety I felt about her and the world around her, a world which clearly wanted to gobble her up and spit out the bones. It seems strange to think back on it now, about the odd fears I had for her, especially since they were completely random and not based on anything tangible other than the fact that clearly, I had Issues.

Here's a good example. You know how most shopping malls have two levels, with a huge open area looking down onto the first floor? I was terrified of bringing Schuyler to that second floor. If we did, I'd keep her away from the edge, because I was convinced that a lunatic was going to run over, grab her from the stroller, and throw her over the railing. I never heard of such a thing happening, much less seen it myself. I didn't even have some urban legend to scare me. Just that thing inside my head which searches for the worst case scenarios and then tries to avoid them before they happen. Even now, I'm not entirely convinced my vigilance didn't prevent a Schuyler-tossing tragedy at some point.

Walking down the sidewalk? A car was going to hop the curb and run her over. Playing in the park? Don't get too far from her (as in, two feet or more), lest a big dog should run up, snatch her in its slobbery jaws, and run away with her forever.

If I took on an unusual amount of anxiety on Schuyler's behalf, she seemed to balance it out with her unblinking appreciation for chaos. Once in a Laundromat, two women began screaming at each other, threatening violence and generally making a scene. When they finally reached a point in the fight where they'd expended their anger and were now just glaring menacingly, the room fell into near absolute silence. Schuyler's little baby chuckle was the only thing to be heard.

When you have a child, you quickly experience the frustration of having your expectations and preconceived notions of How Things Shall Be blown out of the water, often with astonishing speed and usually a small measure of brutality. In my case, my longest standing heartbreak as a parent has revolved around the sad tale of Jasper.

His story began during Julie's pregnancy. When she suggested Jasper as a possible name for our unborn child if it turned out to be a boy, I realized it wasn't an important point to cover, since I knew we were having a girl, a fact that frankly brought me relief. Secretly, I'd wanted a girl. I remembered the kind of little boy I had been, and my brother as well, and I had no desire to have a destructive little me clone living in my home. The joke was on me, of course, since I was ultimately blessed with a daughter who was pretty like her mother but also a little troublemaker like me.

For five months I kept the baby's sex a secret from Julie, in part by mixing up my "he" and "she" rather than trying to just say "it" all the time. With "it," you screw up once and it's over. I have to say, I did a pretty good job of it, but it became trickier when we discussed names.

As I said before, we'd chosen "Schuyler" pretty early on, thanks to a waitress in Kalamazoo. But a boy's name was problematic, particularly since Julie had an early favorite that she was simply unwilling to give up.

Jasper.

You thought "Schuyler" was bad.

It could have been worse, I suppose. She could have chosen Corky or Quasimodo, and besides, I didn't really have to fight Jasper too hard since I knew the argument was purely academic at this point. But I couldn't just say "Oh, yeah, Jasper's *great!*"

For one thing, she'd see right through it. More important, I had a nightmare vision of the sonogram tech being wrong and being handed a slimy little boy in the delivery room, smiling sadly as Julie whispered, "Oh, Jasper!"

The Jasper conversation came up as we were fantasy shopping in a baby clothes store, and as we talked, I found myself looking at a funny little serious-faced teddy bear on the shelf. He was one of about a dozen bears, all of them slightly different, and I liked him immediately.

"Okay," I said to Julie. "I'll tell you what. I'm going to get this guy and put him in my car. He can ride around in the car seat and I'll call him 'Jasper' and see if it grows on me."

"You're going to ride around talking to a teddy bear?" she asked, bemused.

"Oh, sure," I said. "It'll be good practice for watching my language, too."

I'm not sure it had that effect, exactly (*"Did you see that dickhead cut me off, Jasper?"*), but I did become very fond of Jasper the Lumpy Headed Bear as he rode around in the backseat of my Volkswagen. I legitimately enjoyed his company, which is probably a fairly good indication as to my mental state during the pregnancy. I never did learn to accept the name "Jasper" as a possibility for an actual human child of mine (and really, would you?), but for a bear? Perfect name. Most of all, I loved the idea that one day, and soon, Jasper would find a place in my unborn daughter's heart.

Then came the heartbreak.

Schuyler was born, and when she grew old enough to deal with toys, she was introduced to her new bestest little friend in the world, the bear who had been patiently awaiting her arrival with all the tenderness and anticipation an overpriced inanimate object could muster.

Schuyler hated Jasper.

To be fair, it wasn't just Jasper. Schuyler hated stuffed animals, every last one of them. I'd been buying them for her since before she was born, with absolute certainty that she'd fall instantly in love with every one of them. I was relentless in my presentation of them to her. She was relentless in hating them. The cool, friendly lion I'd bought for her in Kalamazoo, when she was barely the size of a Tootsie Roll? Thrown to the floor. The funky giraffe and matching dragon (because really, what goes together like giraffes and dragons?) I'd found at the snotty little toy store down the street in New Haven? Not even a second glance. Even Cookie Monster only got token attention, and then only as long as it took her to realize he wasn't going to crumble snacks into his gaping maw. After that, nothing waited but abuse for poor Cookie Monster. And we actually have a video of Schuyler opening a box on Christmas morning, seeing the doll we'd bought for her at one of the Manhattan museum stores, and then coldly shoving it back in the box.

As for Jasper, he was rudely tossed aside; Schuyler refused to look at him. I can't begin to tell you how many times I tried to make their relationship work. I couldn't help myself. I suppose that in my mind, her rejection of Jasper was tantamount to turning her back on a brother. Or perhaps even me, really. As time went on, many of

Schuyler's stuffed animals were put away, but I refused to give up completely and always left a few of them out for her.

Including Jasper. Particularly Jasper.

My wait for redemption in Schuyler's eyes had taken a few months. Jasper's would last far longer.

I could say so much about that next year, from summer 2000 until July of the following year. The easiest way to describe that year would be to simply say it was a lovely year in ways that feel very improbable and far away to me now. We were living and working in a new town, one for which we all actually had positive thoughts. Schuyler continued to grow and absorb and face every new moment with wide-eyed wonder followed shortly by a look of "Now what?" I was usually standing there with the same expression, but it was a joyful kind of chaos, which might just be the very best way I can describe life with Schuyler, then and now. During that year, everyone was happy and healthy, and the future stretched out before us with nothing but promise.

When our world changed and Schuyler's monster began to make itself known to us, it wasn't sudden and dramatic. It is only in retrospect that I can identify the moment at all, and it arrived dressed in a simple question from Schuyler's pediatrician.

4

Disquiet

One of the first things we had to do when we arrived in New Haven was, to choose a pediatrician for Schuyler. Aside from the Yugoslav doctor in Detroit who had examined her shortly after her birth and a grumpy but straight-talking old doctor who saw her a few times, this would be her first regular pediatrician, and all we had to go on was a list provided to me by Yale. The doctors were all Yale associates, so it was safe to assume none of them got their degrees by way of correspondence courses or shady medical schools on unheard-of Caribbean islands. *("Fortunately I graduated before the junta!")* We had no other information to go on than their names, but when I saw the name "Simone Simon," I was instantly charmed and made what was probably one of my better decisions based on the most arbitrary criteria imaginable. It wasn't because she had the same name as a famous old movie star, either. I was totally unaware of that connection at the time. No, her name just made me giggle.

Dr. Simon was a sweet and sympathetic doctor who loved Schuyler the instant she met her. She was young and unpretentious, which frankly made her unlike any other doctor I'd met at Yale. One thing we liked about her almost immediately, besides her cool, vaguely British accent (from some vestige of empire, perhaps South

Africa), was the fact that she herself was a mother of very young children. Her advice tended to be less academic and more from the trenches, even sharing with us her secret loves and hates in children's television. Most of all, she was funny.

"You know, when I was younger, I had always intended to be very modern and progressive and hyphenate my last name," she said one day when we somehow got on the topic of how we came to be Rummel-Hudsons. "But my maiden name was Simon, and the man I married was also a Simon. So I would have been. . . ." She paused and smiled as she let us fill in the blank.

"Simone Simon-Simon?" I finally said. She laughed and gave a little clap. I could tell it was one of her life's most cherished ironies.

We were seeing Dr. Simon every six months or so, and every time we visited, Schuyler got a good report. She was small, in the 20th percentile for her age (which if you're not in on the parenting lingo, means that 80 percent of the one-year-olds out in the world were bigger than her, making her small but not freakishly so), and she was missing a few of her developmental milestones, but they weren't troubling things. Indeed, Schuyler never crawled, but one evening we watched as she rolled over to the futon, pulled herself up to a standing position (which she'd mastered only very recently) and without fanfare, she took one step, and then another. She fell over a few times until she got the hang of it, and then that was it. She was walking. After that, she was hoofing it everywhere.

In July 2001, when she was eighteen months old, we took Schuyler to Dr. Simon's office at Yale for her routine checkup. Schuyler was changing, no longer a plump, furry little baby but slowly transforming into a little girl. Her hair had become a strawberry blond and no longer curled thick on her head, but fell in lazy waves across her face. Whatever dark moods had plagued her during her first six months had moved on, and now Schuyler rarely cried, but had a ready smile and an outgoing, flirtatious attitude. Now that she'd discovered walking, Schuyler rarely stood still.

Dr. Simon was in her usual good mood (I'd call her "cheeky" if that didn't make me feel like an Austin Powers–wannabe poser), and she played with Schuyler as she went through her procedures. Dr. Simon figured out early on that Schuyler would be as cooperative as you wanted her to be, so long as you negotiated with her a little. Want to stick that cold thing on her chest? Let her listen through it before you try to touch her with it. Poke a light in her ear? Better shine it in her face first.

At this particular visit, however, I became aware of a change in Dr. Simon's manner. She was still smiling and talking sweetly to Schuyler, but she was asking her a lot of questions, too.

"Where's Mommy?" she asked, and Schuyler pointed happily at Julie. "Where's Daddy?" She got that one right, too, I'm happy to report.

"Schuyler, can you tell me who this is?" she asked, pointing first to Julie and then to me. Schuyler just pointed again and laughed. Well, of course, we thought. How could she ask an eighteen-month-old a question and expect an answer?

We'd never had a kid, and never been around babies much. So we had no idea what we were supposed to be expecting by this age. Dr. Simon wrote a small novella in Schuyler's file, then gave her a book to thumb through on the floor while she talked to us.

"So tell me, Mum and Dad," she said; that's how she always addressed us. "Does Schuyler have any words? Is she saying anything?"

"Um, no, not really," I said. "Should she be?"

"Does she ever babble? Like she's trying to put sounds together into words?"

"No, she doesn't," Julie said, her voice lowering ever so slightly. I could see the warning lights on the dashboard of her mind starting to blink. "She sometimes says things like 'aaaah-oooo,' all vowels."

"Does she ever produce consonants?"

"She makes *m*'s sometimes, but she doesn't really seem to be saying anything."

"Does she ever try to imitate your speech?"

"Not verbally, no," I said. "Just gestures."

Dr. Simon looked down from her notes to watch Schuyler for a moment, and then back up to us.

"Mum and Dad, has she shown any progress toward speech at all?"

I glanced at Julie and then down at Schuyler, and then looked hard at Dr. Simon and said a very, very difficult thing. I've said harder things since then, but this was the first, and it's one that stayed with me.

"No," I said. "No, she hasn't."

The next week, we were back. Dr. Simon said Schuyler's speech delay wasn't the part that concerned her, as a lot of kids are late talkers and turn out to be just fine. When I mentioned it on my blog, I got a number of responses, all along the lines of "my Uncle Karl didn't talk until he was twelve, and now he fixes tractors and eats with a fork without help from anyone!" or, "they say Einstein didn't speak his first word until the age of thirty," or my personal favorite, "the reason she's not speaking is because she's trying to tell you not to put her in day care!"

No, the thing that worried Dr. Simon was that Schuyler wasn't trying to put any sounds together at all. Most kids apparently try at an early age, and even if they end up sounding like those little Jawas from *Star Wars* until they are five, it's the effort that doctors look for. The fact that Schuyler's speech consisted of almost nothing but vowels and the occasional (but never appropriately placed) soft consonant was troubling to Dr. Simon. She scheduled the first hearing test for the following week.

Consider for a moment how serious this was for us. For a week, we'd been worrying about Schuyler's speech—or the lack of speech. Was our daughter deaf? Was that the world we were entering? For a week, I'd been imagining a world of sign language and big plastic hearing aids and sad faces, and it frightened me. This wasn't a time for silliness.

Not until we saw the cymbal-playing rabbit and the bear with a drum.

The tech smiled when we arrived and laughed with Schuyler, who was on her best behavior. She led us into a soundproof room and explained how the test would work. We sat in front of a blank wall, on which were mounted two small speakers. On top of the left speaker was a toy rabbit with a pair of cymbals. (Yale is apparently too cutting edge to settle for the more traditional cymbal-smashing chimp. I mean, come on. A monkey? Get serious.) On the other, a bear with a snare drum.

The tech told us she would be in the booth, watching Schuyler. She would play a series of tones from each speaker, starting loud and gradually decreasing in volume. When Schuyler reacted to the tone and looked at the speaker, the toy would do its thing. The whole thing was obviously geared toward amusing the under-two crowd, but I have to admit, the first time the rabbit started jumping around, I think I snickered, too.

It wasn't a definitive test, she explained. All it could do for certain was prove that a subject was *not* deaf. If she looked every time, it meant she could definitely hear. But failure to look could mean anything, or nothing. It could mean the cymbal rabbit and the drum bear didn't intrigue her. Boredom could and often did defeat the test more often than deafness. It was simply a place to start testing.

The test began strongly enough. The tone would sound, Schuyler would look up at the speaker, the critter would do its dance, and Schuyler and I would both laugh. Julie was still too nervous about the outcome to join us in our amusement, but then, she was legitimately afraid that Schuyler might have a problem.

I felt as if I knew better. Somehow, I'd managed to convince myself that she was okay.

But as the tones decreased in volume, Schuyler's reactions

diminished as well. She eventually stopped looking altogether. I glanced out at the tech, who wasn't smiling anymore.

Schuyler failed the test.

When we got in the car, I looked back at Schuyler in her child seat, torturing her Cookie Monster by flopping him around by his arms. She wasn't deaf, that much was clear. She reacted to voices. I said her name and she looked up at me briefly, flashing me a quick smile before returning to her interrogation of her Muppet prisoner.

Could she be hard of hearing? Could the reason she never tried to approximate our speech be as simple as never hearing us clearly? It was entirely possible, I had to grant that. Schuyler was, at eighteen months, no longer a baby, really. Her face was beginning to lose its roundness, although she would have those cheeks for life, and she was addicted to walking now, shunning her stroller most of the time. At day care, she had been promoted to the next level. An infant? Pah. Schuyler was now a Waddler, by golly, with all the responsibilities and privileges that came with her new station.

It was easy to see the little girl she was turning into, but at the same time, she remained inscrutable. She made sounds, but they were incomprehensible, just long vowels with no consonants, like a baby wolf tentatively learning to howl. Were they random noises, or were they her closest approximation of the low roar resounding inside her deaf ears? It was impossible to know for sure.

Dr. Simon authorized the next round of tests, and we were left to worry.

As we waited for the second round of tests, our lives moved on. It's funny to think back on a stressful time when in your memory, all you did was fret, only to go back and read a journal or a diary (or in my case, a blog) and see that you were in fact also living your life at the time.

We decided to move out of the house on Whitney. It had always been too small, but when Schuyler was a little baby in a crib, it was worth the hipness of the place. We slept in the bedroom, which had these huge stylish glass doors through which we could see the whole apartment, and Schuyler slept in her crib in the living room. Now that she was mobile, however, the place was ridiculously small.

We found a house in downtown New Haven that suited us grandly, albeit in polar opposite ways from Whitney Ave. The new house was on Howe Street, which I found out later had been the main thorough-fare for prostitutes in New Haven, working the gray area between horny, moneyed college students and home sweet home crack houses. The area had been cleaned up and was now delightful, but you could still feel the history in the air, particularly late at night when errant Yale students wandered aimlessly about, searching for what passes among Yalies as trouble. The hookers seemed to be missed.

The house on Howe had been built in 1855, which to me, being from Texas, seemed impossibly old. I liked to imagine the original in-habitants sitting in my living room, trying to decide whether or not they should vote for Abraham Lincoln. I hoped it was full of ghosts. It was the only house on the block, nestled among a pizza parlor (with authentic grouchy old Italian men who vaguely resembled the two old guys in the balcony on *The Muppet Show*), a pottery studio, and a slightly seedy falafel shop that was open an hour later than the bars and thus attracted drunken Yalies almost every night until three A.M. The proprietors were constantly fighting or screaming at someone; once, Schuyler and I walked up to the house just in time to watch someone get Taser'd by the police. Schuyler was thrilled, of course. She actually clapped her little hands in delight.

A woman who was housed in the mental health halfway house up the block had once lived in our place and was still convinced it was hers. She'd wander up to the door periodically and try her key, and then slowly shuffle away. When confronted, she would nervous-ly mutter that she needed to get her mail, and then later, that we had stolen her house. Her husband had purchased it, she said, which would have been a more compelling argument had she in fact ever been married.

Schuyler was thrilled about the new location, naturally. So was I. Julie simply said, "This place is going to make great blogging material for you."

The owner of the house on Howe was a carefree gentleman who seemed very much like an ex-hippie except for the fact that he lived in Westchester County, New York. That would make him a pretty fancy hippie. He was carefree and laid-back, aside from being somewhat baffled by the building he was struggling to maintain. We called him "the Dude." Our first real exchange after we gave him the deposit set the tone for the rest of our time under his roof.

"So, um, can you just write up a lease and bring it back with you?" he said. "We can sign everything then and be all set."

I wasn't sure I heard him right. "Wait," I said. "You want us to write our own lease?"

"Well, yeah," he said. "I don't really know much about that sort of thing."

"Oh, okay," I said. "Neither do I, really."

He thought for a moment and then suggested we simply take our current lease and use it as a model. "You could even copy it and, I don't know, just white out the names or whatever." Since our current lease was written mostly in either dense legalese or actual Martian, we opted for something simple. I knew I was going to like living in the House of the Dude.

When we first moved in, the Dude told us that the upstairs half of the house was going to be rented out to a Chinese student named Poo, but as it turned out, Poo was unable to leave China for the semester, so our place remained sadly Poo-free. Given my adolescent sense of humor, it probably worked out for the best.

The date for Schuyler's next hearing test was fast approaching. Julie was bringing home books from work with titles like *The Einstein*

Syndrome: Bright Children Who Talk Late, which was probably irrelevant but something of a comfort to us. Bringing home *Wow, Your Kid Is Really Screwed Up* wasn't going to do anyone any good.

That September, only a few months after we first began worrying about Schuyler's lack of speech, she was administered a second hearing test. This test was more comprehensive. It consisted of measuring the physical reaction of her body itself to sound stimuli. Tiny sensors were placed in Schuyler's ears as she slept, and as tones were played, the sensors measured her ears' physical reactions.

It didn't take long for the results. Only a few days after the test, we discovered that Schuyler had passed with flying colors. Not only could she hear, but apparently, according to this test, her body's physical reaction to sound was even better than average. We both knew she wasn't deaf, but there's a difference between knowing with your heart and seeing it on a fancy report printed on Yale Med School letterhead.

It was good news, but it opened up a whole world of questions. We'd begun, during that summer, to begin to deal with the idea that Schuyler might be hearing impaired and could be entering a community of people with similar problems. It was a hard thought, but it was also somewhat comforting, knowing there would be people waiting for her if she ever did become a part of that world.

With the test results, suddenly we were back to having no idea what was wrong.

The doctor who administered the hearing test was unconcerned when we spoke on the phone. "Sometimes kids just don't have anything to say yet," she said. I wanted to believe that was true. But I had a nagging suspicion there was more at work.

A few months before, Dana watched Schuyler for us for an afternoon and took her over to see her family. Schuyler made friends and charmed everyone the way she always did, and a good time was generally had by everyone. But as they were getting ready to leave,

Dana's mother quietly told Dana, "I think there's something wrong with her."

When Dana told me about that, I reacted with irritation. "Thanks," I said. "That's real goddamn helpful." But my anger wasn't with Dana, who was one of the very few friends I've had during my lifetime whom I could always trust to be absolutely straight up with me.

I wasn't angry because I thought she was wrong. I was angry because on some level, I was afraid she might be correct. I had looked at Schuyler a number of times over the past few weeks, and in those brief moments of absolute clarity, before all my defensive mechanisms kicked in, I had thought to myself, *Something's not right.*

I had my first dream about Schuyler talking that fall. Shy of her second birthday, Schuyler appeared in the first of what would become recurring dreams of her talking. Her personality was becoming so strong and so outgoing and just so unfailingly positive that it was becoming harder and harder to reconcile that little person with her total lack of vocabulary. In my dreams, and strangely in the dreams of many people (friends and strangers alike), Schuyler spoke. She speaks in my dreams to this very day, and I have no doubt she'll do so for the rest of my life.

In this particular dream, she and I were sitting together eating lunch, when she suddenly looked up at me and simply said, "Rabbit." That's it, just the one word. I have no idea where that came from, but for the next few weeks, when I would talk to her and sound out words for her to attempt, I said "rabbit" a lot. I'm not sure I believe in the prophetic properties of dreams, but I wasn't going to rule anything out.

Nothing happened, of course. Schuyler watched my lips, and sometimes she tried to sound something out. I could hear she was getting the vowels right, but that was all. She was scheduled to begin seeing a speech pathologist within the next few months, which was as quickly as she could begin receiving services. Dr. Simon had also put her on a waiting list to be evaluated by the Yale Child Study Center, but we were warned that the list to get in was long. Schuyler probably wouldn't get an appointment for at least a year, probably two. In the meantime, we'd all continue working with her and trying to break through whatever walls were keeping her words from coming.

As our concern for Schuyler continued to grow, a funny thing was happening to me, the selfish guy who could always be counted on to take care of himself, if no other way than by walking away from insurmountable problems. The more worrisome Schuyler's situation became, the more deeply I fell in love with her.

That sounds like a sweet, Good Father thing to say, but it wasn't that simple. In the almost two years since she was born, and particularly in the past few months as a sort of dark cloud had appeared on her horizon, my emotional state had changed from primarily one of hope to mostly one of fear. That fear had once been a shapeless, vague thing. If I read about little children meeting some horrible tragic fate somewhere in the world, in the little movie in my head, there was Schuyler in the starring role. But now, that worry had a form. Something was keeping my little girl from talking, and I was helpless to change it or even figure out what it was. Julie and I didn't know it yet, but we were looking the monster squarely in the eyes. We hadn't yet been properly introduced.

Within that worry, I existed in a state of love unlike anything I'd ever experienced in my life. When Schuyler was with me, I couldn't look away from her. I would watch her as she slept, her tiny hands twitching and fidgeting, working their mysterious spells. This love was daunting to me. It was the rest of my life, this love. I would never have the option of choosing whether or not this was a relationship that worked for me. I was Schuyler's prisoner now, and it was in that captivity that I had achieved my life's joy.

5

The Saddest Place in the World

In October 2000, we received a visit from a friend I had made on-line through my journal, a writer from Ireland named Caoimhe. (That's pronounced *KWEE-vah*, by the way. Well, of course! How else would you say it?) She was visiting the States to attend a conference for online writers, along with Dana and myself and a number of my favorite writers and friends. While she was in New Haven, she wanted to visit New York City and see another friend of ours, a popular on-line writer and personality named Nina, who was unable to attend the conference. I piled into the car with Julie, Caoimhe, and little ten-month-old Schuyler and drove down to meet Nina at the grandest, coolest, most *New York* location we could think of, one which would require no directions other than what we were told by our eyes and which would be certain to impress everyone.

So it was there that Schuyler and I found ourselves on a chilly October afternoon, looking up at the biggest thing in the biggest city either of us had ever experienced. As impressive as the World Trade Center could be from any direction as you approached it, it wasn't until you stood at the base of the towers looking up that you could truly appreciate the enormity and seeming impossibility of their existence. I had seen them before, during a conference and performance with my college trombone ensemble five years before, but it was still hard to be jaded. For Schuyler, not even a year old and still tooling around in her stroller, it was well and truly blowing her tiny little mind.

We found ourselves alone in the plaza. Nina hadn't shown yet, and Julie had taken Caoimhe inside on a quest for coffee. Schuyler and I played around the fountain under the giant spherical sculpture and chased birds around with her stroller, to the annoyance of cool Manhattanites and faux-cool tourists around us. We had a hot dog and played and danced, and it was on this evening that I heard for the very first time the braying, hysterical laugh that Schuyler still hasn't lost. I've heard that laugh a thousand times, but on that night, between the towers as we played and ran and lived antlike in their looming magnificence, we heard it for the first time. That's one of two things I remember vividly about that night.

While we waited for Julie, I pushed Schuyler's stroller up to the long, graceful columns of the North Tower until the bumper touched the wall. I reached down and removed her tiny gloves so she could reach out and touch the surface with her bare hands. She stared up at the long, sleek metal pillars as they fanned out into long vertical lines that blurred together long before reaching their end at the top. The tower seemed to sway gently beside its twin in the sky, an optical illusion created by the clouds moving overhead. We then ran across the plaza, scattering pigeons as we went, until we arrived breathless at the South Tower. As I bent to catch my breath, Schuyler leaned forward to touch the cool, smooth surface, her eyes again straining overhead.

That is the other moment of that day I'll remember. Schuyler's hands, impossibly small and delicate, touching the towers, so improbably big and forever.

Julie was working at a bookstore in Waterbury, Connecticut, when the first plane hit. She was scheduled to lead a tour group of elementary school kids through the store, and by the time their bus rolled up, she was waiting for them, pulling the teachers aside quietly to inform them that something horrible was going on in the city, but no one seemed to know exactly what it was just yet. The tour was given and the kids departed, and for the rest of the day, Julie and her co-workers caught scraps of news from customers and from a radio in the back receiving area of the store. It wasn't until she and her friends walked to Chili's after work that they finally saw the images for the first time. They drank beers and shook their heads as they viewed the explosions and the collapsing floors and the clouds of rolling dust, over and over again, with no context and out of sequence. Julie sat silently, watching a carnival of unimaginable imagery playing out on a soundless television in the noisy bar of an unremarkable chain restaurant, a banal American Everyplace intruded upon by Apocalypse.

That morning, I was sitting in a AAA office in New Haven, renewing my car insurance, when one of the agents announced to the office that his wife had just called him and told him a small airplane had just flown into the side of one of the World Trade Center towers. As my agent put together my policy, the others joked about what kind of dumbass pilot doesn't notice the twin towers in front of him. A few minutes later, the same agent announced that his wife heard on television that it wasn't a small plane after all, but an airliner. Shortly after, his cell phone chirped again. By now we were listening to him for more news, and so we all heard him say loudly, "Holy fuck."

United Flight 175 had crashed into the second tower.

By the time I had arrived at my office on the mental ward, mayhem had landed with both feet. I turned the key and stepped onto a ward buzzing with activity. Yale-New Haven Hospital was close enough to New York to see a large number of the thousands of injured people expected to head our way after the New York hospitals were inundated. Beds were being wheeled into empty rooms. Voluntary patients were being discharged, standing at the nurses' station with their belongings in hand, waiting to be sent out into a world that was suddenly scaring the shit out of each and every one of them. And us.

I went to my office and tried to get to the CNN Web site, but nothing was working. The servers were swamped. The only thing I could get to was a discussion board I sometimes frequented, so I reloaded it over and over, watching as people posted what they knew, and what they didn't know. It was a crazy stream of panic, a swirling mix of unbelievable rumor and inconceivable fact. One plane, two planes, maybe more. An explosion at the Pentagon caused by perhaps a helicopter, a crash on a Washington, D.C. freeway, a fire at the White House, an explosion at the Supreme Court building. *NBC Nightly News* reporting a car bomb outside the State Department. Some group called the Democratic Front of Palestinian Liberation had claimed responsibility. All air traffic was shut down. A third explosion at the World Trade Center, causing the top of one of the towers to collapse down to the thirtieth floor. No, the whole tower. Gone. One person wrote from overseas, "The republic is falling."

I didn't read that last part until later. I had left my office and walked down to the patient area for a moment to take it all in. As I stood there, a low moan rose from the patients and staff gathered around a television. I rushed over in time to see the south tower folding into the roiling cloud of dust. When the north tower collapsed twenty minutes later, the sight was greeted with silence. We were already adjusting to a world in which such things happened.

The nurse standing beside me shook her head. "We're not going to have any patients from this," she said. "Not a goddamned one." By the end of the day, the voluntary patients would begin returning and the extra beds would go back into storage.

When I picked up Schuyler at her day care, she was surprised by the long, suffocating hug I gave her. When we got home, we all watched television in silence. She was quickly bored by the solemn talking heads and played quietly in her room.

Julie and I stayed up late that night, listening to Peter Jennings on an *ABC News* radio feed. I couldn't stop thinking about all the people who didn't come home to their families, the ones who weren't lying awake in bed right now. Citizens of the world and children of God, they were out there in that horrific place. They didn't hug their kids that night. They lay in rubble or in the remnants of an airplane fuselage. No one knew how many. No one knew much of anything, we were bereft of information but floating in our fear and our anger.

"I'm scared," Julie finally said with a crack in her voice. "How the hell does something like this happen here?" Then again, more quietly, "I'm so scared."

Julie finally fell into an uneasy sleep. I got up and crept into Schuyler's room to kiss her slumbering head good night. I paused for a moment and then scooped her up and brought her back to bed with me.

I kept telling myself, "That's it, I don't want to hear any more about this," only to turn on the radio and listen to the endless analysis that had been playing nonstop for a week after the attack. We couldn't turn away. Our need to understand what had happened outweighed our desire for our hearts to stop breaking and rebreaking every time we heard more stories. We watched the news on television almost full-time now. Unavoidably, Schuyler watched the images as well, but without understanding. She saw an exploding airplane and was simply dazzled by the fireball, reacting with her curious half smile and a reaching hand. She touched the screen as it lit up, and I resisted the urge to pull her hand away as if there were a poisonous snake before her. I figured she had time enough to be afraid later. She had the rest of her life to live in this broken world.

On our way home from running errands, I found myself asking, "Do you want to go see it?"

"Yeah, I do," said Julie quietly. "I need to see this." Without a further word, I turned onto the Merritt Parkway and headed to New York. It had been ten days since the attack.

Entering the city was easy, much easier than I thought it would be. It wasn't until we were traveling down the Westside Highway that we started to notice a change. Passing the aircraft carrier *Intrepid* museum, we saw throngs of people congregating along three long walls running down the sidewalk. Paper covered the walls; there were hundreds of missing persons posters, for blocks. Julie didn't start to cry until we saw them. Police were everywhere, along with emergency and military vehicles. Fat military helicopters patrolled the skies.

The farther we headed south, the harder it became to ignore the hole in the sky.

When we reached Canal Street and could go no farther by car, we parked on a side street, pausing to change Schuyler's diaper. As we were sitting there, a pair of fire trucks raced up and stopped right beside us. Giant flags hung from their ladders. Firemen stepped out in their full gear, and suddenly we felt as if we were in the presence of celebrities. These guys were the biggest heroes in America, but to us they just looked exhausted and sour. We asked if they needed us to move our car.

"Nah, you're fine," one of them replied in flat tones. They were there for regular firefighting duties, but it was hard to imagine they weren't thinking about it.

About "it." It. One word to encompass the entire event and the whole place, this saddest place in all the world. Thinking about It, looking at It, smelling It. This It was the biggest It in the world.

We walked, pushing Schuyler ahead of us in her stroller. I didn't know the city well enough to know exactly where the towers had stood, but you could get a fairly good idea from the looks people on the street were giving in furtive glances to the sky. They were still looking for them, a week later.

As we got closer and the wind shifted, we were hit by the thing I had feared the most. It's impossible to describe that smell. Hours later, back in New Haven, I sat up late trying to describe the scene on my blog, and I realized with a start that I could still smell it on my clothes and in my hair.

On the streets of Manhattan, there was no escaping it. We turned down a corner and suddenly it was all around us; one moment it was faint, the next it was the whole world, a world of nothing but that smell. It was a burnt smell, warm like an animal, and sickly sweet. It was the smell of the most awful things in the world. It filled me with panic, and my first glimmer of understanding.

In the midst of it all, Schuyler was oblivious. She was happy to be outside, to watch the people and the lights and the near constant flow of emergency vehicles going past, the only ones on the streets this close to the site. Schuyler was fascinated by the stillness that had suddenly replaced New York chaos, and she saw the sky ahead of us. The way to the site was obvious. There was a great light streaming up from someplace nearby, up into the hole in the sky. Light, and smoke.

There were others on foot, mostly local residents, as far as I could tell. They walked slowly, aimlessly, like phantoms in a place already swirling with too many ghosts.

When we left New Haven, we hadn't discussed the wisdom of bringing Schuyler to this place. I know that must seem pretty irresponsible now. Aside from anything else, the air we were breathing couldn't have been good for any of us. At the time, however, all I knew was that we were a family, an American family, and while the world would go and get complicated soon enough, right then it was simply the place we needed to be, the place that a short year before had become a cherished memory and was now smashed to ruin. I didn't know if any of us belonged there, but if we did, we all did.

It wasn't until we started to meet with crowds of people that I began to get a better understanding of why Schuyler needed to be there. People stopped to admire her, a great many of them, and she dutifully and with great cheer delivered her standard *"cute baby who never cries or shits or does a thing in the world wrong"* routine. She had no words, of course; she was almost two years old, but small for her age. No one seemed to expect her to speak, certainly not in this place where words were too small.

The next set of police lines marked the edge of where we were allowed to go on foot. Beyond these, only residents and rescue workers were allowed. Periodically, one of the cops moved a barricade long enough for a big truck to roll through, its flatbed trailer piled with sadly recognizable twisted metal. Schuyler and I had touched that metal the year before, although the base of the towers where we'd laid our hands against the cold surface wouldn't see the light of day for weeks or even months.

It was here that Julie hesitated, perhaps sensing the horrible *It* that lay just out of view. She was more quiet than I'd ever seen her. As I stood waiting for her, I felt a tug on my jeans. I looked down to see Schuyler smiling up at me. I bent down to her level.

"How are you doing, monkey?" I asked her. She reached out to hug me, which she'd been doing a great deal lately. The gesture carried all the meaning in the world to me, although probably no more to her than *"Thanks for bringing me here instead of another boring night at home."*

A policeman walked up to us as I held Schuyler. His face looked drawn.

"It breaks your heart, don't it?" he said. "I've got two kids at home, and . . ." He stopped abruptly in the midst of miming a hug, unable to continue. He looked back down the street at the lights and the smoke and shook his head. I told him about Schuyler's previous visit to the World Trade Center and how she touched the towers. As I spoke, another truck rolled by, carrying the huge, twisted steel beams. Some of them were actually flattened in spots. They looked like rubber bands.

"It must break your heart every time you see that," I said to him.

"Every time," he replied quietly. We told him how proud we were of him and his fellow officers, but his thanks was muted; he was somewhere else in his heart, somewhere a few blocks away.

Beyond the trucks shone the lights. Bright lights, and cranes, and slowly boiling smoke tumbling lazily from what lay beyond. We'd reached the corner of Greenwich and Duane, and the crowd of people was bigger. Before I could see past them, I saw them taking photographs, and I saw their ashen faces. I looked down the street, and for a moment, my eyes weren't grasping what they were seeing.

At first I thought I was seeing tall, darkened buildings, but the smoke poured out of them, slowly and persistently. Something else was wrong, too. The lines of these buildings were wrong. There were no straight lines, just lumps. When I looked closer and saw the jagged beams sticking out, I realized what I was seeing. Julie had already figured it out; she turned away, finally giving in to her tears. Not delicate tears, either, but great shuddering sobs. She walked away so Schuyler wouldn't see.

"Oh. Oh. Oh." I said it over and over again, unable to stop or say anything else. I was looking at two piles, the farther one slightly higher than the other. They were impossibly big, rivaling the buildings around them. I'd seen photos of how they looked during the day, but at night they were simply hulking black forms, horrible for what you couldn't see. It seemed impossible that such a thing could ever be removed, that the bodies and the smell and the smoke, this mountain of steel and glass and blood could ever be swept clean. It seemed as unmovable and permanent as the towers had seemed the year before.

Men in hard hats walked away from the scene, their grimy faces unreadable.

A female police office walked up to us, bending down to look at Schuyler, who was thrilled to have someone new to flirt with, having become clearly annoyed with her weepy parents who were sucking the joy out of this adventure.

"Well, hello there!" said the officer. "Look at that smile! You are just like sunshine to me right now!" She reached out and touched Schuyler, who responded with her wheezy, goony laugh, the one we'd first heard here a year before. The officer smiled, but tears were forming in her eyes, big ones. She didn't even wipe them away, she just played with Schuyler and let them fall. When she said goodbye and Schuyler reached out to hug her, the officer closed her eyes and gave herself over to the embrace.

I was suddenly glad we'd brought her with us. There wasn't a thing in the world I could do to make this any better, but Schuyler could. She was sunshine.

We left after that, walking away from the city's smoking wound. I turned a few times to look at it again. Julie did not.

"America when will you be angelic?" wrote Allen Ginsberg. I think about the people who died all those years ago, those faces on desperate, hand-lettered posters and ethereal voices crackling over cell phones. I think about all those souls, all those young lovers and sad lonely people, the greedy and the generous, the pragmatists and dreamers and gentle mothers and rowdy fathers. They were just like me, and probably like you, too. They weren't angelic. None of us is.

Even as I write that, however, I know it's not true. I do know an angel. I watched her bless doomed towers with tiny hands and grant absolution to police officers whose hearts were breaking. Schuyler's an angel and also a bit of a devil, a fragile flower who speaks in a howl. She remains, now as she was then, the reason I give a damn.

6

The Holland Thing

Evaluator's Notes:1-21-02—Based on today's evaluation, Schuyler is eligible for Birth-to-Three services. She is demonstrating delays in all areas of development except for personal social skills which are age-appropriate.

Seven months before that bittersweet evaluation, four months before the world went mad and a few weeks before Dr. Simon asked the question that started our search for answers to Schuyler's enigmatic silence, I had a great idea for a Mother's Day gift for Julie. Schuyler and I were going to give her something special, something perfect.

"*Mama.*"

Schuyler was eighteen months old. She should have been talking, or at least trying, but we weren't really aware of that then. Well, I think we knew deep down it was time, otherwise I wouldn't have made such a big deal out of it for Mother's Day, spending all that time torturing poor Schuyler.

"Mama. Mama. Mama!" I repeated over and over, for weeks leading up to the day. Anytime Schuyler and I had some time together, I'd say it to her. Every single time she'd look up at me with a big smile and say nothing at all.

I have no idea what I eventually gave Julie for Mother's Day that year. But it wasn't *"Mama."*

By the time we were beginning to have Schuyler evaluated for services like the Birth-to-Three program, it was becoming clear there was a problem. I just had no intention of letting that problem define my daughter. I refused to let it eclipse her engaging disposition and all the fascinating little pieces that formed a whole, vibrant little enigma.

As Schuyler grew, it became more obvious that she was the kid in the room who didn't speak. When she tried, she could produce vowels and inflections, but only the softest and most occasional consonants. Schuyler's speech resembled that of a deaf child; she spoke as if she heard the words correctly in her head and was unaware of the broken sounds coming out. In addition to sending us on the wild goose chase of repeated hearing tests, it also filled us with dread for Schuyler's social development. We had no idea what was going to happen to her, but one thing was becoming clear. She was going to be the Weird Kid.

Which is why we were both taken off guard by what happened. Schuyler, in all her exuberance and happiness and strangeness, became a little rock star.

I remember dropping her off at day care one day and arriving while the rest of the kids were dancing around to some wild Mexican music the teachers were playing for them. As soon as we walked in, a small crowd of kids ran over and took Schuyler by the hand, leading her away to join the fiesta. She didn't look back, which I selfishly resented just a little. I don't know if it's only me, but I suspect most parents appreciate just the tiniest bit of separation anxiety. Schuyler has always been a heartbreaker in that respect.

The kids pulled Schuyler into their dancing circle, surrounding her with the strangest air of reverence and crying out her name in their little toddler voices like they were at a rock concert. *"Ki-lah!*

Ki-lah!" They moved around her at arm's length, their fingers just touching her; I was reminded of the last scene in *Close Encounters* when all the little rubber aliens led Richard Dreyfuss onto the ship. Schuyler danced and twirled in their midst, occasionally getting knocked over and swimming in a sea of little slobbery kid germs, but holding her own.

The day care workers told me it was always like this, and as she grew older and changed schools and towns, it was always the same.

The Weird Kid was like no one else around her. She was broken somehow, we knew that. But she wore her brokenness like a veil of stars.

Anytime I wrote in my blog about Schuyler and the possibility that she could be deaf, or later that she might have a learning disorder, or even simply that she was different from other kids, one thing I could always count on was that someone would send me the Holland thing. The more serious Schuyler's situation became, the more copies I received in e-mail, dozens of copies of the Holland thing.

Special needs parents know exactly what I'm talking about.

About twenty years ago, a writer for *Sesame Street* who had a son with Down syndrome wrote a short essay about how she perceived life with a special needs child. In her essay she compares this unexpected situation to planning for a vacation in Italy, only to have the plane land in Holland instead. At first she's disappointed in the differences, but eventually she comes to appreciate the wonderful aspects of Holland and realizes it is every bit as swell as Italy.

The Holland thing is very popular among therapists and many parents with kids who are different, and perhaps for some, it is a comfort. In particular, I can see how it probably speaks to and helps parents with kids whose futures are locked in by their disability. I think there's a great deal of the philosophy of acceptance driving the Holland thing, and I get that. The original author was writing about having a child with Down syndrome, and I doubt she intended for it to get dragged out by well-meaning chirpy optimists trying to get their parent friends with broken children to turn that frown upside down. I also doubt she intended for it to come across as a subtle request to cheer the hell up already, although I am not the first special needs parent to note that this essay seems to be given out to us almost exclusively by people who are not in that same slow boat to Amsterdam with us.

It was simply the wrong thing for us. The fact of the matter is, Julie and I worried about Schuyler, and as we did so in our own ways, we started to fracture. We had no guidance, no answers, only a child who seemed with every passing day to be more and more alien. Julie and I were beginning to offer very little in the way of comfort to each other. It went without saying that the Holland thing wasn't doing much for us, either.

The same people who wrote to me offering up the Holland thing often took issue with my use of language. The further we got into this world of special needs parenting (and I absolutely loathe the term "special needs," but it is so deeply ingrained in the vernacular that avoiding its use is a losing battle), the less patience I had with the sugar-coated terminology that seemed *de rigueur* among parents and writers. I found it to be a distraction and a false comfort. Did softening my language really help Schuyler? On more than one occasion, I received e-mail from blog readers asking me some variation on "How do you think Schuyler will react one day when she's older and she reads that her father thought she was 'broken'?" I couldn't answer that, of course, but the one thing I could say for sure was that she won't reply, "What? You mean there's something wrong with me?" Everyone in our family looked Schuyler's monster squarely in the eye, and no one was foolish enough to think that dressing it up in pretty language would somehow blunt its bite. Broken things are things to be fixed, and Schuyler was both fearless and stubborn. After everything she'd been handed and had knocked down with cheerful obstinacy, I was never afraid that realistic

language was going to be her undoing. We chose clear-eyed blunt-
ness over affected sensitivity because it was right for Schuyler. She
never had much use for soft gloves or pity.

I guess my biggest problem with the Holland thing wasn't so
much the fact that people were trying to tell me my growing panic
over Schuyler's delay was somehow inappropriately gloomy, or that
a sunny attitude was what I needed to make things better. I think I
was bothered by the fact that the Holland thing called for nothing
less than acceptance.

There was something wrong with our daughter, and no one
could tell us what it was. We weren't about to accept a damned thing.

Our appointment was pending with the esteemed Yale Child Study
Center, but as we feared, it would be months, maybe a year or
longer, before they would get to see her. Until then, once it had been
established that her hearing was okay, Dr. Simon turned over the
search for the keys to Schuyler's head to the therapists from Connecticut's Birth-to-Three program.

All these years later, I'm not entirely sure how I feel about Birth-
to-Three. I asked Julie how she felt about them at the time, and she
also has mixed feelings. In retrospect, the services they offered
Schuyler were ultimately not very effective. It wasn't their fault;
they were trying to help, and I can honestly say that of all the people
who walked through Schuyler's life during her first three years,
there was no one who tried harder to reach her than the therapists
of Connecticut Birth-to-Three. From the very first time they met
her, they worked to build a communication bridge with Schuyler,
and they didn't slow down or give up until the day she turned three
and left the program. They approached Schuyler's problem with the
single-mindedness and persistence of religious missionaries, not doctors. The problem, I think, was the broadness of that mission. In the
end, although they tried so hard, Schuyler's brain was beyond their
scope.

"From birth to age three your child has a lot to learn," said the program's literature, "but not all children are learning as well as they can. Your child deserves a good start in life. The mission of the Birth-to-Three System is to strengthen the capacity of families to meet the developmental and health-related needs of their infants and toddlers who have delays or disabilities." They evaluated their clients in the home and provided services wherever that child normally spent the day, whether at home or day care or wherever. With Schuyler, that meant our apartment.

Her evaluation showed a number of areas of concern beyond her near total lack of speech development. They were things we'd noticed to some degree, but it was both a relief and at the same time disconcerting to have professionals take note of them. I suppose I was waiting for them to tell us she was perfectly normal and would no doubt start talking at any time. Instead, they saw the other little cracks, too.

Using a system called the Mullen Scales of Early Learning, which assessed language, motor, and perceptual abilities in very young kids, Birth-to-Three determined that Schuyler was "delayed three standard deviations below the mean in all areas of development (fine motor, gross motor, cognitive, receptive and expressive language)." In addition to her speech difficulties, they observed that she exhibited low muscle tone and drooling, leading them to suspect that poor development in her facial muscles could be responsible in part for her speech difficulties.

Two therapists entered Schuyler's life at this time. Maggie provided speech and occupational therapy. She took to Schuyler immediately and was friendly but persistent with her. Maggie was the first professional to whom Julie broached the subject of an idea she'd been having for a while.

Julie wanted to teach Schuyler sign language. It was an unusual idea, I suppose, considering the results of Schuyler's hearing tests, but it made perfect sense to Julie. Schuyler had things to say, that much was obvious to us all, and while her frustration at not being understood was clear, we didn't think she understood *why* we were having the communications failure.

Maggie wasn't very supportive of the idea. She had been using a picture exchange system, but it was quickly becoming boring to Schuyler, who was beginning to refuse to do it, or to do it very reluctantly, as if she found it to be stupid and perhaps even condescending. (Perhaps I was projecting a bit because I pretty much felt the same way.) Maggie was afraid that if we were trying to encourage Schuyler to talk, giving her another mode of communication might be a step in the wrong direction. When presented with a method that was physically easier for her—signing—Schuyler might give up on working to actually speak.

"Schuyler's Birth-to-Three person said some people don't recommend sign language for kids with speech delays," Julie said to Dr. Simon the next time we saw her, following our meeting with Maggie in which she'd expressed her reservations. "Like they'll become dependent on it and won't be pushed to learn how to talk."

"Yeah, there's still a lot of controversy about that idea," Dr. Simon said. "And I suppose it could be true for some kids. But the thing we have to look at here is how to provide Schuyler with a way to communicate. Her speech delay is like a wall that's keeping her from moving forward in all these different areas of her development. Now, we can try to climb over that wall, or even knock it down. And we'll keep trying to do just that. But until we know what's keeping her from talking, I think we ought to empower her to at least go *around* that wall and find another way to tell us what she needs for us to know."

Despite Maggie's distrust of Julie's plan to teach ASL to Schuyler, in the end it was Julie who showed us all the way. Schuyler took to signing quickly, and even with her poorly formed hand signs (a side effect of the fine motor issues she was having), she quickly developed a small but useful basic vocabulary. To her credit, Maggie overcame her initial objections and agreed to learn ASL along with us.

Schuyler's other therapist was a young, pretty physical therapist named Amy. Schuyler often rebelled against Maggie's disciplined approach, as she would later strive to confound almost all of her subsequent therapists and evaluators, but her loyalty to Amy never wavered. Amy, for all her youth and perkiness (two qualities I have always found to be suspect, flinty geezer that I am), had figured out how to reach Schuyler. She simply never let the therapy feel like therapy.

It wasn't as simple as tricking Schuyler into thinking she was playing rather than working. Schuyler was too smart for that. She would cooperate with therapists and evaluators, but it had to be on her terms. It was similar to the game we played during dinner where I would say "Don't eat that!" and she would suddenly scarf up whatever food she had refused to touch only seconds before. She knew I was getting her to eat it. She just wanted to do it her way.

More than anything, even the signing, Schuyler's need to choose for herself—sometimes in opposition to what others were saying— was the most important thing we learned during this time. Schuyler was a friendly, boisterous little girl with a kind and generous spirit, but she shared a trait with her father, one that Dana once told me was my defining quality above all others.

We don't like being told what to do.

Schuyler was mute, with a small collection of ASL signs and not a single verbalized word. She made sounds, but they were just the faintest approximations of words, with almost no consonants at all. She wasn't in any way distant from us, however, not as far as her socialization was concerned. Still, her lack of language and her unique approach to the world on her own terms resulted in an enigmatic little girl, one whose basic needs were now better served thanks to her limited sign language but whose internal world of imagination remained tantalizingly out of reach.

We couldn't quite live in her world, although we could glimpse it from time to time. It was a world with some interesting inhabitants. Like Superfly.

Schuyler had attended a number of day care programs, finally landing at a private center held in the home of an enthusiastic woman named Faith. One of the things we liked about Faith's center was that Schuyler was one of only a handful of white kids. In our area of Connecticut, that was no small feat, and it made me feel a little better about her chances of *not* growing up to be some kind of mute Martha Stewart. Diversity in New England often seemed in short supply.

Once a month, Faith's kids would board a bus and visit one of the cool modern "touch and slobber on everything" children's museums that have become so popular in this country. At the end of the trip, a member of the museum staff would read a book to the kids, and then would hand out a little gift bag with items related to the story.

One month, the story was one of the Miss Spider books. I wasn't familiar with them, although I don't like spiders one bit and couldn't really get behind a story about this kindly arachnid who had tea with all her bug friends. It was clear to me that she was lulling them into a false sense of security before she devoured them all.

At the end of the Miss Spider story, Faith's kids received a gift. They were all allowed to pick a big plastic bug from a bucket. One little girl picked a ladybug, another grabbed a big beetle, and another got a grasshopper. When it was her turn to choose, my delicate little daughter, my fairy princess, had eyes for only one bug friend.

Schuyler picked a fly. A big, scary, poo-eating housefly. God help us, she loved him.

I first met him that evening when Julie picked me up to go to dinner. As I came out of the apartment and hopped in the car, they were waiting for me, throwing the fly at each other. Schuyler had always made strange attachments to some of her toys while totally rejecting others. That night, her heart belonged to a giant plastic fly.

I don't remember why we started calling him Superfly. Schuyler didn't call him anything, of course, but she clearly knew his name. For weeks after she brought him home, I had only to mention Superfly to send Schuyler off in a mad search to find her friend. As soon as she had him in hand, she'd attack me with him, lunging at me and squealing with laughter as I cringed and cried out in terror.

"No! It's Superfly! Get away from me! Ahhhhhh! *Superfly!*"

It wasn't a hard dramatic moment to fake, either. There was something disconcerting about watching my sweet little baby girl laugh maniacally, a giant plastic housefly thrust in my face. Schuyler played the victim with just as much gusto as she did the Evil Flymaster. If I managed to get Superfly away from her and started making my own sinister Superfly buzz, she would erupt in laughter and clumsily run away, fully expecting me to chase her. Me, and Superfly.

It was all very charming, save one disturbing aspect of the Superfly experience. When Schuyler would get sleepy, she would go to her room and grab one of her little blankets, dragging it back into the living room. She would then take one of her dolls and lay her on the floor, covering her with the blanket and tucking her in. It was her clever, wordless way of letting us know that while of course *she* wasn't sleepy and could easily stay up another two or three hours, she could perhaps be persuaded to go to bed, since her little friends were so tired.

So it was one night soon after her museum trip that Schuyler very sweetly tucked her giant fly under her blanket, patting him on his sleepy little fly head.

"Is Superfly sleepy?" Julie asked. Schuyler looked at us both with a serious expression and nodded somberly. As we carried them both off to bed, I found the sight of his big bug eyes peeking out from under her little pink blanket to be more than a little creepy.

I loved her all the same, however, perhaps more than ever. My daughter, my delicate angel. Just a sweet little girl and her beloved housefly.

In the summer of 2002, at the suggestion of Maggie and with the full support of Dr. Simon (who was still trying to get us into the Yale Child Study Center), we paid several hundred dollars out of our own pockets to have Schuyler independently evaluated by the Child Development Center at Southern Connecticut State University. It took the better part of a day and mostly involved a speech therapist who appeared to be about twelve years old sitting in a room full of toys with Schuyler and observing her at play, as well as interacting with her to measure her responses and cognitive abilities.

A few weeks later, they mailed us the results of their study. Dr. Simon, in her own report a few months later, tactfully summed up SCSU's conclusions. *"A speech and language evaluation at the Center for Communication Disorders, at Southern Connecticut State University, supported Schuyler's speech difficulties."*

In others words, they spent several hours observing Schuyler, followed by a further few weeks to compile their data, and they came to the conclusion that Schuyler couldn't talk. Thanks, guys.

Schuyler was by now becoming weary of the evaluations. She was growing quickly, transforming from a toddler into a little girl, right before our very eyes. Still small for her age, she was nevertheless growing tall and lanky and rowdy, with a taste for Converse hi-top sneakers, short hair, and perennially grass-stained jeans. She was also developing into a tenacious little kid with a ready laugh and a warm disposition but absolutely no patience with testing. This was going to be a problem, we could tell, because that autumn, two big evaluations awaited her.

In November, as part of her transition from Birth-to-Three to a public school early intervention program, Schuyler would have a comprehensive evaluation by the New Haven Public School System's Early Childhood Assessment Team (ECAT).

And in December, the sparkling gates of the Yale Child Study Center would finally swing wide for us.

The ECAT test was performed by some of the most earnest child development researchers you ever did see. Julie stepped into an office to provide answers to a verbal evaluation of Schuyler's abilities utilizing the Vineland Adaptive Behavioral Scale, and I followed Schuyler into a playroom, escorted by a no-nonsense researcher and her assistant. The room was full of toys, and they observed her independent play, interrupting with instructions now and again. I could tell Schuyler was becoming profoundly annoyed.

"Schuyler," said the researcher, after repeatedly referring to her as "shooler" despite my polite corrections. "Can you put all these marbles back into this jar?" She stood next to a short table with a large plastic jar, and a huge assortment of marbles in a large bowl. Schuyler looked displeased at the researcher, but when she looked back at me and saw me nod encouragingly to her, she began half-heartedly putting the marbles away.

When she was done, Schuyler enjoyed a few moments of the researcher's congratulations. She glanced over at me with her curious little half smile, and then calmly picked up the jar and turned it over, spilling what must have been hundreds of marbles onto the hard floor. They shot away from Schuyler's feet like the Big Bang, and she laughed triumphantly as the researcher sputtered and ran about trying to pick up marbles.

Schuyler didn't make any friends on the ECAT team.

The team determined Schuyler to be functioning in a low range developmentally. The language used to describe our daughter was becoming both alarming and alien. The repeated conclusions with no real answers and the chilly reports were beginning to work on us, albeit in different ways. My heart broke a little more and my spirit leaked away with every professional, medical statement detailing how strange and flawed my daughter was.

I loved Schuyler intensely and perhaps defensively, too. I told

myself I didn't believe there was anything seriously amiss. But sometimes I was able to step out of my fatherly fog of denial and hypersen-
sitivity and observe her as she danced mysteriously with her shadows,
almost unable to take her eyes off them, or simply fail to respond directly to other little kids, even when they flocked around her. It was
then that I knew in my secret heart that there was something wrong.

One day, as autumn settled into New England, we took Schuyler for
a drive and found ourselves at a beach. All the beaches in Connecticut look out onto Long Island Sound rather than the ocean itself, so
the waters were almost always calm. As we walked out onto the
sand, it became clear even to a former desert-dweller like myself that
the tide was out, leaving huge areas of the beach uncovered and creating little tidal pools. The ground itself teemed with life; tiny little
snails and crabs oozed and trundled around, and thousands of teeny
tiny little jets of water squirted from the sand into the air.

As I dug with the toes of my shoe for the clams or sea monkeys or
whatever was making these little water squirts, Schuyler ran over
excitedly. She looked up at me and jabbered something in Martian,
her consonant-free words sounding like the earnest conversation of
a cartoon ghost, variations on "oo" and "ah." It was clear that Julie
and I had a choice to make. We could keep her back a few steps so
she'd stay clean, or we could allow her to thrust her clean little
hands into the black, stinking mud to discover all the tiny citizens of
the beach for herself. It was never really a serious choice, not once
we saw the look of utter amazement in her eyes when I picked up a
tiny crab and put it in the palm of her hand.

Schuyler lived in a world far removed from our own. But every
so often, she let us come see it for a few moments, and on days like
the one at the tide pool, she joined us in ours.

We visited the Yale Child Study Center four times during the
month of December 2002. After the year that we'd waited to get her

in, a time frame that I thought was almost inexcusable, I must give them credit for taking their time with her once we finally got there. Once we were in the door, we were rewarded with their undivided attention.

The entity that was to become the Yale Child Study Center was established in 1911 by Dr. Arnold Gesell, considered by many to be the father of child development in the United States. Over the course of the twentieth century, the center had a reputation for innovative approaches to child development issues and was considered one of the top research institutes in the world. During her days as a law student at Yale, Hillary Rodham Clinton volunteered at the Child Study Center, studying the latest research on childhood brain development. And now, thanks to my employment at Yale and my fancy pants insurance benefits package, I was finally able to walk those hallowed halls with Schuyler, who was clearly not as impressed as she was expected to be.

We were playing on a circular bench, running around on it in a way that the senator and former First Lady would have undoubtedly disapproved of, when Schuyler's assigned researcher found us. Her name was Betsy, and she was young and soft spoken and earnest in a way that I suppose you might become if you spent your childhood being called Betsy.

From the first moments they met, Schuyler and Betsy seemed to genuinely like each other. After introductions and a surprise hug from Schuyler, Betsy led us to a playroom with a large mirrored half wall, behind which, we later learned, Yale interns watched and took notes. Betsy was nice enough, and she was clearly very dedicated to her work, but from the very beginning I knew she was going to have trouble with Schuyler. As soon as they began to explore the toys, Betsy began asking Schuyler questions and directing her play.

"Is the doll hungry, Schuyler? Can you feed the doll? Is the doll sleepy?" I could see that Betsy was trying to sneak some evaluation past Schuyler, and bless her heart for trying. Schuyler wasn't having any of it. Instead she drifted from toy to toy, idly fooling around but not really committing to any particular activity.

As I sat there attempting to be invisible and not interfere, I tried to watch Schuyler with dispassionate eyes, the way her evaluators saw her. Like a child trying to navigate the swimming pool without holding the side for the first time, I tried to let go of my hopes and preconceived feelings about who she was and who I wanted her to become one day. I tried to watch her and see her as they did, as they had to in order to correctly evaluate her.

What I saw was a child who was happy and friendly but not always socially engaged, almost never making eye contact with her evaluators. I saw a kid who didn't seem to have questions but rather just moved through the world as a passenger, always reacting, always observing. I saw a little girl who was fascinated, to the point of near hypnosis, at the sight of her reflection in a mirror, and who danced with her shadow instead of playing much with others. I saw Schuyler as a mute three-year-old who couldn't grasp potty training and drooled frequently.

I saw a broken little girl, and I had no idea what was wrong. I didn't trust Yale, because I didn't trust anyone with Schuyler, and yet I was pinning all my hopes onto them to find an answer.

Schuyler went back three more times, either with Julie or with us both. Betsy told us she'd have a report (and hopefully a diagnosis) in a few weeks. We didn't hear from her for several months.

I can only speak of my own feelings with any authority, particularly during this time when Julie and I continued to draw inward, away from each other. I know that Schuyler's deepening mystery and unresolved silence was eating away at Julie's strength and causing her to doubt her abilities as a parent. Julie now says that with every visit and evaluation, a little piece of her heart and her hope was taken away. If Schuyler wasn't doing something correctly, Julie took it as a personal failure. Perhaps she wasn't reading to her enough, or playing with her enough, or playing correctly.

Julie felt isolated, I think. I wish I had been a better supporter, but my own anxieties were working on me. At one point, Julie found a child care center claiming to be associated with the Jean Piaget learning system, which emphasized exploring a child's own cognitive development in a less rigid time frame and using individualized goals. Once we'd placed Schuyler there, however, Julie felt the same condescension and judgment we'd seen elsewhere, and we took her out after only a few months. Julie felt like all they saw was a little girl who liked to play with her shadow, and they seemed mystified. I can see now that it was taking a toll on Julie every bit as heavy as the one it took on me.

As for myself, all I can say for sure was that I was trying to make peace with the situation, but I wasn't having much success. I didn't feel like we were in Holland, enjoying the exotic hash bars and legal hookers or whatever it was that was supposed to be charming us about this place. I felt like we were on Mars.

No matter what ultimately turned out to be her obstacle, I was beginning to understand that Schuyler was going to break my heart. That was inevitable, regardless of her condition. Even in a best case scenario where she discovered her voice and got past her developmental delays and grew into a lovely and smart young woman who continued to love her father with intense and unwavering affection, she'd still leave one day. She'd still move away and fall in love with someone who would either love her badly and wound her little heart or love her well and take her away from me.

My life with Schuyler, which both enriched and enslaved me, was occasionally more than I could handle. But I did my best. I did it with love, stupid blind father's love. It was the only tool I had sometimes, but while it was rarely the only tool I needed, it was at the very least the one that led me through the dark until I found my way.

7

"Nothing Makes Us
So Lonely as Our Secrets"

In autumn 2003, Julie and I were in the car, taking a long, lazy autumn drive through rural Connecticut. Schuyler was sleeping in the backseat, and we found ourselves discussing how our lives had been shortly before her diagnosis. It was a time neither of us had ever cared to revisit, so now that some time had passed, we were both a little surprised that we were tip-toeing into that minefield.

As we talked and revisited those rough times, it became clear there was something Julie wanted to tell me. She was getting weepy and hesitant, and she wouldn't look at me directly. Finally, she began to cry. I sat there in that "helpless guy" mode you go into when a woman you love begins to cry and you just don't have a clue what's going on.

"I've been carrying something around with me for a couple of years," she managed to say finally. "I didn't think I was ever going to tell you, but I just feel terrible about it. I just need to tell you, I hope you'll forgive me."

She then started sobbing, and it took a minute or two before she could continue. I waited, now fully terrified at what she had to tell me.

Finally she managed to say it. "Back when everything was so awful and you were so depressed, hell, when *we* were both so depressed,

I . . . I was having an affair with John." She paused and let out a breath. "God, that sounds so stupid, like a bad TV movie."

She stifled more sobs and continued quietly. "We knew it was a mistake and we stopped after . . . after I moved back in. We knew it was stupid, it's just things were so bad, you know? I just started talking to him a lot about everything and it just sort of happened. I'm so, so sorry, Rob. I don't know how to ask you to forgive me."

We drove in silence. I didn't look at Julie, instead watching the Connecticut countryside roll by. When it came to avoiding eye contact on a road trip, New England was very generous with the scenery. At that moment, Julie and I were in a good place, better than we had been in a long time. I needed to choose my words very carefully.

"Please tell me what you're feeling," she asked, glancing over at me nervously.

I looked at her at last. "Would you be surprised if I said I feel relieved?" I said, smiling just a little before beginning.

"I guess this is a good day for confessions . . ."

Dr. Paul Tournier was a Swiss physician, a Universalist, and a Christian philosopher, and I have to admit, even that much I only know because of Google. The only thing I really knew about Paul Tournier before I looked him up was the quote I ran across some time ago, a quote that made me think about, well, all of this.

"Nothing makes us so lonely as our secrets."

When we moved from Michigan to New England, our new baby in tow, we weren't concerned with being lonely. Rather the opposite, in fact. I'd left Texas three years before in large part because I needed emotional space. I had only been divorced for a short time, after a suffocating ten-year marriage, and to be honest, I'd embraced my new freedom with a kind of narcissistic fervor, thinking mostly of myself and without a great deal of consideration for anyone else.

I'm not going to beat myself up over it too much; after ten years in a marriage to a perfectly nice woman who just happened to be as wrong for me as I was for her, I suddenly had only myself to answer to. I'd been married so young that it really was my first time on my own, and it took me a while to adjust. By the time I left Texas to be with Julie, I'd worn out my welcome with my family, particularly my brother. He and I had always had a complicated relationship. Since the death of our father, and perhaps before then, he had come to think of himself as the head of the family, and when I reached a point that I suddenly wanted to go my own way and not necessarily the way he thought I should take, it drove a wedge between us. It didn't last; he found out his wife was going to have a baby within days of Julie's historic "Peeing of the Stick," and we put our differences aside almost immediately. His son was born two weeks after Schuyler.

After Schuyler was born, Julie was feeling that same need for some emotional distance from her family. We'd moved to Detroit so she could have the baby close to family, but it soon became apparent it wasn't going to work out. There was a great deal of tension between Julie's family and myself, and for that I think there was plenty of blame to go around.

On their part, they had a very difficult time accepting that their baby girl, the only daughter of three kids, had married a divorced agnostic who'd left college before graduating and didn't even have the courtesy to be a midwesterner.

As for me, I didn't get a sense early on of how becoming a member of the Rummels didn't just happen because I married Julie. It was a process of assimilation and evaluation that could take years. I realized it would be a very long road to fitting in, and whether it was arrogance or simply fatigue, I didn't want to play. In retrospect, I probably made it pretty difficult for Julie's parents to reach out to me, and by the time they tried, we'd generated some exceptionally bad blood between us.

That bad blood spilled rather dramatically during our first

summer in New England, in 2000. Our departure from Michigan had been messy, with Julie's parents helping us move while at the same time expressing their unhappiness. Looking back, I suppose I can't blame them. I'd been less than the catch of the day when Julie married me, and then two months after giving them their first grandchild, we abruptly moved away. By the time they came to visit six months later, everyone's resentment had grown exponentially.

So here's the wacky TV sitcom-esque incident that got the next few years off to such a dramatic beginning. By the time Dave and Sandy came to visit, utilizing their time-share options to stay in a local hotel on the beach, Julie and I had settled into our "I work days, you work nights" schedule. It wasn't great but it was what we needed to do, at least for a while. During those nights, I would often take Schuyler out with my friend Dana. She and my boss were my only friends in New Haven, and I spent a lot of evenings hanging out with either of them.

Dana and I took Schuyler to eat in an unexciting chain restaurant, because let's face it, a six-month-old baby isn't a great dinner companion when you're at a fine dining establishment. The big chains were accustomed to crying, fussy babies.

They were also apparently good for travelers from the Midwest who weren't all that adventurous in their restaurant choices when visiting Exotic New England, which is how we found ourselves sitting in an Applebee's in New Haven with Julie's parents just a few tables away. I saw them and went over to say hello. They were cordial enough but didn't ask us to join them.

At the time, I didn't think anything of it; I was there with Dana and my baby, after all, and Julie knew where I was. It wasn't until a week later, after refusing offers to let them take Schuyler for an evening if they wanted, that Dave and Sandy told Julie they didn't want to take Schuyler from me because they didn't want to "enable" me and my nights out carousing with Dana while their daughter slaved away in the cruel sweatshop of retail bookselling.

"You know, Julie," said Dave, "when the cat's away, the mouse will play."

You can imagine how well that went over. Julie and I both took turns losing our tempers at them, and by the time they left Connecticut, none of us were on speaking terms. When her parents returned to Detroit, they told their version of the events to Julie's two brothers. Her older brother reacted, perhaps predictably in retrospect, with loyalty to his mother and father. Looking back now, I suppose a case could be made that his response was admirable in its own way. But not by me. I felt as if yet another bomb had been tossed into the midst of our little camp. The whole thing quickly spun out of control.

The irony of where this ugly family spat landed a year and a half later would escape them mostly because they never knew most of what happened. Well, not until they read this, anyway.

Looking back, it's hard to pinpoint exactly when things began to unravel with Julie. I think on some level, we sensed something was wrong with Schuyler, but once the hearing tests began and she started missing developmental milestones, Julie and I grew apart in a hurry.

In talking to other parents of broken children, I've heard the same story, so perhaps we weren't complete failures. I can't speak for other couples, but for us, I think the hardest part of having a child with special issues comes from the need for comfort. We could do anything, face any tough issues that came up, if only we could escape that world every now and then. Perhaps we all need to have someone on the outside to make that escape with, someone who's not there with us. We had no definitive answer to face, no medical diagnosis stating "*this* is what's wrong, and here's what you need to work together to accomplish in order to fix it." There were only unanswered questions and frustrations, and when we looked at each other, I guess what we saw was someone who didn't feel one bit of sympathy for the other. *"I'm in the same boat,"* we seemed to say. *"Don't look to me for any answers."*

As it became more and more apparent that there was something wrong with Schuyler, and as it became less and less clear that we'd ever know what it was, much less be able to help her, we lost our way. I don't know how else to say it. We were sad, and we became disconnected.

It was a bad recipe. It really was, and we both knew it. When we were together, we spent all of our time and energy on Schuyler, making sure she was happy and trying desperately to find the key that would open up her locked mind and give her the voice we were both convinced was there but simply blocked somehow.

When we were apart, we were with our separate friends.

I wasn't there the night in late 2001 when Julie had the last big ugly blowout with her parents and her older brother. I wasn't there when they said things to her that hurt deeply and left her feeling betrayed. Moreover, I can't tell you why they were so angry with her. It will remain a mystery to me forever, one of those moments where a bad situation grows legs and walks around much longer than it should. It devastated Julie.

She stood there with the phone in her hand and cried so hard that no sounds came out, just quivering shoulders and great gulps of air. She didn't know what to say. Just at the time when she felt as if the world was beating up on her own daughter, she suddenly felt more alone than she'd ever felt before.

One reason she felt so alone that night was that I was out of town. The only person she had to turn to was her friend John, a young man whom she'd met while working at the bookstore, and whom I'd met a few times. She called him and he came over, and they drank and she cried, and before it was all over, she'd found a source of comfort, and ultimately more.

What happened between Julie and John occurred because she felt that the people she needed the most were suddenly and inexplicably absent from her life. I can't speak for her family, but I can say with utmost certainty that I betrayed her by not being there, either figuratively in our relationship or literally.

Because I was out of town. With Madeline.

In retrospect, I can't honestly remember how I met Madeline. She was an artist, and a talented one, with a taste for vivid colors, and she was funny, with a sense of humor very much like my own. We had worked together one summer in Michigan while she was dating someone I supervised at the music camp, that much I know for certain. I remember seeing her when she would come by to meet him after work, and I recall flirting with her just to tweak him. The two of them even attended our wedding. To be honest, I don't remember when she caught my attention and kept it, but it was certainly years before, maybe even before I met Julie.

Madeline and I had become friends at some point, the kind of friends who exchange the occasional e-mail and then go a few months without a word, only to pop back up when some random event reminds them of one another. It had been a few years since I'd spoken to her last when I got an e-mail from her one January, telling me she was now living in Baltimore and working as an associate curator at an art museum. She was traveling with an exhibition that was making a brief tour up the East Coast, and she'd be in New Haven for a couple of days. She invited us to come to the exhibit.

Julie and I took Schuyler to the exhibit, and whatever tensions existed between Julie and myself, we nevertheless had a pleasant enough time. Even so, I found myself watching Madeline the entire evening. She was younger than me, almost a decade younger, and there was a world of difference between the Madeline I'd once known and the woman she'd grown into. It occurred to me that given the chilly state of things between Julie and myself, it was probably just as well that Madeline was leaving town the next day.

So naturally, the East Coast was hit by a blizzard that evening.

Madeline called me the next day and said the museum staff was going to be stuck in New Haven for at least another day. "I'm bored," she said. "Want to take me to a movie?"

"You had better say no. Say no, say no, say no, good lord she's beautiful, say NO you ass, say no, say noooo. . . ."

"Absolutely. I'll come get you in an hour."

That's how it happened. That's how I found myself sitting beside this impossibly pretty woman in a darkened movie theater, how at some point I felt her press her shoulder against me and wondered if it meant what I thought it meant, how I found myself leaning back into her to see if she'd pull away, how I turned to tell her something about the movie and was suddenly kissing her, how I found myself sitting in the car with her after all the other moviegoers had left and snow covered our windshield, listening to the shouting voice in my head, the one that could see the future and didn't like how it turned out, and how that voice faded until all that was left was the startling new reality of Madeline and the sense that I wasn't alone and I wasn't unloved and come what may, I was, for just one moment, more than a helpless observer to Schuyler's wordlessness and Julie's unhappiness.

That one moment was important. I may have been Asshole Husband, but I wasn't Tragedy Dad. Not at that moment.

It was a moment that repeated itself, over and over, until that day that I was out of town when Julie needed someone and found someone.

And it wasn't me, on either count.

I can't tell you why it happened. I can say the more of a failure I felt as a father, the more I wanted to run away from that responsibility. I can also say that Julie and I were so preoccupied with the surprise turns our lives had taken that we weren't terribly saddened by how all our time together seemed to be about taking care of Schuyler rather than each other. I can even admit that Madeline was beautiful and I was a dog, if you like. Most of all, I can say all of that and still not get it entirely right.

I also can't tell you when it began to go wrong with Madeline, either. She had spoken a great deal about being together, about leaving our lives and starting over, and then at some point that escaped my notice at the time, she had stopped talking about the future. I didn't see it immediately, which made it all the more stunning when it collapsed.

I suppose I owe something to Madeline's low tolerance for alcohol. I had driven the five hours from New Haven to Baltimore and had arrived to find her drinking wine in her living room, almost as if she'd forgotten I was coming. It was clear that something was wrong. It never occurred to me that the something wrong was her inability to juggle the pieces of her life while she was drinking.

When I arrived and she was drunk, she was unable to hide her new lover from me.

When her phone rang and she answered it without looking at her caller ID, she wasn't entirely aware of my presence in the same room when he called. When he presumably asked how her day had gone, she answered, "Bad day. There was no you in it." And then she looked up and realized that I'd heard, and that was it, I suppose. She didn't tell me immediately, but by the time I climbed back in my car, she'd told me all about him, how they worked together at the museum and had put in long hours late in the evening setting up a special exhibit, and how he'd rubbed her sore shoulders afterward, and how that had spun into something else, something wild and dangerous and not at all unlike a snowy night in New Haven the year before.

Well. Karma is a boomerang. And when it whips back around, it smarts.

Looking back, I can see now that the cloud that fell on me wasn't about Madeline, not entirely. Did I love her? I could hedge and say that at the time I thought I did, but now that I've had time to think about it, I could see it wasn't actually love. But the truth is yes, I did love her, although I never intended to. I tried for so long to keep her at an emotional arm's length. Being a cheating husband was bad enough without being stupid and falling in love. But the world is messy and chaotic, and the heart is retarded. Yes, I loved Madeline, and her betrayal, while richly deserved, hurt me badly.

It wasn't just that, though. There was something else, something I'd been running from for over a year.

I was a failure to Schuyler.

As I left Baltimore for the last time and drove north in the dead of night, the voices I'd repressed for months started clamoring. Schuyler wasn't getting better. No one knew why. I was missing something. She needed a father who could help her, one who could see what was wrong and fix it like a father does. It wasn't my failure as a husband that was dragging me under the waves like a drowning swimmer.

It was my failure as a father.

I was convinced that if given a choice, Schuyler would ultimately be better off with a Ghost Father, one whose imaginary attributes she could invent and build as needed through the years. Ghost Father would be infinitely preferable to Living Failure Dad, with all my faults and inadequacies there for the world to see. I don't know how to make sense of this to anyone else. It doesn't make sense to someone in a healthy frame of mind. And yet to a depressed person, it makes all the sense in the world.

It made perfect sense to me as I drove across the Delaware Memorial Bridge at three o'clock in the morning and stopped at the top of its 175-foot-high span, the only car on the bridge or the highway for miles in either direction. It continued to make sense as I put on my hazard lights and stepped out of the car.

I'd faced depression as a young man. I knew I was prone to it, as was my own mother and her mother as well, the maternal grandmother who had killed herself by parking her running car in the

garage years before I was born. I was familiar with the voice in my
head that could paint such a convincing picture of the Ghost Father
that I'd never stop to consider if it was accurate.

It wasn't until I stood on the bridge on a moonless night, looking
down into the blackness, that I felt how much that depression could
drive me.

I don't want to be overly dramatic. I didn't stop the car and get
out so I could hurl myself into the abyss. One hundred and forty-
two people have jumped to their deaths from the Delaware Memorial Bridge since it opened in 1951, including one gentleman only
two months before I stopped my Volkswagen that night in the dark
and stepped out. I don't think I ever truly intended to join them.

I stepped to the edge and peeked cautiously down into the darkness, not because I wanted to jump, but rather because I needed to
know if I wanted to jump. I stood there, taking in the moment. I noticed the lack of sound, just the wind and the ticking of my hazards
and the occasional creak from the bridge itself. I noticed the fire ex-
tinguishers placed at regular intervals on the bridge and the thick
cables running up into the darkness. I put my foot on a horizontal
cable and imagined the fall, the rush of air and then the moment of
impact, the water's surface as hard and as lethal as concrete. I
thought of my car parked there, hazards blinking sadly, waiting for
someone to figure out my story by its inexplicable presence.

Mostly, I thought of Schuyler, and whether she would be better
off with a phantom father or a failure of one. I don't think it was ever
a question I didn't have the answer to. I just needed to look it in the
face and know for sure.

I got in my car and drove on. I arrived in New Haven as the dawn
was breaking. When the sun comes up, everything feels different.
Not better, necessarily. But different.

A few days later, Julie moved out.

Well, I'm no picnic. Living with me can't be a total joy under the best of circumstances, and my depression at that time was seriously threatening to overwhelm me. I perceived myself as a failure and was convinced Julie and Schuyler would both be better off with me as a memory. When I stood on the bridge, I confronted that choice, and while I didn't exactly have a Capra "I want to *live!*" moment, at the very least I chose to leave that decision for another day.

Julie didn't know what to do with my depression. She had no frame of reference for it. I came home and told her about the bridge and about how I wasn't sure I wouldn't be a better father as a dead memory rather than a living failure. She simply couldn't deal with my issues on top of her own problems. So she made two decisions, both of which were difficult for her.

She decided to move out for a while.

And she decided to leave Schuyler with me.

The second decision doesn't seem to make a great deal of sense on the surface, and yet, looking back, I think I understand it. Part of the reason she left Schuyler with me was simply fatigue. Taking care of Schuyler and worrying about her was taking its toll on Julie. With every evaluation and every one of Schuyler's missed milestones, Julie was feeling the same sense of despair I was. When she finally needed a break, she had to step away from it all.

In later years, Julie would explain the other reason she left our daughter with me. She knew Schuyler and I needed each other. Julie couldn't deal with Schuyler's mystery at that moment, but she felt instinctively that I needed to focus on someone else and would be there for Schuyler. Most of all, I needed Schuyler. Simply put, I needed Schuyler and the unconditional love that she and she alone gave to me. Julie couldn't help me, but Schuyler could, and Julie knew it.

She was right. It seems strange to say it now, but Julie's decision to move out and leave Schuyler with me was a gift. I learned a very important thing.

Even when you're depressed, your kid's still got to eat.

She's still got to eat, and poop, and play. She still needs her meals prepared and her clothes washed and her imaginary friends doted upon. And I gave her that, all that, and everything else she needed. I took advantage of a program for Yale employees and went to see a counselor, and while she didn't exactly help me (she suggested I start going to church), the mere act of going to talk to her felt like a step in the right direction, back into the light. I didn't feel better, not yet, but I saw that even when you feel the weight of sorrow pressing down on you, it was still necessary to live your life.

In taking care of my little girl, I felt my feet touch the ground again.

"You know what?" I said to Schuyler after a few nights alone as we sat on the living room floor eating grilled cheese sandwiches and watching a dinosaur movie. "This isn't so bad. We can do this, can't we?" She nodded matter-of-factly with just a moment's glance, engrossed in the prehistoric monster action on the screen.

By the time the weekend drew near, Julie called and asked if she could see Schuyler. I could hear the hurt in her voice and asked if she'd like to take Schuyler for the whole weekend.

After Julie picked up Schuyler, I sat quietly for about half an hour and then made a phone call to Madeline, who had been asking if we could see each other. She felt horrible about our last encounter. In her heart, I think she knew it was over, but she either wasn't ready or didn't know how to move on, not just yet. Neither did I, apparently, since after we spoke, I hopped on the train to New York.

Madeline and I spent the day in Manhattan, wandering the streets quietly, hand in hand like nothing was wrong and everything was going to work out somehow. We had an amazing dinner at a too-expensive restaurant. We walked some more, down random streets we didn't even see, not ready to step out of the moment.

At Grand Central Terminal, when it was time for me to get on my train, Madeline impulsively returned to New Haven with me, to my now empty house. The next morning, I drove her to the train station, held her for a long moment and kissed her goodbye. I watched her walk down the long passage to the train platform, and I knew in that place in the center of my chest, the one with the sharp but not unbearable pain, that I would never see her again.

I was right.

Julie brought Schuyler home later that day, and didn't leave. She'd been gone for a week and a day.

I'd like to say there was a tearful scene full of epiphanies, but the truth was simpler. We discovered that week that neither of us could live without Schuyler, and we didn't particularly want to try to live without each other, either. Julie and John talked and decided their friendship was more important than the rest of what they'd had but had never felt terribly comfortable with, and that was that. I talked to Madeline on the phone one more time, when she informed me she was pregnant, and not with my child. I discovered bits and pieces over the years, about how the father of her child left her and how she found a new direction in her life in raising her little girl by herself, but it was all information gained from a distance.

Julie and I slowly reconnected. There was no romantic rededication, no stirring reaffirmation of our commitment, nothing but the quiet realization that we really could lose it all. Our sadness and our confusion had gotten the best of us, and we'd lost our way. We'd both stood on the bridge, it seemed, and we'd considered the possibilities that lay with self-destruction before stepping back and putting our feet to the road again.

Schuyler needed us, and we needed each other.

We were about to discover just how much.

8

The Answer That Was False,
and the Answer That Was True

N ot otherwise specified'?" said Julie. "I don't think I understand."

It had been several months since Schuyler had visited the Yale
Child Study Center, but we'd finally received Betsy's report in
the mail, along with a friendly, handwritten note apologizing for
the delay. Now that we finally had Schuyler's evaluation in hand, we
were faced with something unexpected, something I didn't think we
would ever see.

We had a diagnosis.

Sort of.

At the end of four pages describing Schuyler's history and her
performance at the evaluation sessions back in December 2002, there
were four lines under the category of "Diagnosis," labeled Axis I
through Axis IV. And there under Axis I, the answer.

Pervasive developmental disorder, not otherwise specified.

When I went online to look it up, I found a disorder more easily
defined by what it wasn't than what it was. It was a "subthreshold"
condition where some features of autism were present, but not

enough to make for an actual diagnosis of autism. It wasn't mild autism, exactly. If autism were a song, PDD-NOS represented a single verse. It was still the same song, not the Easy Listening version. Just a part of autism, a slice.

One paragraph stuck out to me from the Yale Child Study Center's site:

> It should be emphasized that this "subthreshold" category is thus defined implicitly, that is, no specific guidelines for diagnosis are provided. While deficits in peer relations and unusual sensitivities are typically noted, social skills are less impaired than in classical autism. The lack of definition(s) for this relatively heterogeneous group of children presents problems for research on this condition. The limited available evidence suggest that children with PDD-NOS probably come to professional attention rather later than is the case with autistic children, and that intellectual deficits are less common.

Julie and I looked over this, and other sites as well. We found comments by other parents with kids who had been diagnosed with PDD-NOS, read how the definitions of what made one kid NOS and another autistic were fluid at best, changing between doctors who had wildly differing opinions. One thing seemed consistent.

No one seemed to know exactly what the diagnosis meant.

Everyone seemed to agree that it was something of a catch-all diagnosis suggesting something from the spectrum of autism. To us, however, it seemed almost like a cop-out.

"Does that sound like they don't actually know what's wrong with her?" Julie asked.

"Yeah, "I said. "I think it sounds more like '*beats the shit out of me but I am a Ph.D. from Yale so I can't say that.*' "

The Yale report stated that after observing Schuyler in diagnostic play sessions (and doesn't that sound like the most fun a kid can have outside of Chuck E. Cheese?), it was determined that her eye contact was fleeting and her social interactions with people lacked reciprocity. "The level of pervasive impairment in Schuyler's communication and socialization is consistent with a diagnosis of pervasive developmental disorder, not otherwise specified," the report concluded.

Most of the report was fairly benign, even warm at times ("She presented as an adorable little girl with short blond hair and a bright smile.") The final paragraph didn't pull any punches, however.

> *Compared to other children with pervasive developmental disorder, Schuyler exhibits more emotional expression; she smiles and laughs. However, her emotional expressions are not directed to anyone intentionally. She does not communicate with intention, show interest in the activities of others, or interact socially with others on a consistent and frequent basis. In the course of this evaluation there were only three occasions when Schuyler interacted with the clinician, and these interactions occurred only after considerable effort by the clinician. In sum, Schuyler struggles considerably with basic social skills and communicating, as well as low muscle tone. As a result, she requires considerable early intervention to address all of these areas.*

Julie and I sat together, feeling deflated. We'd gone looking for an answer, but this felt incomplete. Betsy's observations about Schuyler and her apparently random, feral social interactions also seemed wildly wrong to us. I knew Schuyler had been a bad test subject, particularly once she'd figured out she was being observed and decided not to cooperate. But I still felt, even as I considered my own defensiveness and total lack of objectivity, that Betsy had gotten it wrong. I knew with almost absolute certainty that she approached Schuyler with a sincere desire to help. I couldn't escape the feeling, however, that on some subconscious level she might have been predisposed to arrive at PDD-NOS, a condition that had originally been identified and defined by none other than the Yale Child Study Center itself.

We read through it a few more times, and then suddenly I just didn't want to look at the damned thing anymore. I was tired of being asked to observe Schuyler and see what was wrong with her. I felt like there needed to be someone in her life who saw her difference without judgment, someone who would hold her up when she reached for the moon. I didn't like the labels that so many professionals were trying to casually affix to Schuyler. In retrospect, I'm not sure how important it was to me whether or not the label fit, or what it might mean for her if it did.

I was glad we had a diagnosis, if for no other reason than it would open a lot of doors for services that would have otherwise been unavailable to our daughter. But in my heart, I was convinced there was nothing wrong with Schuyler beyond the inability of the rest of the world to open the right doors for her. Schuyler was there, she was this amazing person inside her mind's silent shell, more intelligent than her doctors could imagine and more interesting than any one of us could yet appreciate. I'd watched her as she puzzled out the world around her, and I'd listened as she excitedly pointed out things that aroused her curiosity. She had questions, and lots of them, and the fact that we couldn't understand them didn't invalidate their existence, nor the urgency with which she was asking them.

I believed the rest of us had failed her. We'd failed by not finding a way to reach her inside her unique world.

The problem is us, I thought. *One day we'll get it right.*

I called Betsy the next day to talk to her about the diagnosis, but she wasn't a great deal of help.

"The good news about PDD-NOS, and the thing I think you should feel relieved about, is that we can say with confidence that Schuyler is not autistic," she said.

It was like her glass-half-full good news mantra, one that she emphasized several times. It was a positive thing to hear, but we'd determined a long time ago that Schuyler didn't possess the early warning signs of autism. She was a vibrant, highly socialized little girl who laughed a lot and didn't seem to have a care in the world. She had none of the obsessive behaviors, socialization problems, or detachment issues that so often accompany autism.

She was simply wordless.

Over the next few weeks, I discovered that having an actual diagnosis somehow added an edge to our interactions with the rest of the world. I'd always had a tendency to become defensive when other patrons at restaurants or public areas would give us dirty looks as Schuyler was being frisky. But now I found that with Schuyler's diagnosis, my reaction to the snotty looks became outright hostile. Suddenly I was saying things like "Can I help you?" or "Is there a problem?" or simply "What? What?" when people would look at Schuyler as she jabbered away loudly in Schuylerese. I could sense it wasn't just her volume they objected to, but also her incomprehensibility, as if she were simply choosing to howl instead of speak. If they listened carefully, they might have found that her howl was more than it seemed.

When she was younger, her speech sounded like a baby's babbling, but for the past year or so, it had changed subtly. Her tones altered now in specific patterns and her pitch moved in ways that were clearly approximating speech. It was like trying to listen to a conversation taking place in the next room, through the wall.

Now that Schuyler had been identified with a thing with a name, I wanted people to be able to look at her and just know, and treat her with respect and compassion right from the start.

Why couldn't they just know?

They couldn't, of course, and that was actually a positive thing. Schuyler gave no obvious outward indication of a problem, but sometimes I wondered. I tried to look at her with different, more analytical eyes after the diagnosis. I wanted to see if there was anything at all, any tic or behavior or physical abnormality that would give her away. It was hard to say.

I thought Schuyler was in most ways a normal three-year-old, with a good disposition and a friendly manner and unlimited energy. She had no words, but she was unwaveringly curious, and her wide eyes darted constantly, never dull, taking in the world hungrily. Schuyler was obviously not autistic, at least to my untrained eyes. But as I watched her, I had to accept that she was clearly different.

Schuyler couldn't talk, that was the most obvious thing. Her lack of speech meant she took on a somewhat mysterious air, like a tiny little Buddha looking on the world with silent but knowing eyes, usually accompanied by a wrinkled nose and a quick smile. But it also meant she was unable to express her joy or her curiosity or most important her frustration in the same way a normal three-year-old would be able to do. That avenue of communication was closed, not just for her but for the people around her as well. The only way she could compensate for that difficulty was by becoming physical in her reactions.

When people would look at her with that expression of "What's her problem?" it made me want to knock them over and scream,

"What's wrong with YOU? Can't you see?"

They couldn't. And I could see, but not just a problem. I also saw a little girl who was different, but one with whom I never had a moment in which we couldn't make ourselves understood to each other with perfect clarity. Schuyler's wordlessness was teaching me to compensate and to pay close attention to all the subtle signals she was sending in all her various ways. She signed, she pantomimed, and when I correctly guessed what she was trying to say, she'd laugh and clap her hands. Life with Schuyler was a little like a never-ending game of charades.

It was also breaking my heart a little, over and over again.

Schuyler's transition to the public schools was not going as well as we'd hoped. She was beginning to show signs of aggression toward other kids, mostly out of frustration at her inability to communicate and their inability to understand. Neither Julie nor I was convinced that her special education class was doing her any good. We'd visited the class and discovered that most of its students were severely disabled. One girl was so prone to extreme acts of self-destructive behavior that she had to be kept restrained in a special chair, one she could neither knock over or use to hop around until she was near something she could reach and destroy. Another little boy suffered from Down syndrome and would, without warning, run across the room and smash into walls. I watched all this during a class visit one time, and my heart broke for the parents of these kids, parents who were searching for far different answers than we were.

Through the chaos, I watched Schuyler as she sat against the wall, quietly thumbing through books and watching the other kids run through their wild, hapless routines. It may not be a very polite way to put it, but she looked for all the world like a child watching the circus. She was too young to understand the pain these kids were in, and too curious to ignore them.

Often it felt like the only time we ever heard from her teachers was when they would call to complain because Schuyler had arrived on the bus with a dirty diaper. This was occasionally an issue because Schuyler was not having any luck with potty training, a hard concept to teach to a nonverbal kid.

The school would also send home the most idiotic little art projects that in our opinion had clearly been done by the teachers. There were times when I wanted to call them and say, *"Yes, I know it must be traumatic when you have to change her diaper, and I appreciate that you can spell my daughter's name in macaroni, but do you think you might take some time to perhaps fix my broken kid?"*

We took Schuyler's Yale Child Study Center evaluation to Dr. Simon, and while she didn't come right out and say it, she made it pretty clear that she didn't think much of the PDD-NOS diagnosis.

"Yeah, I don't know," she said doubtfully. "I think Schuyler does remarkably well with the nonverbal aspects of development and seems to *want* to communicate very much. She doesn't exhibit any of the socialization issues I might expect from a PDD spectrum patient. Her comprehension level is very high, and her frustration level is quite low."

She sat down in her office chair and pondered the report while we waited. Her mind seemed far away. Finally she placed it on her desk and sighed.

"There's something else I think I'd like to explore, if you're agreeable to it. I'd like to send Schuyler to a specialist. I interned with an excellent neurologist here at Yale named Laura Ment, and she's still in the School of Medicine. I think I could get her to see Schuyler."

Dr. Ment was a very calm presence. I could see how her style would be a good fit for Dr. Simon. She sat with Schuyler for about half an hour and simply played with her, not directing her activities or getting in her way. When she sat down with us and looked over the report, she agreed immediately that the PDD-NOS diagnosis wasn't the last word on Schuyler.

"PDD-NOS can be a helpful diagnosis as far as it goes," she said. "But it can also be an indication that there are deeper issues that need to be explored, and some of them may be physiological or even neurological in nature. I'd like to start with a hearing test."

"She's had a few tests already," I said. "Two, I guess."

"She's had a test to measure whether or not her ears are physically registering sound, and it looks like she passed that one," said Dr. Ment as she consulted Schuyler's file, which was growing to the point that it was beginning to spill out of its folder. "The next test for her is one that measures her brain's response to those physical changes. I'd like to schedule this brain stem hearing test for early July, and if she passes that, I think we should do an MRI."

"An MRI?" said Julie warily. "Really? That's like a brain scan, right?"

"That's exactly right. If Schuyler's problem is neurological in nature, the MRI is probably going to tell us a lot. It will take a series of scans that will create a detailed picture of the structures of her brain itself. It's not the first procedure we run because it's expensive, and it can be very traumatic for young children and for their parents, too. They have to remain completely still for about an hour, so we place them under anesthesia. It's delivered intravenously, and that's not much fun."

We looked at each other nervously. Dr. Ment smiled and touched Julie's hand. "Let's do the hearing test first and see what it says, how does that sound?"

We'd been through hearing tests before, and so I didn't expect it to be bad. But then, I didn't expect Schuyler to require a sedative, either; I assumed that she'd need to be awake for the test. I certainly didn't expect to see the sedative arrive in the form of a giant syringe. Schuyler's eyes grew cartoonishly wide when she saw it.

The tech saw her reaction, and ours, too, I suppose, and she quickly said, "No no no, this isn't an injection, it's medicine. We administer it orally, just with a syringe."

That seemed strange until they began to give it to Schuyler, and then the reason became clear. This sedative was extremely nasty. The syringe was necessary in order to shoot the medicine so far back into her mouth that she couldn't spit it back out, which based on the smell would have been the appropriate response.

Schuyler gagged and squirmed and cried and generally hated us all for a few minutes before she grew tired. Twenty minutes later she was asleep, and the technician was applying tiny electrodes to her head, finally slipping a pair of huge pillowy headphones over her ears. The test measured her brain waves and their response to the signals being sent by her ears, signals that the brain will respond to regardless of consciousness. The technician ran through the test in a short period of time, and before she even removed the electrodes and the earphones, she was able to look at the results and tell us that Schuyler had passed with an almost perfect score.

Her brain could hear.

Schuyler woke from her sedated state in a foul mood and staggered around like Otis the town drunk for a while, but by the end of the day she was no worse for the experience. Two days later, we returned to Yale–New Haven Hospital for Schuyler's MRI.

The most difficult thing about the MRI appointment was that Schuyler figured out exactly what was going on almost instantly, and after the battery of tests and evaluations she'd already endured, and particularly after the butt-flavored sedative at her last appointment only a few days before, she wasn't having any of it.

When we arrived at the room where the anesthesia was going to be administered, we had to wait for about half an hour. This wasn't a good way to start; Schuyler heard the hum of medical machinery, and when it was time to enter, she balked, stopping at the door and refusing to go in. She didn't even cry at first. She planted her feet and grabbed the door frame and shook her head vigorously, her eyes wide with uncharacteristic terror.

She did not want to go into that room. She was correct not to.

Okay, look. I knew she needed this procedure. I was aware that it opened up a whole new realm of possibilities for answers. We both knew how important it was. But I didn't anticipate having to watch as the nurses tried to insert that impossibly large IV needle into the back of her tiny hand. I certainly didn't expect to help them by holding her down as she screamed and flailed, her eyes locking with mine as if I were betraying her. I thought that was going to be the worst moment I would ever have to endure with my little girl. I was wrong; the worst came moments later when, after three tries, the nurses finally slid that needle into a vein and the anesthesia hit her system. In the midst of her straining and screaming, Schuyler suddenly went limp, her last cry choking off with a gasp.

It felt like nothing in the world so much as holding a person as they died. That's when I lost my composure.

That was hard. Even knowing it was for her own good, it was hard to hold Schuyler down and look into those tearful eyes as they jabbed that needle into her hand, hard to do all that and still feel like a good parent.

I shouldn't be too melodramatic, however. As bad as the preparation was, the MRI itself only lasted about thirty-five minutes. Schuyler slept off the anesthesia in her stroller, and we were on the couch watching SpongeBob a few hours later. I think Julie and I were more shaken up by the experience than our daughter was. Even as we were leaving the hospital, Schuyler held up her arm to any stranger who would make eye contact and showed off the Blue's Clues Band-Aid on the back of her hand as if it was a Purple Heart.

Which really, I suppose it was.

After that experience, and also following a rough few weeks at work (including a shouting match with a doctor about, well, how I wasn't shouting at him), we decided it would be an excellent time to take Schuyler home to Texas to see my family. She'd been once before, as a baby, but this would be the first time she'd actually be able to interact with anyone in a meaningful way.

The trip itself wasn't memorable for any particular events. We sat in my mother's yard in her swing and watched Schuyler play with my brother's son, Scotty, who was two weeks younger than Schuyler but at least four inches taller and ten pounds heavier. Schuyler held her own. We watched the sun set and the early summer storms roll in from the west, flashing menacingly but far away. I took Schuyler into the lot behind my mother's back fence and looked for horny toads. They were supposedly rare but we found one eventually. Schuyler whispered "wow" appreciatively at his fierce appearance, even pointing out he was missing one of his two big horns on the crest of his skull, no doubt lost in some monumental reptilian battle many summers before.

The trip to Texas was significant for one reason. It was the last time we'd spend time with Schuyler, laughing and filled with a sort of nervous hopefulness for the future, without knowing her monster was in the room.

When we finally met that monster, it lay waiting to pounce from between the lab coats of two nervous and sad-faced doctors.

Considering how long we'd searched for it, we were taken completely by surprise.

When we walked into Dr. Simon's office and I saw Dr. Ment standing in front of the light board displaying Schuyler's MRI scans, I watched her face carefully. It bothered me that she didn't make eye contact. Dr. Simon began speaking, softly and nervously.

"So it took a few weeks to make a clear determination, but we do have what I think is safe to call a definitive answer for you, based on the results of Schuyler's MRI scan. We've been in consultation with a geneticist at the University of Chicago who is probably the leading expert in this area. I've asked Dr. Ment to come so she can better explain what we've found."

Dr. Ment faced the light board, still not looking at us. Dr. Simon quickly stepped back, no longer wanting to be in front of us. I felt Julie squeeze my hand.

Schuyler played at our feet, quietly hooting as she engaged in conversation with one of Dr. Simon's dolls.

"Schuyler suffers from a form of brain malformation known as polymicrogyria," began Dr. Ment, apparently deciding that the best approach was simply to lay it out for us. "Her particular form is called congenital bilateral perisylvian syndrome.

"Now, breaking that down, 'congenital' means Schuyler has had this malformation since before she was born. It developed while she was still a fetus, and was fully formed at birth. The good news about that is it isn't going to get any worse. The brain she has now is the one she's always going to have. The bad news is, it's never going to get any better, either."

I was still stuck on the word "malformation." I glanced at Julie and saw her resolve slipping. I'd never seen her eyes so wide.

"'Bilateral' means the malformation affects both sides of her brain in roughly the same place, so the normal redundancies you might expect to kick in from the other hemisphere of the brain aren't available. If you look,"—she pointed to some dark gray areas on the cutaway photos of Schuyler's head, oddly recognizable by the shape of her mouth—"you can see the affected areas, which are consistent with CBPS. These areas include some fine motor skills, which explains why Schuyler's hands are still very awkward, and it most seriously affects the speech areas." She pointed and paused. "Those speech areas appear to be completely impaired."

"We do apologize for the amount of time it took to arrive at a diagnosis," said Dr. Simon, "but this disorder is extremely rare. Right now, new cases are being discovered all the time, but I could still only find fewer than a hundred documented cases out there."

"As soon as we figured out what we were looking at, we contacted Dr. William Dobyns in Chicago," said Dr. Ment. "He's been the leading researcher in this area, and he confirmed the diagnosis yesterday."

There was a pause. We had no comments or questions and instead just tried to take in everything that had just been told to us.

Schuyler's brain was deformed. She wasn't developmentally delayed. She was broken, and they would never be able to fix her. This was it.

Dr. Ment continued, her voice softening. "There are some things you should expect from this condition. First of all, no one can ever say for sure, and I encourage you to continue with speech therapy and keep working on her language. But you need to start preparing yourselves for the possibility that Schuyler's speech may never progress further than it has right now." I felt Julie stiffen beside me.

"Most CBPS patients suffer from a similar range of difficulties, but there is a wide variation between the best and worst cases. I'm hopeful that Schuyler represents the best case spectrum. If so, I think it is reasonable to expect that she very well may be able to live independently one day."

Julie was crying now, trying to hide it from Schuyler but falling apart quickly. Dr. Simon could see we didn't have long. "I'd like to schedule a consultation with Dr. Ment and a geneticist in the next few weeks so you can sit down and have a more comprehensive look at what all this means," she said. "Now is probably not a good time to go into the details. This is hard stuff, I know. And I am so, so sorry this was the news we had for you." I could tell Dr. Simon felt horribly for Schuyler. It suddenly occurred to me that she'd probably had her own tears already.

Schuyler climbed into my lap and played quietly with my hand, making me clap it on my leg and against my other upturned palm, laughing to herself.

"I know when you get home, the first thing you're going to do is go online and look this up," Dr. Ment said. "I just want you to be ready. It's going to be pretty rough."

And it was.

When we got to our cars, I said miserably, "Jesus Christ, I have to go to a staff meeting, I totally forgot."

"Do you have to go?" Julie asked sadly.

"Yeah, I do." That was probably a lie, but I needed to be away from all this for an hour or two, and sitting at the back of a darkened conference room while pretending to watch a PowerPoint presentation sounded like a good place to do it. "I guess start calling everyone, and I'll be home as soon as I can." We embraced without another word, holding on a little longer than usual and clutching a little more tightly before parting. I gave Schuyler a little wave through the window as they pulled away.

When I got to the meeting, it had already started. I slipped into the back of the room. My supervisor, Jim, saw me and immediately knew something was horribly wrong. He looked at me and shrugged, his eyebrows arching dramatically. I took out a notepad and turned to a blank sheet. I paused before writing. I had no idea what to say. Finally I scratched out a few words and tore out the sheet, folding it before handing it across to him. I watched his face fall as he opened it and read.

"Schuyler's brain is deformed. She may never talk. It's bad."

After the meeting, we exchanged a few words and then I excused myself and slipped away to my office. I knew he was telling our bosses what was going on, and I was glad; it wasn't a conversation I was looking forward to having with anyone.

I sat at my desk and pulled out the sheet Dr. Ment had given us. It listed the ugly string of cold medical terms that gave a name to the thing inside Schuyler's head, the tiny monster that had been living there all along, squeezing her brain and fogging her thoughts since the day she was born.

I typed the monster's name into Google and found a handful of articles.

I read through them. The first one I read carefully, printing it as I did so. The rest I skimmed, unable to face the totality of it all just yet. Select words jumped out over and over, words I hoped would only be in some articles, words I wanted to be disputed among different doctors. Words I didn't want standing anywhere near my daughter.

Partial paralysis of the face, tongue, jaws, and throat. Difficulties in speaking, chewing, and swallowing. *Grand mal* seizures, often very serious. Joint deformities. Tendency to drool. Mild to severe mental retardation. *Retardation. What was that? Seizures? Retardation? Retardation. God, make that word stop. . . .*

I stood up and left the room, not stopping to talk to anyone. Jim had informed everyone who needed to be told, and no one tried to engage me. They could see it wasn't the right time. I felt dizzy and stopped at a vending machine for a Dr Pepper. Once I had it, I suddenly didn't want it, but I carried it with me anyway.

I took the stairs two at a time and burst out the back door of the clinic. The sun had almost finished setting while I was in my meeting, and the air was already cooling down. I got in my car, tossing the can onto the passenger seat, but instead of heading toward home, I found myself driving in the opposite direction. I had no idea where I was going until I got there, pulling up in front of an old Gothic church I'd driven past countless times. It was at least a hundred years old, probably older.

I pulled up and shut off the car, sitting in the twilight without a word. I stayed frozen in place, holding in a great swell of emotion I didn't immediately recognize. I was suddenly aware of the can on the seat beside me, and that's when I grabbed it, opened the car door and stormed out, rushing to the front of the church. I paused for a moment and then threw the unopened can as hard and as high as I could, aiming up at the darkened stained glass panes near the steeple high above, waiting for the smash and the sound of glass crashing below, the only sound I wanted to hear.

The can impacted against the glass but didn't break it. The soda tumbled back to the ground, bouncing off the stone steps below and erupting in feeble spray, hissing softly.

"Why? Why? What the HELL did she ever do to you?"

I heard the voice, choked with tears and rage, barely comprehensible, like a mockery of Schuyler's own speech, and as if watching from behind one of the two-way mirrors Schuyler had looked into so many times while being evaluated and tested, I understood that the voice was my own.

"What did she ever do to you? What reason could you possibly have for doing this to an innocent little girl?"

I spun around for a moment, looking for someone to engage, as if God might appear to me, but I was alone. As I spun, I lost my balance and fell to one knee as if drunk. My glasses flew off into the grass. As soon as I was down, I kept going, putting my face against the ground and closing my eyes. There was silence around me now; the can had spent its carbonated energy and all I could hear was the faint murmur of traffic.

"I don't understand," I said quietly, rolling onto my back and looking up into the darkening sky, its last streaks of color fading behind the church. "Don't do this to her. Do it to me, don't do it to her. Please. Please. I hate you, God, I hate you so much. Please leave her alone. Hurt me instead."

I cried then. I cried for the future, for the life I had always imagined for my little girl, a life that would never ever be what we'd imagined it to be. I cried as I imagined her one day collapsing into seizures, her uncomprehending eyes finding mine before she lost consciousness, the question of how I could let this happen to her forever unspoken. I cried for Julie and I cried for Schuyler, for the day she realized she was different and broken. I cried at the word "retardation" and the atom bomb of low expectations it carried with it. I cried at the idea of Schuyler growing old in our care and never knowing a life on her own terms.

I lay in the grass as the sky grew completely dark, I lay there until I felt God wasn't watching me, if indeed he ever had been. God, my enemy, the bully who'd reached down and damaged my angel's mind. I didn't know much at that moment, but I knew God wasn't watching.

At last I stood, found my glasses and walked back to the car, never looking back at the dark stone church as I drove home to my family and our monster and the future.

Part Two

A Monster Revealed

9

Monster

It all starts within a teeny tiny brain, in the transparent head of what looks like a guppy but will one day be a child. It is in this unthinkably alien and yet most human of human worlds that the monster is born.

No one knows for sure why it happens. It might begin with an infection, perhaps one so slight that the mother never even knows it happened. It may start with an episode when there is a lack of oxygen going to the fetus during the second trimester, maybe from a brief entanglement of the umbilical cord. In some cases, it very likely takes place in the realm of the very very small, where the monster reaches out and damages or mutates a handful of very specific genes on a chromosome. In many cases, the monster forms at the very same instant the baby begins her life, the result of a genetic disorder with recessive inheritance. In a perverse mirror image of that enchanted evening, you may see a stranger across a crowded room. That soul mate carries half a code that is meaningless by itself, but when plugged into the other half that you carry, creates the thing that will forever change a life, and all the lives that spin around it.

The monster has a family name, an imposing handful of syllables that doesn't feel natural on the tongue no matter how many times you say it. *Polymicrogyria*. Despite its heft, however, the word breaks down into very easy pieces. Poly, or "many." Micro, or "small," and gyria, which are the folds in the surface of the brain, the things that make a brain *look* like a brain.

A typical brain is composed of many different folds, but in a brain afflicted with polymicrogyria, there are too many of these folds and they are smaller than they should be. These tiny squiggles are the monster in its most basic form—it is the closest thing to a face the monster has—and yet these imperfections, visible only on an MRI or CT scan, will be very difficult to see, even for an experienced radiologist. Since these diagnostic procedures are expensive and often traumatic, there's no guarantee that the brain scans will ever be run on a child whose monster prowls on more delicate feet.

The difficulty in detecting and then recognizing polymicrogyria is one thing that makes it hard to diagnose and treat. Another is the wide variation in its manifestations. One teenaged boy carried his monster for eighteen years before it was detected by an MRI, run as a result of a hockey injury. His head was fine, but not fine. He'd grown up with a speech disorder and a learning disability and had compensated for both, but it was only on the edge of adulthood that he found out why.

Other children born with polymicrogyria don't live past their first few weeks.

Polymicrogyria is not a disease. It's a descriptive umbrella for a number of disorders, all caused by the deformity of the gyria. These monster siblings live in different areas of the brain, with some variations in symptoms and severity. They all share some common traits, however, and all are incredibly rare.

They all typically cause some amount of global developmental delay, feeding difficulties (sometimes resulting in fatal aspiration), respiratory issues, fine motor dysfunction, seizures (occasionally life threatening), and mental retardation. Most are bilateral, meaning they hit both sides of the brain nearly symmetrically. The usual polymicrogyria manifests itself into a number of these similar disorders, rare and cloudy monsters with similar-sounding names, like a brood of identical blond southern children with alliterative biblical names like Jacob and Joshua and Jordan.

Bilateral frontoparietal polymicrogyria. Bilateral mesial occipital polymicrogyria. Bilateral diffuse polymicrogyria. Bilateral parieto-occipital polymicrogyria. Bilateral parasagittal parietooccipital polymicrogyria. Bilateral frontal polymicrogyria. Unilateral perisylvian or multilobar polymicrogyria.

And bilateral perisylvian polymicrogyria, also called BPP and known in that cruel summer of 2003 as congenital bilateral perisylvian syndrome.

Schuyler's monster.

In a family of disorders as rare as winning lotto tickets, BPP is the most common of the polymicrogyria clan. It stands out from its brethren by way of partial paralysis of facial muscles, resulting in speech difficulties and excessive drooling; in some cases it can lead to feeding problems for a baby. It lives in a deeply grooved area on either side of the brain called the sylvian fissure and impairs both the speech areas and those controlling fine motor skills. BPP is sometimes accompanied by cerebral palsy, causing even greater motor difficulties and loss of control of voluntary muscles. None of this had manifested itself in Schuyler in any dramatic form.

But Schuyler's monster brings with it another terrifying weapon, one that may be worse for the observer than the patient, but can also in rare cases snatch life away from its sufferers.

Seizures.

It begins with an electricity storm.

When the nerves of the brain are called upon to transmit an electrical signal, they do so by moving salts quickly from one side of the cell's membrane to the other. This movement spreads like a stadium crowd doing "the wave," from one end of the nerve to the other.

The storm is likely to occur in certain areas of the brain, such as the temporal lobe and the motor cortex, where nerve cells are especially sensitive to abnormal levels of electrical transmission. Some patients report warnings from their brain, such as peculiar smells or problems with their vision, but when one of these or some other event actually triggers a seizure, things happen quickly.

Mercifully, the first thing that usually happens when a seizure strikes is a loss of consciousness. If it is an absence seizure (pronounced with a wacky French accent for maximum effect), that loss of consciousness will not be accompanied by any associated motor symptoms. The subject will just stare, with perhaps a few subtle motor movements, for perhaps five to ten seconds and will then continue on with no memory of the event. Absence seizures are often the first sign of PMG in a patient, but it's not the worst of it. It will normally take a few years for the patient to progress from absence seizures to the type most people know and fear the most. When it arrives, the monster of all seizures lands with both feet.

When a *grand mal* seizure begins, a sound will escape the patient's mouth as she collapses and experiences what is often referred to as the "epileptic cry," a haunting and agonized howl created as the diaphragm contracts and forces air through the contracted vocal cords. The patient becomes rigid, extending her arms and legs and arching her back, falling down as she does so. She will experience jerking movements in her arms, legs, and trunk muscles, and may involuntarily pass urine or feces.

After the seizure has run its course, the end brings confusion, as well as sore muscles, a King Kong–sized headache, difficulty concentrating, and extreme fatigue. The patient may sleep for hours, a deep healing slumber as her brain picks up its shattered pieces and puts them back in place.

If the seizures don't stop after twenty or thirty minutes, the brain's neurons can be damaged. Over a period of time, such damaging seizures can eventually bring significant brain damage and even death.

But this is rare. Seizures don't usually kill. They terrify, they confuse, they can cause head and bodily injuries from falls, and they will break hearts, but they don't typically take life, only wreck it instead. When the *grand mal* seizure is over, the patient moves on as best as she can, taking the monster with her.

Patients suffering from bilateral perisylvian polymicrogyria develop symptoms at different times, and with differing degrees of severity. Some are profoundly impaired, some develop cerebral palsy, some cannot eat without the aid of a feeding tube. Some die in their sleep from a condition similar to apnea, and some are hit as infants with debilitating seizures that ruin their young brains before they even have a chance to dance in the world.

Others show very little effect at all. No doubt thousands never even find out they have it.

In summer 2003, at the time of her diagnosis, Schuyler suffered from a virtually complete speech deficit, as well as some difficulty chewing some foods, weak but not paralyzed facial muscles that resulted in messy eating and some drooling, and some fine motor impairment that kept her from signing very precisely but didn't particularly affect her ability to get around or feed herself or play hard. Her personality was vibrant but her cognitive abilities were still a huge unknown. She was significantly delayed in almost all areas of development, including toilet training. Perhaps most significantly, she had yet to experience any seizures.

Typical onset of seizures for polymicrogyria patients occurs between the ages of six and ten. Schuyler was three.

There was no way of knowing if a bigger monster lay in wait for her.

10

Hard Times Give Me
Your Open Arms

I awoke on Valentine's Day 2004 to snow. For the past seven years, that had been not only expected, but pretty much a given. On this morning, it was a surprise. After the week I'd had, it was a nice surprise.

It was snowing on Valentine's Day in Texas.

Austin is our setting. Our new home.

I wanted to burn down the whole world.

The weeks in Connecticut following Schuyler's diagnosis in the summer of 2003 run together in my memory, so much so that when I go back and read the things I wrote at the time, it's almost surprising to see that our lives went on normally. We got up in the morning, we went to work, we did the same things we'd always done, but in something of a haze, I think. We were given the news and just released back out into the world, with very little in the way of follow-up. A sad little handshake and we were gone.

That lasted about a week, during which we obsessively looked up everything we could find on the Internet. In 2003, that wasn't much. Schuyler's condition had been identified ten years before by an Argentine neurologist named Dr. Ruben Kuzniecky. (It was originally called "Kuzniecky's syndrome," as if that was any easier to pro-nounce.) In the decade that followed, a great deal had been learned, primarily by two doctors, Dr. William Dobyns at the University of Chicago and Dr. Christopher Walsh at Harvard, but most of their findings weren't generally available to members of the slobbering public like us. We found enough information to scare the crap out of us, but not really very much that was of any use to Schuyler.

After about a week of trying to make sense of what we'd found, I finally broke down and e-mailed Dr. Simon and Dr. Ment. "We don't know what to do now," I wrote. "I feel like we've been handed this big scary thing and been set loose. We're lost now. Please advise on the next step."

The next step was apparently to visit a geneticist at Yale, someone who could explain this from a different perspective. As soon as we met him, I had a pretty good idea what this geneticist was all about. I got the feeling that he wasn't a terribly sociable person and wasn't necessarily concerned about Schuyler as a person, but rather as a ve-hicle that transported a brain and gave it something to do. I also saw from the beginning that while Schuyler the little girl might have been invisible to him, Schuyler's brain was another matter. He'd done his homework before seeing us, so he knew exactly what he was going to see, a rare brain disorder (although he said the number of diagnosed cases was probably closer to one or two hundred by then) that he was very eager to see up close. The very first thing he did was begin asking us to sign consent forms so he could send everything off to Dr. Dobyns and get Schuyler into the study project being done in Chicago. Schuyler had a celebrity brain, and I don't suppose it ever occurred to him to consider how much less thrilled we were about that than he was.

Despite my irritation, however, I found myself liking him. He had a no-bullshit approach I found oddly refreshing. He didn't ap-pear to give a damn about my daughter or my family, but he didn't pretend to, either. I wasn't in a hurry to provide him and his colleagues with their next medical journal article, but at the same time, I got the feeling he would give us some answers.

I think he wanted to, although he didn't have much more to tell us than we had already found on our own. He wasn't terribly concerned about mental retardation, since she was so high functioning. I wasn't sure why I was comforted by the opinion of a genetics expert on the topic of Schuyler's behavior, but just hearing that after a week of worry was a relief. He didn't pull any punches abut her lack of speech or the possibility of severe seizures, but at the same time, he was completely unconvinced she'd had any absence seizures.

"There's a lot of crap out on the Internet, and most of it's wrong," he said. "I'd just stay away from it altogether if I were you."

I understood that, having contributed quite a lot of crap to the Internet myself, but at the same time, what we'd found online was pretty much the only information we'd had available. I wasn't entirely sure what he wanted us to do, aside from send Schuyler's stuff off to Mount Olympus and patiently wait for FedEx to deliver unto us the stone tablets sometime in the undetermined future.

If there was one thing we'd learned from Schuyler's saga, it was that we couldn't just wait for someone else to come along and take care of her.

It's funny how the simple passage of time changes things.

In the month following that meeting, life moved on. It felt as if it shouldn't at the time, like the whole world needed to stop what it was doing and recognize the shift in the universe, when an innocent little girl who had nothing but smiles and laughs and love for a rough world was repaid with a broken brain and a scary, uncertain future.

But the world didn't stop, or even pause. It went on, because that's what it does, and Schuyler went forward most of all, as perhaps I should have expected her to. She understood on some level that things were different, I suspect. She seemed to know that the house felt sadder, more desperate, and I imagine she felt the change from our tenacious search for an answer to the paralyzed new "be careful what you ask for" atmosphere that had settled in its place.

Furthermore, she understood on some level that *she* was different, and had been reaching that understanding for some time. She understood, but I don't believe she was ever frightened by it. She would watch people conducting conversations with a sad sort of wonder, but she also made herself understood well enough through signing and miming and dogged persistence, and she almost never stopped smiling. As I struggled to pull myself out of the funk that descended after the diagnosis, I watched her with wonder. I didn't know many people with fewer reasons to laugh than Schuyler, and yet I knew no one who laughed more.

I had written about the diagnosis on my blog, and the response was overwhelming. I received a few ugly, anonymous e-mails, and one blogger wrote how Schuyler's condition was God's divine retribution against her sinner of a father, but mostly what we received was support and love, from people we had never met and whom we would probably never meet, people for whom Schuyler had become a real person through the things I wrote about her and her situation. I received hundreds of e-mails within twenty-four hours of posting about the diagnosis. I sensed more than politeness from most of them. I felt real pain from these people, I understood that in some way, they had become emotionally vested in Schuyler and were also grieving in some way for the little girl they had always imagined Schuyler becoming.

The diagnosis brought us all to a place where we had to accept that there wasn't a solution for Schuyler's problems. Nothing was going to fix this. As our family moved through this new world, however, I began to notice other children with their own problems, and I found myself imagining their lives. One day at the mall, Schuyler and I saw a little girl who was about Schuyler's age but easily twice her weight. I found myself wondering about her future. This girl was different, and because she wasn't what our culture sees as beautiful or even acceptable, she was going to have a future filled with pain and harsh realities. In her own way, she'd won the same evil lotto as Schuyler, the same one a lot of kids win.

When Schuyler saw me looking at the girl with sadness in my eyes, she silently took my hand and gently kissed the back of it. She was the one with the monster in her head, but even then, she was the one teaching me how to make my way in this new world.

Not long after that, I received an e-mail from a parent in Europe whose nineteen-month-old child had been diagnosed with BPP only a few hours before. This father had gone on the Internet to look for more information, just as we had only a month before, and in his search, he found my words of frustration instead. His e-mail was full of shock and anger, and most of all hurt. It felt familiar. I read it and I remembered the panic, and the hurt. I didn't have any answers or wisdom for him, but I shared his feelings. They were mine as well.

The panic was gone, and my anger and my fear had been put in little boxes. I carried it all with me, and it made me sadder than I think the people around me realized. I was trying to put the diagnosis and its resulting despair behind me and move on to the next thing, whatever that might be. I watched Julie struggle the same way. Bit by bit, we were making the monster a part of our lives.

I don't actually remember how Julie and I first heard about the Magic Wings Butterfly Conservatory and Gardens in Massachusetts, although I suspect Dana told us about it. A few weeks after the diagnosis, on an impulse, the three of us piled into the car and headed north.

Julie and I stepped into the main conservatory room, Schuyler walking between us, and stopped, holding our breaths. We were standing in a greenhouse, warm and full of plants and paths and a koi-filled pond with a burbling waterfall. Of course, there were butterflies, about four thousand of them. They flitted lazily through the air, landing on feeders or leaves or visitors. The visual effect was stunning. Taken one at a time, the butterflies were tranquil. When seen *en masse,* they became a frenzy of motion, completely silent but suggesting cacophony. We walked slowly down the paths, Julie and I silent in our thoughts as we had been for weeks, and Schuyler wide-eyed and breathless at the sight of so many butterflies.

I watched Julie carefully. I saw the sadness in her eyes beginning to melt away. She carried Schuyler and held out her arm, pointing to some of the impossibly big specimens and hoping one would take advantage of her offered hand and alight there. I saw how in this place, maybe the most ethereal place we'd ever been, Julie wasn't the mother of a broken child. Schuyler didn't speak, but neither did we. Neither did anyone.

We sat down on a bench and watched the butterflies swirl around us. One landed on Julie's bare shoulder, and she laughed as its feet tickled her skin. A few minutes later, another landed on her forehead. Schuyler sat still for as long as she could, but eventually she began following the butterflies as they flew lazily past, quietly stalking one until another caught her attention.

When did I become so serious? I thought as I watched Schuyler and listened to Julie's laugh. *When did I turn into such a sad person?*

I walked over to a little bronze fairy sculpture that held a feeder, consisting of a small glass bowl and a sponge soaked in sugar water. There were a few butterflies sitting on the sculpture's tiny hand, and as I held out my camera to try to get as close a photo as I could, a giant *Blue Morpho* landed on the back of my hand. He was huge, and yet barely registered any weight at all. I held my breath as he slowly opened and closed his wings. A few seconds later, he took to the air.

I looked down to see Schuyler watching me, a curious little smile playing at the corners of her mouth. Neither of us made a sound.

Autumn is my favorite time of the year, even with its accompanying melancholy, and fall in New England is like nothing you've ever seen before, even more beautiful than Michigan and without the accompanying dread of potential frozen death.

Fall 2003 felt different, though. The change in the weather and the autumn smell in the air served as a reminder that things were moving forward, with or without us. We'd taken Schuyler's diagnosis to her school in order to try to get her into a different class, but her classroom teacher seemed to take the request personally. She resisted, and in the end, we withdrew Schuyler from school altogether while we awaited a review by the school district. Classes started for everyone but her.

One of the things that had attracted us to Connecticut was its reputation for good schools, but now that we were in the glamorous world of special needs education, I felt as if I'd leaned against the front of some shiny new building, only to have the front wall fall over and reveal that I was on a movie set.

Every special needs child in this country's public schools is entitled to a periodic meeting with school officials and teachers to develop an IEP, or Individual Education Plan. The purpose of the IEP is to develop a course of study that is tailored to the student's particular needs, but judging from our experience, most special needs kids in New Haven seemed to end up in large mixed classes like Schuyler's. The most severely affected kids understandably attracted the most attention, but as a result, the only real individual attention Schuyler received occurred during her occupational, physical, and speech therapy sessions, none lasting more than half an hour or so every week. The teachers themselves appeared to be committed to their work but seemed tired, and at times jaded. Schuyler's teacher used a lot of sarcasm with her kids, and while I'm obviously a great believer in the therapeutic and spiritual benefits of smartassitude, I'm not sure how well it works on a kid with Down syndrome.

During the few weeks between our admittedly petulant decision to remove Schuyler from her class and the review that would hopefully place her in a more appropriate setting, she spent her days at

Faith's day care. Schuyler was not quite four years old and was still not potty trained, a fact that was perhaps understandable considering the communications barriers we faced, but still troubling. Faith decided to focus on making this happen for Schuyler, and as a result removed Schuyler from her diapers and put her in plastic underpants so she could feel when she'd gone and learn to prevent accidents. This technique probably worked well with kids who were both more verbal and less stubborn than Schuyler.

We should have been more involved. I blame myself completely.

A case of mild diaper rash became serious, and from that developed into a staph infection and a painful abscess. When we took her to see Dr. Simon, she took one look at it and called the Yale–New Haven Hospital and arranged for a surgical team to meet us when we arrived. I never thought we'd have a worse experience in Dr. Simon's office than the diagnosis meeting, but there it was.

The surgery itself only took a few minutes; by the time we'd finished filling out all her paperwork, she was lying in recovery, her tiny body floating in a giant bed. Over the past few months, I'd been aware of how tall she was getting, tall and slender and very grownup looking. Now suddenly she looked like a little mouse. It took about an hour for her to regain consciousness, and when she did, a transformation took place. Something sinister took hold of our sweet little monkey. Her eyes grew dark, her mouth opened into a little square, the tiny tendons in her neck bulged and her face turned purple as the wail escaped her mouth. For the next six hours, Schuyler expressed the purest and most primal rage you could imagine from an undersized little girl not yet four years old. I was impressed.

Schuyler cried without ceasing, she howled in pain but mostly in anger. Not anger really, so much as wrath. You can call her nonverbal, but never let it be said that Schuyler was unable to communicate that day. She punched at anyone who came within reach. She kicked, thumping loudly against the bed and arching her back every time she put any weight on the offending butt cheek. She was so persistent in her fury as she tried to remove the IV from her tiny little foot that the nurses eventually had to wrap a splint to the side of her foot, with the tubes tied firmly in place. This had the effect of giving her a little peg leg. Tiny Ahab was not amused.

We shared the room with another little girl who'd been transferred to New Haven from another hospital in Danbury where she'd had her own room. She wasn't too happy about sharing one now. Her family looked like every upper middle class New Englander we'd ever met, which is to say they appeared to have stepped out of a Lands' End catalogue. Every time one of us made a sound, we could hear the annoyed sighs from the other side of the curtain. At one point, a machine that administered antibiotics to Schuyler's IV began to softly beep. It continued for a few minutes, and then suddenly a head popped around the corner of the curtain. It was Lands' End Dad.

"I'm sorry," he said, sounding a bit like a young Thurston Howell, "but do you think you could stop that beeping? It's really very annoying."

I looked at him and smiled my very best *"ha HA, and aren't YOU a gigantic dumbass!"* smile. "You know, I'm not a doctor, actually. I wouldn't have the first clue how to make it stop." I pointed to the offending console.

"Oh. Oh! Right! Wow, I'm really sorry!" It had actually never occurred to Lands' End Dad that the sound might have been coming from some piece of actual medical equipment rather than some personal beeping device, something we were setting off just for our own amusement. His daughter was transferred to a private room shortly after that.

We stayed with Schuyler for most of the evening, long past visiting hours. Julie reluctantly left so she could go to work the next day, and I crawled into the huge bed beside Schuyler, whose anger had finally depleted her energy. She lay miserably beside me, curled under my arm as if she were seeking protection. I sang her to sleep, a Kelly Joe Phelps song about how sadness is part of life and comes with us to remind us of where we've come from and what we're reaching for. It had been on my mind lately.

Schuyler awoke the next morning to a room filled with balloons and flowers from dozens of my blog readers; I'd posted a note the night before. We'd slept fitfully and watched the sun rise together the next morning. Schuyler's foul mood had passed completely. She ate her breakfast as if it was the grandest feast ever served to a princess with a bandage on her ass, and when the nurse returned to check on her, Schuyler tried to brush her teeth for her, laughing the whole time.

The discharge nurse gave us instructions on taking care of the wound, and suggested I go home and get some sleep.

"Well, I'll be watching her, so I guess I'll have to wait."

"Don't you have any family in the area?" she asked.

That question seemed to be coming up a lot lately. It had been working on my conscience since the diagnosis, but I didn't realize it until that moment.

"No," I said. "It's just the three of us."

The annual online writers' conference I periodically attended was held soon after, and this year it took place in Austin.

It had been years since I'd been there, but I had many memories of Austin from my college days. It's the capital of Texas and yet unlike the rest of the state in some significant ways. Home to the University of Texas, Austin is a fairly liberal and wildly individualistic outpost in an otherwise very conservative state. Returning there now after all these years, I was reminded of how much I felt the town's sensibilities matched neatly with my own. When the conference was over, I left Austin but couldn't get it out of my head.

I knew Julie had become disenchanted with Connecticut. Living in New Haven was expensive, and despite advancements in our jobs, we simply couldn't seem to make enough money to live without eating bugs and grass by the end of the month. (Perhaps I exaggerate.) If I hadn't worked for Yale and been the recipient of a very nice health package, I'm not sure if we would have ever gotten an answer to Schuyler's silence. That had always been the incentive to stay, but now that the diagnosis had been delivered, there wasn't much left for Yale to do for us.

Still, we'd always been proud and happy to raise Schuyler in New England. It was a place that was interesting and historical, and we'd always liked the idea of her growing up on the East Coast. New Haven had been the place we were going to make our own, and Schuyler's own, too. It was to be her very own Yankee Adventure.

Ever since the diagnosis, however, the town had just felt cold and uncaring and a million miles from home, from family. Julie had made a few enduring friends at her bookstore job, but not many, and I had somehow managed to avoid all the social networking and hipster friendships that one is bound to encounter working in a mental hospital. In four years, I'd made a handful of friends, and one of them was my boss.

Schuyler was embarking on a hard journey, we all were, and now we were doing so without the benefit of a single extended family member to offer any kind of comfort or help. Julie and I talked, and not for long, before we decided. It was time to move.

When Julie and I talked about moving, we discovered something that we'd both felt and probably sensed that the other felt as well. Since the diagnosis, we'd been losing our hope. We'd felt it leaking away gradually but steadily, and we weren't sure how much longer we could hang on. Schuyler had been assigned to a new class at a different school, but there was no indication it was going to be any better for her. We knew that being special needs parents would be a challenge that was going to take everything we had. We just didn't think what we had would go so quickly.

Once we made the decision to move, things happened quickly, frighteningly so.

I'd made a friend in Austin named Tracy, a young writer and political activist with whom I'd actually sparred a bit online from time to time. In person, however, we got along well, and when Julie and I announced that we were looking to move to Austin, Tracy immediately began putting together job leads for me. One jumped out at me immediately, as a helpdesk technician at Apple, Inc. I applied and was given an interview over the phone. I flew back to Austin to meet them and found a workplace with cubicles full of art and snotty political slogans and funky action figures, populated by hippies and hipsters alike. I didn't see a single tie in the place. When they extended a job offer, I accepted immediately.

I loved New England. It wasn't working out, but I loved it all the same. Leaving Dana behind was difficult; she'd been an amazing friend to us for four years. I hated goodbyes, and when Apple told me the job would require me to attend training starting in about two weeks, I swallowed my sentimentality and packed up my VW Bug to the roof. I've always felt guilty for leaving as suddenly as I did, but I'm not sure I would have had the courage to just pull up and move like that if I'd hesitated.

While Julie finished packing our stuff and getting ready to move, I drove to Austin at the beginning of December 2003. I rented a room in a nice old house owned by a shy, stylish gay couple and began my training at Apple. I spent three weeks learning how to fix Macintosh laptops over the phone, and I missed my family more than I thought possible. When I called Julie, she told me Schuyler was signing "Daddy" almost constantly. At night, I dreamed about Schuyler, the same dream that had haunted me ever since the diagnosis, the one where she talked to me and told me everything was going to be okay.

I'd wake up alone on an inflated mattress in a rented room in a strange town, and the little three-foot-tall hole in my world felt emptier than ever.

The day before Christmas I flew back to New Haven, and after celebrating the holiday on cardboard boxes instead of furniture, we piled into Julie's car—three humans, a farting black pug named Lulu whom we'd gotten shortly before the diagnosis, and just about everything we owned that we couldn't part with.

And just like that, we were gone. Four years of our lives, dissipated like smoke.

Like a table that looks great in the storefront but turns out to have one leg shorter than the others, my new job in Austin was a wobbly situation almost from the beginning. That's the funny thing about first impressions. Sometimes they aren't just wrong. They're wildly wrong.

Apple was a bad fit. I think I knew it from the beginning, but I needed it to work out, so I kept busy, first in training and then later on the phone, and I tried to ignore the fact that the funky cubicles were still cubicles, and the hipster nerds working in them were still corporate drones with quotas that had to be reached. It was a world in which everyone but me seemed to have been employed at some point, and I really tried to make it work.

Just so you know, I did try. And I might have even worked it out, if I hadn't gotten fired by a computer.

A funny thing happens at Apple if you get sick during your first month of employment and miss more than two days of work. Let's say you're new and maybe sort of irresponsible and don't really read your employee handbook very closely. (In my own defense, this was Apple. No one reads the manuals at Apple.) Let's also say you get the flu and are out of the office for three days. You call in and everything, it's not like you just stop showing up. But still. Three days.

On that third day, the gigantic Human Resources computer

automatically generates a letter with the words "Involuntary Termination Notice" printed across the top. Not being programmed for absolute heartlessness, the HR computer then prints this notice and mails it from the main office in California to Austin. That letter arrives two days later, and the first you hear about it is when your supervisor shows up at your desk with an embarrassed expression and an empty cardboard box.

A few days later, I woke up on Valentine's Day and stepped outside with Schuyler in my arms to greet the snow flurries falling unexpectedly on the trees and the bushes and my big stupid unemployed head.

By noon, the snow melted away. My sinking suspicion that moving to Austin was quite possibly a huge mistake did not.

11

Schuylerese for Beginners

One morning shortly after losing my job in Austin, I looked up from my breakfast to see Schuyler emerge from her bedroom, hair in a wild tangle and tiny hand rubbing her sleepy eyes.

There in her arms was Jasper.

At some point in the night, for reasons known only to her, Schuyler had gotten up, grabbed her long-suffering teddy bear, and taken him back to bed with her. Now she was carrying him with her as if they had never been anything but best friends. The only thing giving away the newness of the relationship might have been that she was actually holding him upside down; she was essentially hugging his butt, with his stubby little tail sticking up into the air.

As she ate her Cheerios, Jasper sitting in her lap (and occasionally being made to eat along with her, his nose smashed into her cereal bowl), I looked at her and smiled. I felt validated now by her love for Jasper.

"Hi, Schuyler," I said. She responded with a quick little wave.

"Is that Jasper?" She looked at him as if for the first time and then nodded.

"Is Jasper your friend?" I asked. "Do you love him?"

She considered the question for a moment and then broke into a sweet smile.

"No. . . ."

That story isn't quite true. Schuyler didn't say "no."

She said "mo."

Schuyler's use of consonants, or lack thereof, was one of the more mysterious and troubling aspects of her disorder. When Schuyler wished to say "no," she came pretty close. She would fix you with a defiant stare and say, *"Mo!"* in a sure tone that left very little confusion as to her meaning. Not only that, but she could sign it, too. She didn't always use the official American Sign Language sign, which looks a little like an ostrich trying to bite you. Instead, she would take the ASL sign for "yes," which consisted of a fist bobbing up and down like a little Señor Wences head nodding in agreement, and she simply changed it so the fist was shaking its "head" instead. Technically incorrect, Schuyler's "no" nevertheless made perfect sense.

When using that sign in conjunction with *"mo,"* Schuyler made her meaning clear.

Now, during this same time period, when she was about four years old, a strange deficiency in Schuyler's vocalization skills became clear. If you were to ask her to identify those who are close to her, she would respond with her vowel-only answers (mommy=*"ah-ee,"* daddy= *"eh-ee"*). If you were to then ask who she was, she would emphatically point to herself and try to say "me," which of course would come out as a boisterous *"eeee!"*

So Schuyler could make the long "ee" sound, and furthermore she could clearly form the "m" in "mo." The mystery to us was her inability to put those two sounds together and say "me," or "mommy," or "moo" when she's telling us what cows say, instead of her adaptive *"Oooo!"*

Whatever the neurological reason, Schuyler simply could not get it. I could get her to say *"mmmm"* and I could get her to say *"eeeee,"* but despite all the work we put in on vocalization with her, she was no closer to putting them together than she had been when we began seriously paying attention to her speech development, before she was two. She had the physical mechanics in place to form the individual sounds, but she wasn't able to put them together.

I had no idea why. It was a mystery, a door in Schuyler's head that remained locked. But still I worked with her. Once we knew what was wrong, we were fixated on trying to find a way around the wall that stood in her way. Polymicrogyria was robbing her of speech, and it was doing so in ways that confounded us. The hardest part of it had less to do with summoning the energy or the will to do everything we could to help her; we'd spent the six months since the diagnosis doing little more than rage against the monster and try anything we could to make things better. The worst part came with the realization that sometimes, there wasn't much anyone could do for her.

If there was going to be a breakthrough, it was going to come from her. We fought hard for her, to teach her sign language and try to give her words that she showed no sign of ever owning for herself, partly because we desperately wanted to defy her monster, but mostly because honestly, what other options did we have?

When we moved to Austin, our choice of an apartment made sense at the time. Literally across the street from Apple, it was close enough for me to walk to work, which I believe I may have actually done twice in my two-month tenure. After I walked out the door at Apple for the last time, cardboard box in hand, the proximity to my former workplace was obviously not the delight it had been. Every day I got to drive past the building and grumble to myself, although honestly, it was a relief not to be there anymore, in that *"wow, I hope we don't starve to death and die"* sort of unemployed relief. Corporate America was a bad fit for me, and deep down, I suppose I'd known it all along.

An unexpected result of where we chose to live, however, came when we went to enroll Schuyler in public school shortly after we arrived. We'd been looking at her school options for a few weeks, including the possibility of immersing her in sign language by having her attend the Texas School for the Deaf. That was ultimately a silly idea, and not just because there was a waiting list for deaf kids who wanted to get in, much less a hearing child. ASL also works differently for hearing kids than the deaf. We eventually determined that something called Signing Exact English, which uses the same grammatical structure as spoken English, would be more appropriate for her, and we started changing our approach to her signing. She still had trouble making signs, especially intricate ones, but she was learning. We sat down and figured out that she had about fifty words, maybe half of which she used regularly. It wasn't much, but it was a beginning. Now we just needed to get her into school and an appropriate classroom setting.

Thanks to where we lived, however, it wouldn't be in the city of Austin. Although we lived in Austin itself, we technically fell within the school district boundaries of a little town called Manor. The pronunciation wasn't what you would expect. Just like Guadalupe Street (*gwad-a-LOOP*) in Austin and Houston Street in New York (I know from sad experience that if you are a yokel and ask a New York taxi to take you to Houston Street and you pronounce it like the city, you'll get a much more expensive ride), Schuyler's new school was located in *MAY-ner*. By golly.

We had misgivings about a small town school district, but we were encouraged by the amount of enthusiasm shown toward their work by the teachers and specialists we met with. I have to be honest and say they didn't seem to have much of a clue what to do with Schuyler, and during those first few meetings, I felt as if we were constantly educating them about polymicrogyria and how to approach it, which was understandable since it was so rare. I have to admit, however, they listened to everything we said and followed our requests closely. Schuyler's special education teacher, a friendly and vivacious woman named Michelle, had no idea how to approach Schuyler's disorder, but she listened to everything we said and consulted with us frequently. It wasn't perfect, but it was already better than we had experienced in the New Haven schools.

The only catch? Once again, they looked to us for instructions on what to do with Schuyler. We had a great deal of hope and were willing to do whatever it took to help her, but the simple truth was that we didn't really know what to tell them.

Inexplicably, and seemingly overnight, Schuyler had transformed into a little girl.

She continued to grow tall and slender, with long, delicate fingers, but she never lost her perfect round cheeks. She looked like a ballerina but played harder than ever. Her full lips and long eyelashes kept Schuyler from ever looking terribly boyish, but most days she came home from school covered in scratches and bruises, her jeans grass-stained and worn. Later, when summer came, she spent much of her free time with Julie at the pool, turning brown like a nut. In my memories of those days, she is always laughing.

Schuyler had become more than her monster; indeed, she always had been, but by the time she turned five, she had developed a very clear set of likes and dislikes. She loved mermaids and ponies and princesses, but she did not yet wish to actually transform her appearance into something particularly girly, save her love of pink and purple.

She also loved dinosaurs, in a way that was absolutely free of fear. If there was a show on television that showed computer-generated dinosaurs, she was transfixed. When the tyrannosaur chased after the little kids in *Jurassic Park*, I could swear she was rooting for the monster to eat them up.

Her monster fixation didn't end there. Before she was born, a friend had sent me a collector's figure of King Kong, maybe a foot tall, that sat on my bookshelf for years. Even as a baby, Schuyler was captivated by Kong and his snarling, ferocious expression. A tiny, two-inch-tall Fay Wray made it clear that Kong was a big monkey, even to little Schuyler.

As she grew older, Schuyler constantly pointed to Kong and then shrugged her shoulders, her way of asking about things in the world around her. I told her that he was a giant gorilla, but that he wasn't bad, just protective of the ones he loved. I don't remember when it might have happened, but she must have seen the original film on television at some point, because she knew that Kong roared and beat his chest menacingly. She didn't do a bad impersonation her-self.

When Peter Jackson's *King Kong* was released in 2005, we hesitated. We knew it wasn't exactly an age-appropriate film, but Schuyler was fearless, and she loved King Kong. It seemed wrong not to take her. Age-appropriate hadn't seemed to apply to Schuyler in a long time, although we did keep her away from movies with realistic, person-on-person violence. Scary dinosaurs seemed remote enough, but still. I thought *King Kong* might be pushing my luck. I took her, but we sat near the aisle in case it proved to be too much.

Schuyler loved it. When Kong burst out of the jungle to rescue Ann Darrow from the tyrannosaurs, Schuyler didn't feel a moment of split loyalty, either to the girl or the dinosaurs. She jumped up in the theater and cheered, pumping her fist in the air for Kong. She never pulled her eyes from him when he was on-screen, and when he died at the end, she turned to me with real concern. Concern, but no tears. She knew better. King Kong was alive and well.

I suppose it's pretty clear why, even in her most feminine of phases, Schuyler has always loved monsters. She has always referred to them, then and now, as her friends. In her mind, I believe she saw them as her protectors. If the world sent oppressors her way, Schuyler's dinosaur friends would be there, along with King Kong, ready to eat them up for her.

It was probably a little unfair. Schuyler wanted a big scary monster to protect her, but what she got was me.

Spring brought renewal of sorts, and promise.

After two scary months of unemployment, I got a lead from Julie, who had returned to Barnes & Noble in Austin (working at B&N is a little like being in a mob family, without the "loads of money" part; you never get out completely). There was an opening for a music manager at the city's big, fancy flagship store and I decided to give it a shot. I interviewed with the store manager, a petite and friendly Irish woman named Mairead with whom I hit it off immediately. Almost before I knew it, I had returned to work in the only job I'd ever really enjoyed in my life, and this time in a fancy pants store which, unlike my previous location in Detroit, actually made money.

Well, I thought. *This is different.*

Having successfully moved me to Austin, my friend Tracy married a man who had the nerve to live in Plano, a suburb of north Dallas, and she moved away that spring. Clearly, from my perspective, that was rude.

I'm kidding, of course. I'd known from the very beginning that Tracy was going to move away and marry Greg, who was the nicest guy in the world, particularly to Schuyler. Plano wasn't that far away, either. It was disarmingly close in a number of ways, as it turned out.

We made other friends, some with kids, even. The friendships that Schuyler made were troubling to me, however. My problem wasn't that she was falling in with a bad crowd; she was four years old, after all. She wasn't going to have to choose between joining the Sharks and the Jets just quite yet.

Schuyler met at least one little girl with whom she made a bond that seemed to mean a great deal to both of them. I have to confess, I was never entirely comfortable with how their friendship manifested itself. Bethany was both younger and smaller than Schuyler, but she was also just about as different from our daughter as a kid could be. Simultaneously strong willed and sensitive, she took to bossing Schuyler around and controlling most aspects of their playtime together. Watching Schuyler get involved in what felt like a toxic friendship made me sad—no one wants their child to be the Lenny to another kid's George—but the relationship seemed to somehow work for the girls. Bethany accepted Schuyler's disability without hesitation, and Schuyler gave her unconditional friendship without pushing back. If there was an element of cruelty to their friendship that made me crazy, it didn't seem to bother Schuyler, who played her usual game of cheerfully (and perhaps passive-aggressively) refusing to play by Bethany's rules much of the time, inspiring much predictable drama, most of which I ignored.

Mostly, it was the three of us, and since Julie and I were working in two different stores with opposite schedules, it was a rare treat for the three of us to be together at the same time.

Schuyler became my best friend, and my social circle.

One evening, I was watching Schuyler at home. We were playing hard and getting extremely worked up, laughing and yelling as we tore through the apartment like pirates, or tornados. Pirate tornados, perhaps. When we finally settled down on the couch, giggling like morons for no reason at all, I decided to take her to the store to buy ice cream and extend our fun a bit longer. There seemed to be so much more running and screaming and laughing and howling left to do. Shutting it down just when the decibels were starting to reach impressive levels seemed a pity.

So it was that we found ourselves in the frozen food section of the grocery store, looking for ice cream. As I pondered the choices, Schuyler played a game that might be called "Sugar-crazed Howler Monkey Runs In Circles." Since we were standing in the freezer section of a mostly unoccupied store, I was inclined to let her be rowdy for a while longer.

A short, older woman walked down the aisle in front of us, eyeing Schuyler with a pinched expression on her face. As she moved past us, the woman rolled her eyes and said loudly, "Wow, I hope you're not planning to have another one!!"

For just a moment, I was confused. I actually thought she was referring to the ice cream. *Is she calling me fat?* Then I realized what she meant and where her eyes were drawn.

"I beg your pardon?" I said. She gave a short sarcastic chuckle and kept walking.

"Wow," I said, feeling my irritation growing. "I can't believe you've never seen a rambunctious kid before."

The woman snorted and said, "Not like her." She pointed down at Schuyler, who hadn't picked up on the conflict (or simply didn't care) and continued playing and hooting with abandon.

The woman walked off. I stood there for a moment, fully intending to just let her go and avoid her altogether. But something stuck in my ear, something that seemed to ring a little louder as I stood there.

"Not like her." This time, I'd heard something new from someone confronted with Schuyler's uniqueness. I'd heard disgust. And rejection. Of Schuyler. I'd wondered for years if I would ever experience it, and suddenly there it was. This woman faced Schuyler's jabbering and hooting and didn't hear Schuylerese.

She heard a feral child.

I sought out the woman, who was by now paying for her groceries. I didn't want a fight, but I wanted her to apologize, and I wanted her to look at Schuyler and see her for who she really was. I'd been so enchanted by Schuyler's otherworldliness for so long that it seemed inconceivable someone else could miss it.

"Excuse me," I said as I stepped up to her. She recognized me and fixed me with a stare, smiling rigidly. "I thought you should know, my daughter isn't just some out of control kid. She——"

"She sure seemed out of control to me," she said quickly. "She acted like a wild animal. If you can't control your kid, you shouldn't take her out in public."

I took a breath. "The thing is, I wanted you to know, she's got a neurological disorder and she can't speak. I know she can get a little loud, but right now that's all she has. She can't communicate like other kids."

I paused. "I was hoping you'd apologize for what you said. I think it would mean a lot to her, and to me."

Her eyes narrowed as she paid for her groceries and grabbed her bags. A small crowd of employees had gathered by now, watching the show. "I don't care what's wrong with her," she said. "If she can't behave like a normal kid then she shouldn't be out in public with the rest of us. Maybe you should have her institutionalized if she can't do any better than that."

I stood for a moment, feeling a rush of emotions. It had been almost a year since Schuyler's diagnosis, and in that time we'd worked so hard to find a way for Schuyler to function in the world like other kids. It wasn't working, we knew that. She sat in a special needs class in tiny Manor, Texas, trying to make herself understood with a handful of signs and a heart full of frustration. At four years old, she wasn't grasping potty training completely. I was looking into the eyes of a stranger who saw Schuyler as someone already beyond help.

Still looking into those eyes, I leaned forward. "You're a nasty person, aren't you?" I said quietly.

And then I said it.

"I hope you get cancer."

I heard a gasp behind me. The woman stopped smiling. She quickly turned and hastened out the door, looking back to make sure I wasn't following her. I looked around at the young clerks, every last one of whom was staring at me in horror. No one said anything. What was there to say?

I took Schuyler's hand and quietly told her that we were going to find another store. As we walked out, I tried not to make eye contact with anyone, but I knew they were staring at me.

When we got in the car, I sat for a moment, waiting for my rapid heart rate to slow down. I'd wished cancer on someone, simply for not accepting Schuyler. I felt evil, and weak, and wrong. But mostly I felt panic and shame. Not just because I'd said such a horrible thing, not entirely, but also because deep down in my secret heart, I couldn't help wondering if the woman was right.

12

To the Mountaintop

One of the more popular bumper stickers around Austin (besides "George Bush Is a Punk Ass Chump") said "Keep Austin Weird." Before we ever moved there, I bought Schuyler the obligatory T-shirt. A college town and hippie haven, Austin was the perfect place to bring Schuyler. It was a place where everyone was weird, which meant no one was.

This was mostly true, we discovered that summer. When we took Schuyler to any of Austin's many cool parks, she played with the other kids and was almost always accepted immediately. Schuyler was made for summer. We kept her hair short as it had been most of her life, a short bob without bangs that would have fallen into her face without the ever-present little plastic hair clips that she loved. We considered letting it grow out, but her ferocious level of play made that seem like a sad world of tangles waiting to happen. She played harder than ever during the summers and never hesitated to make a new friend to join her in her playground adventures. She always found one, too. Sometimes they asked why she didn't talk, and we explained that her brain didn't work like other kids', but she understood what people were saying to her (which we thought was probably true, although it was hard to know for certain) and she could talk with her hands, which was also true to some extent. The other kids would ponder this for a moment, and then move on.

In a town like Austin, every kid was different in some way. *That girl is five and has blue hair. That boy has two mothers. That girl can't speak and talks with her hands. That boy is a Muslim.* The kids in the park would process the thing that was different, make whatever minimal social adjustments were necessary, and then move on to the business at hand, usually involving taking over some choice bit of playground real estate.

For the first time, we didn't catch many parents looking at Schuyler warily, as if whatever she had might be catching. Austin felt like the ideal community for raising Schuyler, and for unlocking the secret of her brain. We took her out as often as we could in order to socialize her, which was good for her but hardly necessary since she remained, as she had always been, the most outgoing and sociable human being I had ever seen in my life. Her monster had taken her speech away, but I sometimes wondered if it had left something in its place, an extra helping of courage and curiosity. Perhaps it had stolen away her shy phase along with her words.

The summer brought a break from school, but when we began preparing for the fall classes, all the old familiar warning bells began to go off. We had another IEP meeting shortly before classes started, mandated by law for all special needs students. Just as in New Haven, these meetings consist of the parents, the teachers who primarily deal with the kid, and all the support staff, such as therapists and the school nurse if necessary. The goal of the IEP is to agree on the student's course of study for the following year. There are mandated yearly meetings, but a new IEP may be called at any time if deemed appropriate. Schuyler had been in school in Manor for less than one semester, the previous spring, so getting on track now was important.

Two things became clear at the beginning of this IEP. The first was that Schuyler's teachers cared deeply for her, particularly her homeroom teacher, Michelle, and another, Robin, who saw Schuyler in her mainstream kindergarten class a few hours a week but who also had a special needs son of her own. We liked them both, although Julie teased me constantly about what she perceived to be my crush on Robin. (Well, it was true enough. Nice of Julie to take it so well, though.)

The second thing that became apparent early on was that if this school was going to provide even remedial services for Schuyler that were appropriate, we were going to have to take the lead and guide them precisely through her particular needs. The school district's special education director was present at the meeting, and I have to say, she was a bulldog for Schuyler. Sweet and pretty and funny on first meeting, Tammy was also tenacious and unrelenting if she sensed hesitation on the part of any of Schuyler's team. We watched silently and wide-eyed as Mrs. Malison, the speech therapist, admitted that she was hesitant to recommend more sign language for Schuyler, in large part because she didn't know sign language herself, certainly not the Signing Exact English method that was being recommended for Schuyler, and she didn't think she'd have time or the resources to learn it.

"You're just going to have to find time," Tammy said. "We'll find the classes for you."

It wasn't ideal, and I still got the sense that Schuyler was being low-balled on her evaluations, but they agreed that communication was going to be her primary issue. It was decided they should concentrate on speech therapy to break the hold of polymicrogyria on her brain and sign language to give her an alternative form of communications. It was also agreed that potty training would be a priority, particularly since Schuyler was beginning to grasp the concept (and no one was happier than I about that) and it provided an opportunity for more two-way communication with her.

Everyone wanted to help Schuyler. None of us knew exactly how to go about doing so.

At summer's end, we spent an evening with some friends from work. After a few beers, we found ourselves discussing religion, and in particular the differences between one of my friends' deeply felt atheism and my own agnosticism.

It's a discussion I've had before, but usually I found myself confronting the old "agnostics are just wishy-washy atheists" point that I've heard so many times. This time, the focus was on the things that the two belief systems do have in common. And they are systems of belief, really; even faith in a lack of something is still faith. And faith is the key. Agnostics and atheists agree on the lack of empirical evidence that God actually exists and has a big plan for us all. Believers get past that lack of evidence because they have big-f Faith, the thing they believe sets them apart from the rest of us. I always found Faith to be weak. It is the act of taking nothing and calling it something, and it may be sincere, but by its very definition, Faith substitutes what the believer wants for what he doesn't know or can't know.

My point was, the greatest difference between atheism and agnosticism was Faith. The atheist sees an apparent lack of evidence and concludes that God doesn't exist. But that lack of evidence is still not proof of God's nonbeing. It is, in its own way, a form of Faith, one that says "I can't see, therefore I have Faith that there's nothing to see."

For the agnostic, the lack of evidence is just as evident, but final conclusions aren't made because they can't be made, not without proof either way. With that lack of evidence, the agnostic (meaning of course me because I am not in fact the spokesperson for agnosticism) leaves open the possibility that there may very well be more at work than we can possibly see or understand.

In the place of Faith, perhaps the agnostic has Hope. It's not something we can substitute for proof the way the believer does, but nevertheless, our hope is a thing that allows us to remain open to the possibilities. There's a Thomas Hardy poem that I quoted every Christmas Eve on my blog, about how the agnostic is unable to make a blind leap of faith, but on Christmas Eve, he sadly and desperately wishes he could.

Our discussion of religion was interrupted by Julie. She stepped out into the late summer evening.

"I'm trying to put Schuyler to sleep, but she's not having it," she said. "She knows we're having fun. Think you can go work your magic on her?"

My magic usually involved lying down with Schuyler and singing her to sleep, and it usually ended with me asleep right along with her. I found her sitting up in the guest bed that had been given to her, sleepy-eyed but stubbornly awake. I lay down with her and laughed quietly with her for a while, and she jabbered softly in my ear about something only she knew. Satisfied that she'd had her say, she curled up beside me and allowed me to sing her to sleep.

It occurred to me that evening in the dark that my own approach to Schuyler and her monster was somewhat agnostic. I couldn't have the faith of the believer to convince me she would talk one day and be able to live the life of a normal child, not in the face of the medical and observational evidence at hand, evidence that suggested she would be in some way different for the rest of her life. But I couldn't have the pragmatism of the atheist, which would lead me to give up on the possibility of defeating the monster and instead completely embrace the alternative life that I could not see or understand but which she would probably have to live.

My agnosticism was strengthened by my relationship with Schuyler. I needed to maintain a place for the possibility that she would speak one day. Some days it was harder than others. On those days, when we would work with her for hours trying to get the sounds to come, and they just wouldn't, it was hard to see those possibilities. But we would cling to them like a drowning swimmer clutching at a life preserver. I couldn't have faith, but faced with the ugly reality of Schuyler's monster, I could have hope, and if that was the best I could do, it might just be enough.

Once Schuyler was asleep, I quietly rejoined the adults in the living room. Julie was holding someone's new baby and rocking him to sleep with a sad smile on her face. Babies were bittersweet for Julie. Holding someone else's infant made her happier than anything I could do for her, but it also reminded us both of our other unspoken loss, the child we'd never be able to have because of the risk of polymicrogyria recurring. We'd accepted that fact the summer before and had resigned ourselves to having an only child, but it was hard.

"Schuyler would make an awesome big sister," Julie said on occasion, and she was right.

The next morning, it all hit Julie pretty hard. She cried for a few minutes, cried for the other child we'd never have, and then she moved on without dwelling on it. That's what we did, we expressed our sorrow and our anger and then we moved on. That's how we dealt with Schuyler's monster and the impenetrable fog of her future, looking in the face of that sad lurking motherfucker known as Might-have-been.

On evenings when I worked late at the store, I would come home after Julie and Schuyler had already gone to bed, and I would go online to see what I could find about congenital bilateral perisylvian syndrome. I joined an online support group for parents of kids with polymicrogyria, but I never posted anything to it. Instead, I watched and read other people's stories of their own children, the kids who suffered horrible seizures and swallowing problems that required them to be fed through a tube and physical impairments that left them in wheelchairs. Every so often, one of them would die, and the messages from their parents were unbearable.

(Tonight, my Tori became an angel. She was eleven years old and had polymicrogyria and microcephaly. We have no idea why, she just would not wake up this morning and the paramedics couldn't revive her. She seemed healthy, but I guess God had other plans for her. I know she's in a better place, but I miss her so much. . . .)

One night in early October, I plugged "congenital bilateral peri-sylvian syndrome" into Google to see what was new. There had to be a better way to get information, but we'd yet to speak to a doctor outside of Yale who knew a thing about Schuyler's condition without first receiving a little primer from us. From what we'd been told by Yale, there wasn't going to be much new information that could help us. Schuyler's condition was static. There was no treatment possible, we'd been told, and while it would never get worse, it would also never heal. But like any stubborn pain in the ass parent, I only accepted that to a point. Late at night when I felt overwhelmed by the enormity of it all, I'd go online and look.

On that October night, I found an abstract of a paper presented in the *Journal of Neurology, Neurosurgery and Psychiatry Online*. I have to confess, to my eyes it appeared to be mostly written in Martian and Bullshit. But one phrase jumped out at me:

Conclusion: Plastic changes of sensory and motor cortex location suggest disturbed cortex organization in CBPS patients. Because the polymicrogyric cortex of CBPS patients may embed normal functions in unexpected locations, functional mapping should be considered before brain surgery.

Brain surgery? Did I read that correctly? Was there now surgery for CBPS?

In retrospect, I can see now that no, that isn't what it was saying at all. I believe it was actually saying the brains of CBPS patients adapt to their circumstances by taking on some functions from affected areas in other parts of the brain, so if you're a brain surgeon, you'd better map out those adapted functions first before you start hacking away at the brain for something else.

But at the time, all I could see was "brain surgery." I sat motionless for a few minutes, letting my thoughts spin into something that made sense to me. Then I Googled Dr. William Dobyns, the only name I knew to look for, and got his e-mail address.

Twenty minutes later, as soon as I finished writing it but before I could second guess myself, I sent an e-mail.

From: Rob Rummel-Hudson
Date: October 1, 2004 12:26:12 AM CDT
To: Dr. William Dobyns
Subject: CBPS
Dr. Dobyns,

I hope you don't think I'm presumptuous in writing to you. I know you must be incredibly busy, so I'll try to be brief.

Last summer, a little over a year ago, at the age of three and a half, my daughter, Schuyler, was diagnosed with CBPS by Dr. Laura Ment at Yale's Dept. of Neurology following an MRI.

During that evaluation at Yale, Schuyler was determined to have high cognitive functions and no early discernible signs of significant retardation, although she was significantly delayed in most areas. She showed no facial paralysis but did (and continues to) suffer from weak muscle tone and a deficiency in tongue movement that caused her to drool. Most importantly for Schuyler, however, was the determination that her speech delay was significant and had shown almost no change in the two years in which she had been working with a speech therapist.

In the past year, she has been in a special needs program in her local public school, which has included some speech therapy (although not nearly as much as I think she needs) as well as some mainstream pre-K classes for part of the day. At home, we have made some progress with sign language; Schuyler knows about forty signs and uses basic ASL for about twenty words daily.

I'm not sure exactly why I'm writing to you, except that ever since the diagnosis, we've felt lost in this. I guess no parent is ready for something like this, and we were no exceptions. Yale made the diagnosis, and for that we are extremely grateful, but they gave us little hope for any sort of significant follow-up and none whatsoever for any kind of treatment. We were told of Schuyler's level of affliction, gently advised against having more children by the Department of Genetics, and then sent out into a world where no one had ever even heard of CBPS.

We've tried to stay current by reading what we can online, but the information out there changes very little, and I just can't believe that nothing more has been discovered since August 2003. At the time of her diagnosis, we read that there were only about 40 diagnosed cases in the world; by the time we met with Yale Genetics, they said they thought the number was closer to a hundred. I have no idea how high that number has grown, but we still feel like we're the only parents in the world who are dealing with this.

I guess what I'm hoping for from you is some sort of direction, even if it's just more current information and maybe a direction we could go in. Your name was the first one given to us by Dr. Ment; I believe she sent Schuyler's MRI to you at some point. I know that meeting with you is probably a long shot, and I don't know what would be accomplished by you seeing Schuyler, but tonight I stumbled across a reference to brain surgery in a very complicated abstract I found online, and I was shocked to see that possibility being mentioned in regards to CBPS. If things have changed since last summer and there ARE any treatment possibilities, I thought you'd be the one to know, and I'd be a bad father to Schuyler if I didn't reach out to you now.

Rob Rummel-Hudson
Austin, TX

I sat staring silently at the screen for a few minutes, lost in my thoughts and trying to push the hope I felt back to a place where I could manage it, and then I went to bed.

Three days later, I received a reply.

Dr. William Dobyns was a very intelligent person, a giant in the field of genetics. I, on the other hand, had only recently been an hour late for work because I had inexplicably left my car keys in the refrigerator. So it probably goes without saying that the better part of Dobyns's e-mail went right over my head, at dizzying heights.

A few things did leap out at me in regular guy English, however. Of all the forms of polymicrogyria, the perisylvian flavor was the most common, making up about 2/3 of his patients, which now numbered

300. He now believed that the causes of the condition could be both genetic and environmental, and the chances of it recurring with subsequent children in families of girls with perisylvian PMG were under 10 percent. And in regard to the brain surgery that had originally caught my attention, he reported that it was only appropriate for intractable epilepsy in patients with very limited forms of PMG.

"To answer detailed questions," Dr. Dobyns concluded, "I would have to see her here in clinic."

I read the e-mail, and then I read it again. I sat in silence. I'm not sure what I thought he would say, but I wasn't expecting him to say that he could see her. Anytime I'd read about William Dobyns, it was in reference to his research work. It had never occurred to me that he saw patients. I showed the e-mail to Julie.

"What do you think?" she asked.

"I don't know. That percentage for recurrence in girls is way different from what Yale told us. I wonder how many other things have changed?"

"You know," said Julie, "I think we should take her. Nothing seems to be working. If anyone knows how we can reach her, it'll be Dobyns. I'm running out of ideas."

There was no way we could afford to fly to Chicago, much less afford to see Dr. Dobyns. We talked about it that evening and went to bed without a plan.

The next morning, I wrote about the e-mail from Dobyns on my blog, concluding my post on a hopeful note.

We've got a lot to think about and to talk about over the next few days, but the idea that someone might be able to help Schuyler makes me feel just about as good as you might think. I can't describe it, and perhaps I don't have to. Nothing tangible, no promises, but a door just opened, maybe even several doors.

Our next step should be pretty clear. We need to find some money to get Schuyler to Chicago. It's time that she and Dr. Dobyns met face to face.

I posted and went to work.

Tracy was in town and we met for lunch. As we sat down at a lit-tle Japanese restaurant near my store, I told her about the e-mail and our plan to try to raise money for a trip to Chicago to see the doctor.

"You should make a fund-raising Web page," she said. "I'd help you set it up, I've done that sort of thing before." Tracy was very ac-tive in Democratic Party politics in Texas, and had run a number of campaign Web sites. She knew what she was talking about.

"How serious is he?" she asked. "What exactly did the e-mail say?"

I took out my laptop and connected to the wireless network in the restaurant. I opened my e-mail, but before I could pull up the message from Dr. Dobyns, dozens of new messages started arriving. "This is weird," I said.

"What is it?"

"I've got like thirty plus e-mails, all from PayPal."

They were donations, from readers, sent via the online money exchange site PayPal.com. Without even asking, without establish-ing a fund-raising site or even finding out how much it would cost to fly my family to Chicago, I had almost nine hundred dollars in donations from people who had never met Schuyler but who had become emotionally vested in her life. I sat looking at the screen in silence. Tracy said nothing, but just smiled and squeezed my shoulder.

It was the first time I truly understood how much Schuyler had come to mean to so many people. It was by no means the last, nor would it ultimately prove to be the greatest.

By the end of the next day, we contacted the University of Chicago Genetics Clinic and made an appointment to see Dr. Dobyns in January.

I didn't want to invest this appointment with too much hope. I'm sure Dorothy told herself the same thing, right up until the mo-ment that the Great and Powerful Oz appeared before her.

13

Bug Fairy

Halloween was always a strange day for Schuyler, or rather for me and my perception of her place in the world. After her condition became more apparent, and particularly after her monster got a name, the day took on an even more peculiar feel, not because Schuyler was different on Halloween, but because she wasn't. It was a night when she was disguised as something else, something strange, but in reality, every day was like that for Schuyler in some way. During the rest of the year, her difference wasn't apparent, not at first. But even before you figured out that Schuyler couldn't speak, not in a way you'd understand, you might sense she was not like other kids. Her speech was incomprehensible, but it didn't sound unnatural. Her tone was smooth and relaxed. If anything, the lack of hard consonants gave her speech the feel of something gentler than human language, the way you could imagine angels might communicate their secrets with each other. She didn't seem broken. She just seemed ethereal, otherworldly.

Schuyler had suffered through some of my bad Halloween humor in her past costumes. When she was not even two years old, she was dressed as the devil, albeit the devil in white sneakers. The next year, she was a very impressive Godzilla monster, again in sneakers.

The following Halloween, Julie finally put her foot down. No more evil-but-cute costumes, she said. She understood the idea that putting sweet little Schuyler in the guise of a scary monster or figure of evil was funny, but I think she was afraid of where this path would lead us. She opted for little bug antennas for Schuyler before I could contribute. I think she was afraid I'd dress her up as Hitler or Osama bin Laden.

Now, our first Halloween back in Texas presented us for the first time with a trick-or-treating experience devoid of that bitter fall cold to which we were accustomed. Schuyler's costume needed to reflect her new environment, but we had no clear idea of what to do, so we let her pick out her own costume. The result was stunning, and it reflected her personality with a clarity that neither of us had ever approached.

Imagine, if you will, a tiny little fairy. She would have a fluttery, gauzy little outfit of green, with shimmering skirt pieces falling lazily at her waist and gossamer bug wings on her back. This fairy, however, would be wearing brightly striped, multicolored tights. She would have sprightly little antennas on top of her shoulder-length, bright pink hair. The wig was the piece she was the proudest of, while I was very happy to contribute the final touch, a pair of Chuck Taylor hi-top Converse sneakers, in a shade of hot pink that matched her hair.

Schuyler had chosen. She was a fairy. A somewhat punkish bug fairy.

Halloween was one day every year when people would look at Schuyler and say, "Oh, look at the little punky bug fairy!" or even, "Oh, look at little Godzilla in her Keds!" But even in her non-fairy life, people would see a happy, vigorous little girl, full of life and energy and a healthily detached approach to the world. They didn't see her monster, or at the very least they didn't see it for what it was.

I was concerned about how long that would be the case. Schuyler had a gentle strangeness about her, like a visitor from some realm where no one spoke but everyone laughed. Would she still have that enchanted quality about her when she was a teenager? An adult? How would the ugliness of the world impact her?

Once we hit the street, Schuyler quickly made friends with another little girl, who it turned out was a fairy as well, albeit a more traditional, less punk-ass fairy. She was a fairy from the good part of Fairy Town, whereas Schuyler's bug fairy had clearly crossed the tracks. Apparently fairies were all the rage in 2004.

I took a lot of photos of Schuyler that night, which should surprise no one who knows me, and aside from a few crabby moments and territorial scraps with the other fairy, almost every photo I took captured Schuyler's glowing, laughter-filled face. I always wished I could laugh like Schuyler. Anyone who knew her during that time might tell you how the thing they remember the most about Schuyler was how she laughed, and laughed hard. She got hurt by the world from time to time, but mostly she laughed and ran and jumped and generally lived her life turned up to eleven.

As we went from door to door, Schuyler and her new fairy friend raced ahead of us, giggling like goons the whole time. At one house, the doorbell unleashed a barrage of maniacal barking from some apparently gerbil-sized dogs inside, and for some reason this struck the two fairies as the funniest thing they'd ever heard in their short lives. They just stood there and laughed, hard. That's usually what Schuyler did—she laughed.

Sometimes I tried to buy that laughter for her. I would try to take on her monster for myself so she wouldn't have to. I worried so she could be free. It was a stupid idea, of course. Schuyler was going to be a happy little girl regardless of how much I wept and fretted and tried to take all onto myself the harshness of God's little gift to her. I tried to accept her joy and her approach to the world for what it was, without thinking too much about what her future might hold for her, but it was hard. Any parent knows how difficult it can be to resist the urge to try to suck up their child's pain and make it their own.

I remembered reading accounts of how some of the more highly regarded faith healers would operate by taking on the person's pain and sickness for themselves first. They would let it infect them and inhabit their person before releasing it to wherever that sort of bad energy goes and is accepted. On one level, it sounded ridiculous to me, but if you'd really pressed me on it, perhaps over a few beers, I would confess to you that I'd always thought it would be wonderful if it could be done, and that I would love to know how to do it myself.

As we drove home at the end of the night, Schuyler sat in the backseat, mentally cataloging her candy haul and jabbering softly to herself in Schuylerese as she considered the quality of each individual piece. I watched her wordlessly. Schuyler was going to turn five soon, and she wasn't where she was supposed to be, not even close. I wasn't concerned that she wasn't going to have a meaningful life, because I believed she already had that. But it was a life lacking in predictability, which sounds great to a free and easy adult but nerve-wracking to a parent. I couldn't say when she was going to conquer potty training, or when her scribbles would turn into letters or when she'd even know what those letters meant. I couldn't see her living independently one day, a young woman who couldn't speak but who had the world's ass kicked anyway as she made her way through it. I knew I couldn't protect her or make a world for her that she could live in for the rest of her life, but the more I tried to face that reality, the harder it pushed back, and the less likely I became to ever make any sort of peace with her monster.

When we got home, Schuyler grudgingly took off her costume, but when it came time to lose the wig and the wings, she refused. When she crawled into bed, she wore her pajamas and her pink hair and her wings, which folded and crunched softly as she rolled under the covers. I crawled into bed beside her and sang her to sleep.

Schuyler knew she was different, although I couldn't really tell you when that happened. More clear was how she wasn't afraid of that difference, not like I was. She behaved like a tourist from some foreign land, trying to make herself understood. She became frustrated occasionally, but not nearly as often as you might expect. Mostly, Schuyler seemed amused, as if the rest of us were engaging in some stupid, jabbery behavior when really, we would all be much happier with some hand signs and excited vowels and a good, loud laugh. At moments like this when I sang melancholy songs to her, at times when I was sad, which was more often than I would let most people know, Schuyler would roll over in her bed or shoot me a look across her shoulder, a look that said "What's *your* problem?"

On any given day, I felt like Schuyler was visiting the rest of us here, a tiny being not of this world but trying as hard as she could to fit in. But it was different on Halloween night, watching Schuyler with her gauzy butterfly wings and her crazy pink hair and that braying, unashamed laugh, dancing to some wild and perfect music that the rest of us weren't allowed to hear. On a night like that, it was even easier for me to imagine Schuyler taking flight, her pink Converse hi-tops leaving the surface of this grand rough world for the last time.

I could imagine, with heartbreaking clarity and hand outstretched, watching Schuyler fluttering happily back to wherever she came from, whatever place in the universe exists where bug fairies speak in laughter and where sad, broken fathers aren't welcome.

14

Note to Schuyler, Christmas 2004

December 25, 2004

Dear Schuyler,

I'm sorry.

I'm sorry you went to bed crying tonight, on Christmas of all nights, because you wanted one thing and we wanted another, and none of us had the tools to communicate those things clearly to each other. We were stern with you, and when we closed your door, we left you crying with hurt and with rage, and most of all I think, with frustration.

Here's a secret. Although it's not just my secret, but your mother's, too, I'll just speak for myself here. I get frustrated, too. And when I get frustrated, when I try to tell you things and for whatever reason you don't understand, my frustration isn't with you, not one bit. It's with me, with my inability to connect with you, and it's with your monster.

My frustration carries with it a large load of guilt. Guilt for giving you your monster with my genes, guilt for wasting so many months and years not knowing there was anything wrong. I played with you as a baby and looked into those arresting green eyes of yours, but I never saw that you needed my help. I *didn't see it for years. The monster was there the whole time, and I never saw it. You were almost four when we found out, and I feel like I wasted all those years.*

Tomorrow morning I'll get up and go to work long before you wake up, and I'll think about you all day. When Julie brings you to work to see me, I hope you'll smile and yell "eh-eee!" like you sometimes do when we see each other again after a separation. I hope you forget we were angry with each other tonight, because I won't, and it'll eat at me all day.

Schuyler, when I was young, I wanted a lot of things, and not many of them were admirable. A lot of them were selfish and destructive, and none of them really did any good in the world. I never thought about the world as a place that I should try to improve. Now that you're here, I have only one true wish in my life. Just one. I'd throw the rest away in an instant, I'd forgo any happiness in my own future if I could only have my one true wish, and that is for you to be happy.

I'm sorry I'm not the father you deserve, a strong dad who's always positive and always knows exactly what to say or do. I'd even settle for knowing the right answer every so often. You should have a father who never loses his nerve and never shouts at you and doesn't close the door on your crying simply because he just doesn't know what else to do. You should have gotten a smart and levelheaded and emotionally stable father—instead you got me.

Sometimes people tell me what a great father they think I am. They say that, based on how much I love you, which is something that is hardly a secret to the world. What they don't seem to understand is that loving you isn't enough, not even remotely so. All it means is that my love for you makes it that much more apparent when I fail you, and that much more obvious that in addition to a monster in your head, you got a weak father who most of the time stands there helplessly saying "What the fuck?" when you need him most of all.

When I went back into your room to see how you were doing, you were sleeping, and your face was sweet and a little sad but no longer screwed up in anger and frustration. I lay beside you and whispered most of these words before kissing you and coming into the living room to write this. What I came into your room to tell you was this:

I'd give anything for you, Schuyler, anything at all to make you happy and to fix what's broken and to set you free in a world that you're equipped to live in. I'd burn down the whole world for you if it would change things. Instead, all I can say is that I'm sorry, dreadfully sorry. I love you so much that my heart breaks in two every night for you. I know that doesn't help you, not one bit, but tonight it's all I have.

Love, Daddy

15

Fighting Monsters with Rubber Swords

Schuyler's appointment with Dr. Dobyns in Chicago was full of hope for us, hope against our better judgment, and against what a year and a half of experience had taught us. We'd learned to be on our own, navigating a new world of Schuyler's disability, and with little information and no road map. We learned that for parents like us in the situation we were in, all you can do sometimes is trust in your fool's hope and keep going. You never give up, and you persevere, not because you're plucky or heroic or even smart, but rather because you hate the thought that there might have been some answer or solution waiting right around the next corner, and you would miss it if you gave up too early. It's hope, and it's stubborn and sometimes it's even stupid, but it's the thing you've got so you run with it. You go into battle against the monster with a rubber sword because, really, what else are you going to do?

It had only been a year since my return to Texas from seven years living in the north; I still kept my giant samurai snow brush/ice scraper in the trunk of my car. You know, just in case. But it had been a while since I'd experienced anything like real winter, and Chicago in January is real winter by anyone's standards. When we got off the plane, we felt the single digit cold through the walkway.

As soon as we got our luggage, we opened our bags and extracted the scarves and gloves and hats that we'd had to search for in a dozen stores in Austin. Schuyler was thrilled to be back in the long coat, hat, and mittens that had been ever present in Connecticut but which had disappeared from her life once we moved to Texas. Stepping out into the cold wind was startling and yet familiar. It felt a little like a homecoming.

We were met at the airport by Erin, an old friend whom I'd met as a result of the blog. (As if I ever met anyone any other way.) Erin was another old school journal writer whom I'd met at that writing conference a few years earlier, and even though we didn't speak much on a regular basis, she was the kind of friend whom you see after a year of silence and it's as if you'd never been apart. I think everyone has a few of those low-maintenance friends, the ones who seem to pop up out of nowhere when you least expect and most need them. That was Erin; as soon as she heard we were coming to Chicago, she offered her apartment as a crash pad. As far as Erin was concerned, it wasn't negotiable. A hotel was simply out of the question.

I think in some way, perhaps even subconsciously, Erin recognized the possibility that this visit might defy our high hopes and desperate wishes for good news. Perhaps she imagined the three of us leaving the hospital with heavy hearts and spending the next two days sitting in a strange, cold hotel room, alone with each other and the invisible monster in the room that had brought us there in the first place. When the snow started falling, we'd be watching it from our hotel room window, and if there was a more depressing way to begin processing bad news, I doubt Erin could think of it.

If we got good news, on the other hand, we'd get to spend it celebrating with a friend. We rarely get trashed and start tearing up the joint, as a rule, so it was a safe enough proposition.

Schuyler was her usual friendly self, opening up to Erin and climbing on her as if my friend had been placed on this earth specifically for her abuse. As she took in the sights of Chicago's Children's

Museum that evening, Schuyler pulled Erin along the whole way, taking her hand and leading her impatiently. She jabbered at Erin in her excited Schuylerese. It was almost like family. It was exactly what we needed. Schuyler was so busy assimilating her new friend that I don't believe she ever noticed her parents' quiet nervousness.

Erin drove us to the University of Chicago Hospital the next morning, through city streets freshly blanketed in overnight snow. Schuyler sat smiling her curious little smile in the backseat. She'd taken my scarf and had created a little cocoon against the cold. We traveled in silence, equal parts anticipation and fear swirling around us.

The waiting room of the Genetics Clinic at the University of Chicago was designed to feel nonthreatening to children, with crazy shapes and funky furniture and little television monitors playing cartoons. The examination room itself lacked the sterility of Yale's facilities but had little for Schuyler to do while we talked. As Julie pulled books out of Schuyler's bag and tried to distract her, the door opened and Dr. William Dobyns walked in. I recognized him immediately from his photos on the Web.

He introduced himself to us and looked at Schuyler with what appeared to be surprise. When he said hello to her, she politely said "eh-oh" back to him and then returned to her exploration of the room. He watched her for a few moments, the look of surprise lingering, and then he sat down to examine her.

As soon as it became apparent this was going to be an actual doctor's visit, Schuyler dug in her heels. She set her jaw and fought the exam, but much of what Dr. Dobyns needed was to evaluate her muscle strength and dexterity. He got plenty of examples of both. I was a little surprised at how irritated he became with her, but I had to remind myself that he was a research geneticist, not necessarily a clinical one. I'd been told by other CBPS parents that he was a brilliant doctor, but that he didn't have a lot of time for polishing his bedside manner. That was fine with me. We wanted answers, not comfort. Or so we kept telling ourselves. What we really wanted was some good news for a change.

Or maybe a miracle.

When Dr. Dobyns was finished examining Schuyler, he sat down with us and opened up his laptop. "I wanted to go through Schuyler's MRI with you so you can see exactly what we're looking at," he said. He pulled up the scans of Schuyler's brain that had been done a year and a half before at Yale. I hadn't seen them since that day in Dr. Simon's office when we got the diagnosis.

I was always fascinated by Schuyler's MRI scans, but honestly, I hated them, too. They were the most tangible, real-world evidence of her monster, but they weren't images of her. They didn't show how she could somehow embrace this mean world, or how she loved to argue with me in sign language, laughing loudly as she did so, just to be a brat. They helped explain why she had no words; they didn't reveal how the words she had, the ones that only Julie and I understood, could have so much power to make my heart simultaneously swell and break when she'd see me at the end of the day, crying "Eh-ee!" and throwing herself at me in what was half hug, half tackle.

Schuyler's MRI scans showed just how much of her brain was broken, and how badly, but it didn't give up any of her secrets. Sometimes her secrets were revealed in her enigmatic laugh behind her mittens, some private joke she couldn't share and that, untold, left us the poorer because of the experience. Sometimes she'd share her secrets in a loud stage whisper, and unintelligible though they might be, we still felt blessed in the sharing. Schuyler's mysteries, even unexplained, were treasures.

"If you look here, you'll see the areas of Schuyler's brain that are malformed," said Dr. Dobyns, indicating the scan. "We see extensive irregular gyral pattern with apparent microgyri." I understood "gyral" to mean the curved patterns in her brain, and where he mentioned microgyri, they were much smaller and tighter. "You can see it here in the posterior frontal, perisylvian, temporal, and parietal lobes with probably mild polymicrogyria in the anterior frontal lobe and probably none in the occipital lobe." As he mentioned these regions with names that sounded like made-up words from a bad television hospital soap opera, Dr. Dobyns pointed to areas of Schuyler's brain, like a butcher with a map of a cow's prime cuts. It was strange, looking at her brain so clinically. "It's clearly most severe in the perisylvian region. Right here."

He pointed to gray featureless areas of the photo, and we both realized immediately that Dr. Ment had tried to shield us from the worst of the news. As we looked at scan after scan, we saw the gray areas, and we saw just how much there was. Not just in the two small spots she'd pointed out to us, but in massive areas. I couldn't believe what I was seeing, now that I knew what to look for. Most of Schuyler's brain was affected. Her monster was huge.

Dr. Dobyns let us look in silence before he spoke again, quietly. "From these scans, I'd estimate that anywhere from sixty to seventy-five percent of Schuyler's brain is profoundly malformed." I stopped breathing and glanced up at him in horror. He nodded.

"Now, this just illustrates exactly how little we still know about the human brain. From examining this MRI, I can tell you that I certainly didn't expect to walk in the room and find a little girl running around and playing like a typical child. I wouldn't expect Schuyler to be functioning at a significant level mentally or physically, but there she is. She looks and behaves like any other kiddo, and she's obviously functioning cognitively at a reasonable level. Those affected areas of her brain are working, they're doing something. We just have no idea how, or what her brain is capable of."

He showed us the areas of Schuyler's brain that control her speech. Completely grayed out, on both sides. He pointed out that in many cases where a part of the brain is incapacitated in some way, other areas will take over. Even in bilateral cases like Schuyler's where the damage is symmetrical, other nonrelated areas of the brain can develop and take over.

"But in Schuyler's case, I'm going to be blunt. There aren't a lot of unaffected areas left to pick it up for her. As I said, we don't know what those malformed areas are capable of, and since they're already performing in a way we wouldn't expect, there's no telling what they might do. Realistically, I think it's time to face the fact that Schuyler's going to need to develop alternative ways to communicate."

We looked at him blankly. He sighed. "She shows excellent promise in developing communication skills through signing or some other form of assisted communication. But she's probably never going to talk. I'm sorry."

The rest of the meeting went pretty much the same. Things we thought we'd understood were worse than we'd thought. The assumptions we'd taken away from Yale were false. Schuyler's monster, never changing, never growing or shrinking, was nevertheless much worse than we'd suspected.

Dr. Dobyns was pretty insistent that Schuyler should receive much more speech therapy, but he made it clear that this was in the hopes of improving her comprehension and communicative understanding. For her own actual communication, she would need to continue learning sign language.

It wasn't quite that simple, however.

Schuyler's dexterity problems with her hands were going to continue to be a big problem for her for the rest of her life, making it difficult for her to sign clearly. Her sign language would be similar to her attempts at spoken words. They would be approximations. The reason for this was that the area of her brain that is located directly above her stricken speech center is the one that controls fine motor skill in her hands. Her monster was garbling her words with one hand and fumbling her fingers with the other.

"I expect that Schuyler is probably going to be a clumsy girl for the rest of her life," he said.

Because CBPS affects the mouth and jaws of its patients, including difficulty swallowing, Schuyler could develop eating problems, some of which could lead to other illnesses, including life-threatening bouts of pneumonia.

"Now, there are several other medical problems to watch for during her childhood. First and foremost are seizures, as you probably already know. I see that she hasn't had any seizures so far, not even absence seizures, and that's a very positive sign. Be aware, however, that the risk of epileptic seizures over her lifetime is probably greater than eighty percent, although the age of onset could vary from now to her teens or early twenties. Now, these seizures sometimes prove to be very serious. In some kiddos with PMG, the seizures can be very difficult to treat leading up to and following puberty, but then they'll sometimes get better with more control and less medication. Since she hasn't had any seizures so far, certainly I'd say no treatment is needed right now. Should she start to have any spells, you should have her evaluated promptly.

"I can tell you I've only had two patients die from their seizures," he added. I think he realized as soon as he said it that it wasn't nearly as comforting as he might have meant it to be.

We sat and we listened, and it all felt familiar somehow. I remembered a summer day in Connecticut, stepping out into the sun after getting the diagnosis from Dr. Ment and feeling the warmth of the late afternoon sun on my face. What I remember most is feeling like something had been sucked out of me, leaving behind a void. Sitting here now, listening to Dr. Dobyns speak and watching Schuyler read her books and jabber softly to herself, not looking at Julie because I knew she was trying to hold herself together and didn't need me making that any harder, it all felt so much like that awful day in 2003. That day, we'd been caught unawares because we had no idea what was wrong. This time, we were ambushed because we had foolishly underestimated the monster and allowed ourselves to think that since we already had the bad news, all Dr. Dobyns would have left to tell us would be something good. I felt as if somewhere in the universe, something hidden and hateful was laughing at us.

"Now, one thing you'll need to do when you get home is you'll need to make an appointment with a pediatric psychologist to make an official, detailed determination of Schuyler's cognitive level. I'd say her normal head size and relatively normal tone and motor skills, save for mildly delayed coordination, are relatively favorable indicators for future development. I found no other abnormalities. Her overall developmental prognosis is still rather difficult to determine due to her young age. However, her normal head size, normal tone, relatively normal motor skills, and excellent progress to date in all areas except speech/language suggest to me that she'll continue to make progress. I suspect she'll end up in the borderline or 'slow learner' range, which is defined as an IQ of seventy to eighty, or possibly the mild retardation range, from fifty-five to seventy."

We of course heard one word loud and clear—the "R" word. "What does that mean?" Julie asked. "She'll still be able to live independently, right? That's what they assured us at Yale."

"How could they possibly say that?" he said, a bit irritably. "There's no way to know that. You need to be ready for the possibility that she's going to be under your care for the rest of her life."

I watched Julie's face as she processed what he said, and I suddenly realized that of all the things I'd heard her say about that day in Connecticut when we got the diagnosis, the one phrase I'd heard Julie repeat the most frequently was how Dr. Ment had said that Schuyler would be able to live independently and have a job one day.

Looking back, however, I have to be honest and admit that Dr. Dobyns was probably correct in his incredulity. In retrospect, given the high emotions that we were feeling during that meeting with Dr. Ment the year before, and how desperate we had been to grab on to some kind of good news, I can see now that it is very likely that Dr. Ment had merely held out the idea of Schuyler's future independence as a possibility. In our sadness and shock, however, we had clung to that possibility. Dobyns was right, there was no way anyone could ever say something like that for certain. In the absence of concrete assurances, the mind builds its own.

At the time, it had been a blow to us, being told that our former dreams of college and success for Schuyler were being downgraded to her ability to get some kind of job and live on her own. For some reason, though, Julie had latched on to this idea as something she could count on. No matter how bad it got, she thought, at least one day Schuyler would be able to make her own life, on her own terms. Now I felt as if that was being pried from her grasp as well.

"Now, I do have some more positive news. I know you were very interested in finding out more about the risk of recurrence if you were to have another child. I also know you were initially told that you had a one in four chance of having another child with CBPS, and at the time, that made sense in light of what we knew. The cause of perisylvian PMG is still under study, and there are some suggestions of acquired or extrinsic causes such as viruses before birth, but these do seem to be rare. I'm aware of significant evidence for genetic causes of perisylvian PMG. Preliminary data from several years ago suggested a recurrence risk in future siblings of up to ten percent. My more recent data suggests that the recurrence risk may be lower, perhaps in the range of five percent, but these figures are still inexact. It may be even lower, but I don't have enough data yet to say for certain. I do think that if you did decide to have more children, those might be odds that are more acceptable to you."

"Yeah, that's great," I said quietly. We weren't going to have another child, I knew that without even looking at Julie. Suddenly we didn't know what we were going to do with the one we had.

The remainder of our Chicago trip was something of a blur. All three of us had blood drawn for further genetic studies, particularly one for something called comparative genome hybridization. I had no idea what that meant, and I realized that suddenly I didn't care much. One more string of medical terminology that, if translated, would just break our hearts a little more. Julie went first so that Schuyler could see that she was going to be okay, then Schuyler had her blood drawn. I went last as Schuyler dried her tears, I suppose so she could get some small measure of satisfaction out of watching me suffer, too.

As we waited downstairs for Erin to pick us up, Julie and Schuyler stayed inside the lobby, escaping the cold. I stood outside. The icy wind made my face numb, and that felt appropriate somehow. I didn't want to feel anything.

Erin arranged for us to visit the Shedd Aquarium and the Field Museum of Natural History, and Schuyler had a wonderful, over-stimulated time. We wandered through the tanks of bizarre sea monsters and dinosaur bones, and it was exactly what Schuyler wanted to see. She growled menacingly at Sue the T-rex and squealed in delight at the whales, and we followed her around with few words between us.

That evening, Erin cooked dinner and invited some friends over. We'd known Jessamyn and Geoff for several years and had them stay with us for a few days in Connecticut one summer as they traveled through New England. We were eager to see them this time because in the interval since we'd seen them last, they'd had a baby. Julie spent the evening fussing over little Katie, and the bittersweet look on her face was too complicated to read. Well, for me it was, anyway, mostly because I was getting drunk.

Heidi was someone else I knew from online, although honestly, not all that well. She wrote a site that was mostly concerned with weight loss, and it wasn't something I followed very closely. Heidi worked as an editor at a children's publishing house, and she thoughtfully brought some books for Schuyler. Somehow, through it all, I forgot about those books until a few days after we got back to Texas.

During the course of dinner, I kept watching Heidi and the way she looked at Schuyler. I wasn't sure how to interpret it, how her eyes found Schuyler every time she made one of her loud proclamations in Schuylerese or otherwise drew attention to herself, which of course with Schuyler was often. Schuyler was her usual gregarious, unselfconscious little girl self, and maybe it was just because I was drinking, but I just couldn't figure out the look that Heidi was giving her. It wasn't annoyance, not exactly. It was a sort of detached observation, like how you might watch a weird bug on your windowsill.

Then it hit me. She's watching Schuyler like there's something wrong with her. She's watching to see how it manifests itself.

I suppose that's when it landed on me with both feet. Heidi was inclined to be sympathetic to Schuyler and to my family, and yet part of her was fascinated and repelled by our broken daughter. This was the future we had ahead of us. Schuyler was growing up, and the older she got, the stranger her affliction would appear. As a little girl she was a unique, ethereal child, and her wordless world was something strange and somehow enchanting. The day was coming, however, when she was simply going to be a broken child, and the world wasn't going to be kind to her any longer.

There wasn't a thing we could do to stop it.

Later that evening, we changed Schuyler into her pajamas and gathered in Erin's living room. We didn't talk, really, but sat together quietly and tried to let the day settle into something manageable. Julie and Schuyler sat on the couch, while I sprawled on a love seat and Erin sat on the floor. Schuyler noticed Erin on the floor and grabbed her pillow and blanket to join her. She took her blanket and carefully draped it over the two of them, and then curled up next to Erin and motioned for her to come closer.

I watched Erin's face as Schuyler earnestly tried to talk to her, and I saw the sadness and the understanding in her eyes. Erin understood the frustration of not being able to understand Schuyler's words, and I think she felt the unfairness of it all. Later she told me that she got a sense then of what our lives must have been like with Schuyler, and why our feelings about God were so complicated.

That night, after the guests had departed and Erin had gone to bed, I sat on the couch with Julie in the dark. We watched out the window as the snow fell, and we tried to talk about how we felt about the whole thing, but it was too big, too soon. I tried to tell her how helpless I felt, but out of nowhere I began to cry. I cried hard; Julie held me and didn't say a word. I couldn't stop.

"I don't know what to do," I said, over and over. "I don't know what to do. . . ."

I couldn't sleep, and I couldn't stop my mind's runaway train path of destruction. Mostly, I thought about God.

When I thought about God and his relationship with Schuyler's monster, I had some difficulties, particularly in relation to the comforting words the people in our lives felt compelled to share with us. I didn't mind the sharing, and I certainly didn't mind when people said they were praying for us. I understood that for them, it was the sincerest form of care, and I was always moved at the gesture. I mean that, too. Not in some condescending, refrigerator art sort of way, but with a recognition of the very powerful sort of energy that must be released into the universe and for Schuyler when someone prays from the heart like that.

To be honest, however, I was also mystified by the act of praying for Schuyler. I suppose there were a lot of ways to view God's role in Schuyler's life, but none of them were particularly comforting. If God set the world in motion and then sat back, unwilling or unable to fix the flaws in his design, then of what value was prayer? And even if we accept the premise that God did actually control our lives and our destinies, even darker possibilities then came into play.

Did God give Schuyler her monster? If he did, what possible good reason could exist for doing something like that to an innocent little girl? And if God didn't do it, who did? Fate? The Devil? Can they really be all that different from God himself? If someone truly believed in the all-powerful Christian God, then they would have to be capable of looking me in the eye and telling me that yes, God did that to her.

"God has the power to help her," they'd said to me, *"if only we believe and pray hard enough."* Well, what did that mean? How was that any different from begging a school yard bully not to beat you up anymore, or pleading with a mugger not to steal your purse or hurt you? Was the act of praying to God to help the little girl that he broke in the first place like negotiating with terrorists? What kind of supreme majestic being demands a certain volume of sorrow before fixing his mistakes?

If that was God, I thought to myself in the dark, then he was a bully. He was the same God who unleashed natural disasters on the poorest people on earth, people who brought tangible meaning to the word "godforsaken." If people believed in a God the Creator who moved in our lives, and if they believed in the power of prayer, then what did it say about all of those tragic people in the world for whom prayer had yielded so very little?

That night, I couldn't honestly say what kind of God I believed in. I thought about a hateful, hurting world with millions of examples of a malicious God, one who seemed to derive pleasure or at least some kind of amusement from the pain of his children. More to the point, I thought simply of Schuyler. I thought about those eyes that I looked into every day of my life, those windows into a soul that might never be free. I thought of her struggle to say what she needed to say, and I considered how hard she tried to keep up and learn, and express what she had learned.

She was a fighter, she had twice my strength and yet it might very well come to nothing. What were we supposed to believe about that? What should we have done with all our hope and all our strength if it wasn't enough? One fine lovely day, I thought with a sinking feeling in my chest, we were probably going to watch her fall to the ground with *grand mal* seizures. I didn't need to understand the nature of God to hate him for hurting my child.

We'd been told that God would never give us more than we could handle, and that he was testing us. Bullshit. If God wanted to teach me a lesson of some kind, then he should have given me polymicrogyria. He could reach into my head and hurt my brain so that I couldn't talk anymore. If God wanted to teach me a lesson, he should have taken Schuyler's hurt and given it to me. I was thirty-seven years old. I'd said enough in my lifetime. *Let me take the hurt,* I'd pleaded, almost in prayer, that night in front of the church almost two years before. *Let me take the silence and the fog and the clumsy hands and God, let me take her seizures. Let me take it from Schuyler. Give her monster to me.*

But that was never going to happen. If God was real, then he chose to give this to Schuyler. It was her burden to carry and fight, not mine, and no matter how much I might wish otherwise or even pray, that was never going to change.

Schuyler's gift from God was her monster, and my gift from God was Schuyler. My gift was precious beyond description, but hers felt like utter ruin.

Two days after our meeting with Dr. Dobyns, we left the comfort and warmth of Erin's home, which had become very much a sanctuary for us, and dragged our luggage and our full hearts out into the snow. I carried our bags to the curb and sat, waiting for the taxi that would take us to the El stop, to the train that would take us to Midway and send us back to our lives in Austin, whatever those lives were going to be.

I sat alone, waiting for the cab and for Julie and Schuyler to join me. The snow muffled the sounds of the city, and it felt strangely like I was watching the world with the volume turned down. I'd had plenty of thoughts swirling in my head for the past two days, and they were starting to come home to roost.

I don't think I'm the person for this. I don't know if I can be that father.

The train ride to the airport was full of heavy silence, from Julie and I beginning to really face the monster head-on and from Schuyler losing her little mind over the city that was sliding by us. The El was Schuyler's latest and most thrilling discovery, a rolling, hissing thing that rattled loudly down the tracks and stopped just for her. It opened its doors for her, and it was even kind enough to let her sad, moping parents along for the ride, even though we were a gigantic buzz kill at the moment. Schuyler had no time for our sadness. There was a city to softly "wow . . ." at. Julie and I were lost in our thoughts.

When we arrived at Midway, we had a long walk to the terminal. We trudged dutifully, our bags hanging off our shoulders and towed behind us as we walked, shrinking from the cold for the last time. Schuyler was free of bags, of course, aside from the oversized Dora the Explorer backpack that made her look like an astronaut. After an hour on the El, she was ready to stretch her legs and run. She spun and circled around us, an energetic little satellite orbiting two tired, brokenhearted planets.

This was the state of our little convoy when we reached the moving walkways. Julie was in her zone and sidestepped the moving sidewalk, but Schuyler and I chose the moving walkway, Schuyler because she'd had fun jumping off at the end on the inbound trip and me because, well, because I am a lazy, lazy man.

Schuyler realized that she and her mother were moving at the same speed even though she was in fact not walking at all, and so she started walking and moving ahead of Julie. "Race Mama," I said, hoping to break the spell. Julie perked up and started walking faster, and before I knew it, Schuyler was actually running down the moving walkway. It was one of those moments that you see what's coming just as it's too late to do anything. I saw Julie walking faster and faster to keep up with Schuyler, and I watched my daughter sprinting, laughing and oblivious to what lay ahead.

I saw the end of the walkway and I knew that she was moving too fast. I knew, even as I called out her name in vain, that she was going to reach the end of the walkway and jump as she had before. And I knew, with a sickening certainty, that she wasn't going to make the landing. She was moving too fast, she was going to wipe out.

Schuyler reached the end of the walkway and with a final burst of speed, jumped into the air. She flew forward, arms outstretched, and with a metallic smack, her feet hit the stationary floor. The sudden deceleration was shocking to her, and for a moment her arms pinwheeled wildly, bleeding off her forward motion and energy.

That was it. She didn't stumble, and she didn't fall. Her outstretched arms were enough to stop her, and her balance and coordination had saved her. I exhaled and relaxed, and as I stepped off the walkway, Schuyler turned and looked, first at me with a big smile, and then down at the walkway.

"Ha!" she cried triumphantly, not just with glee but also with a touch of menace, with that faux-evil edge that her laughter sometimes acquired in some hard-earned victory. She glared at the walkway for a moment, giving it a dirty look but with a crooked smile to assure the walkway that she had most certainly kicked its mechanical butt. Then she spun and continued her erratic, mothlike trajectory down the concourse.

I watched Schuyler laughing and spinning, and I felt as lost as I'd ever felt in my life.

I'm failing you, I thought. *I can't fix this for you.*

16

The Island

So it goes, I thought on the plane as I watched the earth slide slowly below, fields of snow scattered like sheets of smoky glass. *It's never going to change.*

We had high hopes for Chicago. Instead we got a grander version of "*Here's what's wrong with your child, it's even worse than you thought, and no one can fix it. Bye now!*" Schuyler was observed, placed on a chart with all the other kids with other monsters and then sent on her way. She was evaluated, as if we didn't already know that she was behind all the other monsterless kids in the world and might not ever catch up. We knew that. We had lived in hope, had moved to Texas and scratched together a new life so that hers could be better, and instead she ended up in one more substandard school. Sitting on that plane, Julie and I rode in silence, lost in the consideration of exactly how little we'd gained in the year and a half since the diagnosis.

And so it goes, and so it goes, and so it goes.

I think most people, or most shallow people like me, anyway, keep a secret list of all the things they'd do if they won money. There are the small award dreams, of course, like a new car or even a house, depending on how responsible you are. (I always took the car in my prize-winning dream. The idea of buying a house frightened me back then. It frightens me still to this day.)

But there are also the Big Lotto dreams, the ones involving huge sums of money and real changes in your lifestyle. One day you're working for The Man and driving a car with rust holes in the bottom, and the next day, you're holding the giant fake check and having your picture taken. You can do anything. Quit your job, buy the company, and fire your old boss. Put your name on a building at your old college, the one that kicked you out for excessive drinking and a 1.0 grade point average. Buy a blimp. Whatever. You can do whatever your newly, fabulously rich heart desires.

Flying back from Chicago and watching the cold world pass silently and soullessly below, my Big Money Dream changed. I supposed it had once been all about special schools and the best speech therapists money could buy. My dream had been about hope for Schuyler, about fighting tenaciously for progress and throwing such impressive fistfuls of cash at the problem that she would not be able to do anything except somehow crush her monster and achieve the life she deserved.

In my new, shameful Big Money Dream, I would take my $200 million payoff, say goodbye to all my friends and family, post one last blog entry, and then take Julie and Schuyler and move us all far, far away, to that mythical and deserted South Pacific island that has served as the subject of so many fantasies and New Yorker cartoons. It would be more beautiful than Hawaii and more remote than Pitcairn.

I would build a little hut on our island, with a thatched roof and perpetually open windows overlooking a crystalline lagoon. That nameless, uncharted island would be our paradise home forever, and we'd spend the rest of our days with Schuyler, a perfect civilization of three. My little girl would know nothing about monsterless kids or where she fell on a sad chart in a geneticist's office, and she'd never have to ponder the holes that a mean-spirited God had punched in her brain.

Schuyler would carry her monster, but she'd never know it, and for all the days of her life, she would only know that her tiny world was one of beauty, and that she was loved by her parents with a passion and a tenderness that enveloped her. Every night, after sitting on the beach with her watching the sunset, I would go to bed and sleep a deep, untroubled sleep. I would never again have that dream, the one where Schuyler spoke to me and told me not to worry, because all the things I worried about had been left behind on the far side of a protecting ocean.

Most of all, until the day I died, she would understand that, monster or no, she was the only child in my life, and not just because of the fear of another monster riding into the world on another innocent brain. She would know that she was the only one I ever really wanted.

The plane tilted forward ever so slightly, and I glanced out the window. The snow had passed behind us a long time ago, and we began descending back to earth, and not to my selfish island, which I desperately wanted but knew was wrong for a million reasons.

Part Three

A Monster Challenged

17

Vox

The next month passed as if we were trudging through deep water. Once again, nothing had really changed, but suddenly it felt as if the monster was bigger than before, and the answer more elusive. Our lives went on, ostensibly as if nothing had happened. We applied for Social Security for Schuyler and were turned down because we made too much money at our lucrative retail jobs. We acquired goldfish, three of them, to whom Schuyler immediately assigned roles for all of us as she always did with any group of three, whether it was fish or dogs or spoons. (I got to be the goldfish with the big bug eyes, naturally.) I had a vivid dream where Schuyler told me she loved me in clear, strong words, and I hurried to the computer the moment I woke up, rushing to e-mail everyone I knew; it was still booting up when I woke sufficiently to realize it had only been a dream.

One day about a month later, I went to pick up Schuyler at school and found her in her classroom. When I peeked in, I saw Schuyler looking at the door, clearly waiting anxiously for me. This was a change from her usual desire to stay in school with her friends for as long as possible before being forced to leave with smelly old uncool Daddy.

When she saw me, she ran over to me excitedly. I saw she was wearing a strange device around her waist like a jogger's purse. It had three large buttons on the top which Schuyler could easily reach down and hit: a green one, a red one, and one with a face. She grabbed at my arm to make sure I was watching and pushed the face button.

"Hi, my name is Schuyler."

"What?" I said. Schuyler's face burst into a broad smile and she pushed the button again. A young woman's voice repeated the phrase.

"Hi, my name is Schuyler."

Well. I didn't see that coming. I sat down in one of her classroom's tiny chairs as Schuyler went through all the buttons.

"Schuyler!" I said. "Are you talking now?"

"Yes."

I wanted to see if she actually understood what she was saying. "Do you want to go home with Daddy now?"

She laughed. **"No."**

"It's something new we're experimenting with," said Schuyler's teacher Michelle. "The school district has a new technology coordinator and she wanted to see if Schuyler would like to try some of these things. This is an entry level device, but it can be programmed with up to twelve responses. We're going to try expanding them over the next few weeks and see how she does."

For a moment, I was back in my recurring dream, listening to her speak for the first time. It was literally the very last thing I expected to hear.

Julie and I were working opposite schedules while we tried to find after-school care for Schuyler, and we would meet at my store for the trade-off, since it was on Julie's way home. Schuyler and I waited for her excitedly. I kept asking Schuyler yes and no questions so she'd keep using the device. When Julie walked in and Schuyler ran up and hit the button to introduce herself, Julie's face lit up. I'd waited all afternoon to see her reaction. Like me, she saw the potential almost immediately.

Looking back on it now after having explored some of the most amazing technology that's been developed in the field of augmentative communication, that first three-button device seems childishly simple. Cleverly called the HipTalk, it was simply a big blue plastic device with buttons on the top surface and laminated overlays with pictures and words on them. When you pressed the button, a recorded voice (in this case, one of the young Manor teacher's aides) spoke the word out loud. Set with three buttons for Schuyler, the HipTalk could say "yes" and "no" and "Hi, my name is Schuyler." That was it. And she was capable of saying yes and no very clearly on her own through the universal language of nods and a shaken head, as well as a very clear "uh huh" and "nuh uh." This device was meant for a very young or very seriously disabled child, and in Schuyler's hands, once she mastered her few words, it was more of an amusement than an actual means for communication.

As primitive as it was, however, the HipTalk was startling to us, if only because the concept it represented was so simple and yet world altering. Schuyler had a voice. Of sorts.

The next day, when we picked her up, the device was set with a number of new buttons, and Schuyler wanted to show them all to us. One now said she was hungry, and another said she needed to go to the bathroom. Schuyler was working hard on potty training at this point, but she was still resistant to going unless she absolutely had to. She particularly hated leaving a social situation to go. When she was showing off the HipTalk to some of my co-workers, she accidentally hit the wrong button.

"I need to go potty." Her face suddenly lit with horror with the realization that she had inadvertently asked to go to the last place in the world she actually wanted to visit. She hurriedly hit the **"No"** button repeatedly, shaking her head vigorously and signing "no," her little hand making the biting ostrich over and over. She reminded me of a politician who didn't realize the microphone was on.

The HipTalk was something of a toy for Schuyler almost from the beginning, but it opened our minds. The school had it on loan for two weeks, but after a day or two, we were already trying to look beyond its limited benefits. I don't know why it had never occurred to us that something like this was out there. I don't know why it never occurred to anyone to tell us.

Once we found the technical term for these devices (Alternative and Augmentative Communication devices), a search on the Web immediately began revealing more options. Most involved larger versions of the HipTalk, with big boards covered with words and pictures. Each button would accommodate a short recording of the word. After Chicago, we were hesitant to get excited again, especially since even these beginner-level devices started at several hundred dollars. Still, it was impossible not to feel like another door had just opened, one we didn't even know was there.

"Worst case scenario," I joked with Julie, "I'll bet we could afford a Speak N Spell."

We had another meeting with Schuyler's team at the school, to go over Dr. Dobyns's report on Schuyler and to discuss the recommendations he made. He actually mentioned Alternative and Augmentative Communication in his report, but with no specific details. We nevertheless took that as a directive and presented it to the school as part of her physician-mandated treatment.

The meeting went much better than either of us expected. Shortly before the Chicago trip, Schuyler had been evaluated by her physical therapist as being in the one percentile for physical development. Let me say that again. One percent. That meant, according to the physical therapist, 99 percent of kids her age had better physical development and motor skills than she did. Kids in wheelchairs, kids with nervous disorders and muscular degenerative diseases? All but one percent of them did better than Schuyler, who just a week or two after that evaluation took her flying leap off the airport moving sidewalk with such skill. I wanted to know how that was possible.

At the meeting, we learned it was possible because Schuyler, in her usual "Fight the Man" form, had refused to cooperate during the evaluation. Rather than send home a report saying something along the lines of "Your kid is a punk and wouldn't do a goddamned thing for this evaluation," she simply marked her at zero for the activities that she refused to do.

"So wait a minute," I said. "She didn't take the evaluation, but you assigned her a number anyway? That number is going to follow her forever, you know. Is that really fair?"

Tammy, the school district special needs superintendent who had fought so tenaciously for us before, shook her head. "At the very least, an explanatory note needs to be included with that report. I think it's clear she's not in that percentile range."

Mrs. Malison, the speech therapist, once again balked at the resources required to include Signing Exact English in Schuyler's plan, despite the fact that Dr. Dobyns specifically mentioned it in his recommendations. Once again, we were told accommodations would be made. Once again, we didn't believe them. Julie slid me a note that said simply, "We'll need to teach her signing ourselves."

There was someone new at the meeting, a woman with a serious expression and a quick cadence to her speech that might have been enthusiasm or might have just been nervousness. She was introduced to us as Margaret, the new technology advisor for the school district's special needs program. She was the person who had sent home the HipTalk, with the idea that some kind of speech device might be beneficial to Schuyler. She had brought a number of other devices to the meeting for us to see.

There were several devices similar to the HipTalk only larger, devices with overlays that could be changed and re-recorded as needed. Margaret thought these simple devices were appropriate for Schuyler, especially since she had no speech at all. She gave one of them to us to take home and try out.

Among the devices she had with her, one kept catching my eye. It looked like a laptop but without a keyboard. Instead, the screen was covered with images of buttons, each containing a word and an image representing that word. While the meeting finished up and all the administrators were finishing the paperwork, I took this strange computer and began to play with it.

The screen was actually a touch screen. When I touched each button, the screen would change, and as I played around with it, I realized every time I touched a button, the device would give me a new screen with new choices. If I hit "eat," food choices would pop up. "Play" would bring games and sports words. The words would appear in a blank area at the top of the screen, and when I touched that area, a vaguely human-sounding computer voice would speak the text.

"Isn't that amazing?" said Margaret. "One of our more advanced kids in the junior high is using that. It really has a huge vocabulary and lots of options for putting together sentences and phrases."

"That's incredible," I said. "I can't imagine what Schuyler would do with this."

She gave a tight smile as she took the device and placed it in a cardboard box with the others she had brought. "Yes, maybe one day. I think that's way too advanced for Schuyler right now. Let's see how she does with the one I gave you. I think that might be more appropriate for her skill level."

Out of the corner of my eye, I saw Julie watching Margaret with an expression that might have been at least first cousin to a glare.

"How does she know what's appropriate for Schuyler?" Julie asked later in the car as we drove home. "How dare she say Schuyler's not smart enough for something more advanced. That pisses me off."

"They do seem to want to go slow," I said. "I don't know, maybe they think they've got a more realistic view of her abilities than we do. Maybe they just don't want to pay for a more expensive device."

"I hate being told what Schuyler can't do," she said. "I don't think anyone's trying very hard to figure out what she *can* do."

The larger device didn't work very well, with frequent malfunctions and buttons that were hard for Schuyler to use. She still had the HipTalk, now expanded to its full twelve-button capacity, and she loved wearing it and bossing people around with her dozen phrases.

I noticed that as she used it, she began to integrate it into the communications tools she already had. It was something to see. One day after Julie dropped her off for me at my store, Schuyler walked up to Christina, her favorite of my employees, and began to sign "cookie."

"Schuyler, tell your cheap-ass daddy to buy you a cookie," Christina said. "You look like a girl who needs a sugar rush."

Schuyler turned to me, signed "cookie" again and then pressed a button on the HipTalk.

"I'm hungry" said the recorded voice of her teacher's aide. When I didn't respond quickly enough, she hit another button for Christina.

"Bye bye!" said the device. She then grabbed my hand and began to pull me away.

As we walked to the café, I realized that even with this primitive device, Schuyler was excited about having words. She was using the device for things like "yes" and "no" and "I'm hungry," words and phrases that until now she used almost constantly in sign language. It wasn't just a matter of being able to communicate more clearly. For Schuyler, it was about being able to do so like everyone else, with a voice.

Even if it wasn't her own.

I couldn't stop thinking about the advanced device. I thought

Margaret was wrong. Schuyler was already moving beyond what the HipTalk could do. How would she handle something that could say anything she wanted, if only she had the skills to use it?

When I got home, I went online and looked up AAC devices using touch-screen technology, and by the time Julie came home from work, I had discovered two companies, DynaVox (makers of the one we'd seen at the meeting) and the Prentke-Romich Company. Both produced small electronic devices of varying levels of complexity. The fanciest models utilized touch-screen technology, advanced language software, and synthetic computerized voices, the kinds of things that would be able to grow with Schuyler into adulthood. Because the buttons were arranged on a screen rather than physically on the device, a multitude of different levels became possible, ranging from four big buttons to eighty-four small ones. And of course, the grammatical architecture of the language meant that every screen would lead logically to another, depending on what the user chose. It would display the words as it spoke them, allowing the user to learn spelling as well. The devices had the capacity to interface with a PC or a Mac and allowed the user to import and play WAV sound files. (I could create Darth Vader clips for her to use for intimidating the other kids, for example. *"It is your destiny to give me your chocolate milk."*) They could control other appliances such as telephones if necessary, and they weren't even very big, about nine by eight inches and weighing about three and a half pounds.

All that power, for a mere seven thousand dollars. Closer to ten, with the warranty.

Yeah, I know. After I read that number and recovered from my head exploding (very painful, by the way), I poked around online and found that for most people, there are two options that make a purchase like this possible, not including the sale of vital organs on eBay.

The first option was quite simply the law. If it was determined by her doctor that Schuyler required an augmentative speech device, the school district had to provide it for her. This sounded like the answer to all our problems, except for one obstacle.

While it could very well be determined that Schuyler required such a device, the exact type of device was up for grabs and to ultimately be determined by Margaret, who so far had shown enthusiasm for the low-end models such as the two-hundred-dollar HipTalk. Given the size of the school district, the chances of their voluntarily spending ten thousand dollars on a device for one student seemed extremely remote. And given a recent (and in my opinion, dickish) Supreme Court ruling that placed the burden of proof in any challenge of a school's IEP decisions on the parents rather than the school, it would be a long, hard fight before there was a chance of Schuyler laying hands on a device, and if we did win, the device would belong to the school, not Schuyler.

The second option, that of the insurance carrier, was eliminated with a single phone call to our insurance company. Not only "no," but "no, we don't even have anything like that listed in our little book, and say, are you making this up? Who is this?" We filed an appeal, but the process could take months, possibly as long as a year, and Schuyler was far enough behind as it was.

We were getting ahead of ourselves, though. I showed everything that I'd found to Julie, and we agreed to follow up. I sent a long e-mail to the local representative for Prentke-Romich, whose devices were receiving excellent marks from every site I visited. We set up a meeting for the following week, in the café of my store. I wanted to see these devices in action and hear what the rep thought they could do for Schuyler.

The more we read, the more convinced we became that Margaret was wrong. We'd tried a lot of things, and we'd been wrong before, but hesitantly, gun-shy from Chicago and a hundred other false hopes, we had nevertheless become convinced that Schuyler needed one of these advanced devices.

She needed a Big Box of Words.

18

The Village

We had moved to Texas to get closer to my family. So it was strange that it was with Julie's parents that a kind of reconciliation took place.

There wasn't a great deal to reconcile with my family. My brother and I had made an uneasy peace when our kids were born, and now that we were back in Texas, I suppose it was easier to forgive me for leaving in the first place, particularly since I returned with a wife whom he actually liked. My sister and her kids were easygoing enough. As for my mother, she and I had always had one of those relationships where we could go for months at a time without talking, only to pick things up as if it had been just a few days. She didn't have a lot of high maintenance requirements for me, and she didn't entertain any from me in return.

It's hard to know what to tell you about my mother. We're a great deal alike; we have a similar sense of humor, and we like our privacy, although I suppose blogging and then writing a memoir is a funny way for me to show it. For my mother, the past was something that she negotiated with every day. Her own mother had committed suicide a few years before I was born, and my mother's guilt haunted her for as long as I had known her. She'd managed to put the poverty of her youth behind her when I was a kid, but it all came crashing down about the same time my father left her. (I'm sure that was not entirely a coincidence.) Left poor and alone, with her two oldest kids living on their own and her youngest, a pain-in-the-ass teenaged son, still very much living at home, she began to drink, and she spiraled out of control in a hurry.

The thing about my mother, however, is this: she might have made mistakes, she might have screwed up in small ways and in some that were astonishing in their breadth and power, but she was a survivor. I came home from school on more than one occasion to find her hiding under the table, crying and barely holding it together, and I would do the only thing I knew to do. I never tried to get her out from under the table. I simply joined her on the floor, and while it wasn't much, it was enough. Eventually she joined Alcoholics Anonymous and quit drinking, and that was that. She identified herself as an alcoholic from that day forward, but I don't know that I ever really bought it, AA philosophy notwithstanding. I never think of her as an alcoholic, but rather as someone who had a problem, kicked its ass, and then moved on. She's more like Schuyler than I think I've ever told her, and even though I poke fun at some of the more ridiculous aspects of twelve stepping, the fact is I'm proud of her. I'll probably make her buy this book in order to read that, though.

As a result of a lifetime of mistakes and redemptions, my mother is an extremely nonjudgmental person, which is swell for me but doesn't make for a terribly interesting story. She keeps her feelings at a slight distance, which is perhaps understandable given the life she's led, but with Schuyler she's completely accepting. Perhaps my mother sees her as a kindred soul after all.

When Schuyler received her diagnosis in 2003, Julie's parents were devastated. Everyone was, really; when my mother found out, she cried, something I hadn't heard her do for almost twenty years, not even when my father died. But for Dave and Sandy, there was more. I'm not sure if it was guilt or just regret for how things had transpired between us in the years since we left Michigan, but when we moved to Texas, I think on some level they felt as if they were going to lose us for good. And while their feelings about me were undeniably complicated, their love for Schuyler, their first grandchild, was simple and huge.

In the end Dave and Sandy reached out to us without guile or condition. They made the drive from Michigan to Texas a number of times, a trip that I know from my Interlochen days is no picnic, and they helped us both financially and emotionally as much and as often as they were able. Ultimately, and I can't believe I'm about to say this, Julie's parents were bigger than I was. But they'll have to buy this book to read that, too.

Julie and I had become spoiled over the years, with the team at Yale and Schuyler's well-meaning day care owner and the countless, faceless readers of my blog, all looking out for our daughter. We had reached a point where we took it on faith that the people in Schuyler's life were concerned about her well-being before any other priority that might come her way. We all made mistakes, and some of them had lasting consequences for her, but we had never run up against anyone who was in the position to balance Schuyler's needs against some other agenda. When it finally happened, I'm not sure we handled it very well.

Let me say that I do believe Margaret, the school district's special needs technology advisor, had Schuyler's best interests at heart. You don't go into special education without some kind of sense of mission, and she clearly wanted to help Schuyler and the other kids in the program.

I suppose there's an inherent conflict built into the system of public school special education programs. In that conflict, you eventually find two forces that, while both working to meet the needs of the students in their care, nevertheless end up doing so from two opposite perspectives. One force is the school, trying to give out the smallest amount of resources to each individual student so more students can be served. The other force is the parents, trying to get as much help as possible for their child, regardless of the cost. Add to that the law, which states that a public school must provide special services to a child who requires them but doesn't necessarily provide the funding to do so, and you've set into motion an inevitable clash.

As I mentioned before, the Supreme Court heard a case in which parents of a special needs child were unhappy with the services assigned to their child in an IEP meeting. The case would determine who carries the burden of proof in a situation like this. In the end, the court decided that if parents, with whatever resources and representation they can afford, wish to fight a school district, with all its specialists and resources at their disposal, that burden of proof falls upon those parents. I don't believe it was the court's finest moment.

In further conversations with Margaret, we made it clear to her that we wanted to explore more advanced speech devices with Schuyler, particularly the upper-end models from DynaVox and Prentke-Romich.

"Well, we can certainly look into it," she said one afternoon when we picked up Schuyler from school. "I can try to contact representatives from both companies to see what they can do about giving us evaluation models. I really don't think Schuyler's ready for the more advanced models, however."

"How do you know what she's capable of until you see how she does?" asked Julie. "So far she's only had these really simple devices, and she's mastering those right off the bat. How do you know what she'd be able to do with the right equipment?"

"No no, I agree completely, and I'm going to try to get my hands on one of those models," she said. "But I really do think one of the simpler devices is going to be better for her."

"If she's evaluated and found to need that device, isn't the school legally obligated to provide the equipment?" I asked.

"That's absolutely true," said Margaret. "And we're totally committed to providing whatever's determined to be appropriate for her developmental level."

"So who makes that determination?" asked Julie.

"Well," she said, suddenly uncomfortable. "I do, actually."

We researched the different devices produced by DynaVox and Prentke-Romich, and more important we read about the software that drove them. Margaret and the school had shown a preference for and familiarity with the DynaVox systems, but the more we read, on both the companies' Web sites and from independent sources online, the more intrigued we became with Prentke-Romich. Their philosophy seemed geared more toward building language skills than simply providing a simple and intuitive method of communication. We contacted the company and set up a meeting with a representative.

We met at the café of my store after I got off work. Tracy Custer was easy to spot when she walked in, devices in hand. She was tall and confident, and shook my hand firmly when she introduced herself. We sat and got right down to business. She asked a lot of questions about Schuyler; like most people, she'd never heard of polymicrogyria, but Schuyler's symptoms closely resembled those of many of her clients, many of whom suffered from cerebral palsy, rendering them similarly nonverbal. Before joining Prentke-Romich, she'd worked as a speech pathologist.

We also discussed the devices I'd read about, particularly something called the Springboard. At around two thousand dollars, it was a lower-end device and was in the range of technology being recommended by Margaret. Both DynaVox and PRC had devices in general areas of development that paralleled each other.

"And her cognitive abilities are unimpaired?" she asked finally.

"Nobody knows," I said. "Dr. Dobyns in Chicago thinks she probably suffers from some cognitive deficiency like most polymicrogyria patients, but no one's really sure how much. The IQ test is almost impossible to administer to a nonverbal subject, not without a lot of subjective opinion being thrown in the mix, and to be honest, we haven't felt like having some sort of label slapped on her just yet. If they get it wrong, she's got that stuck to her for life, you know?"

"Tell me this, Robert. What do *you* think?"

"About her cognitive ability?" I asked. I was momentarily taken aback. Everyone seemed so eager to tell me what they believed about Schuyler's abilities, but it occurred to me that very few people ever bothered to find out what I thought.

"Yes, do you think she suffers from any form of retardation? I find the parents usually have a pretty realistic idea, especially the ones who get involved enough to start researching AAC technology. What do you think?"

I hesitated for a moment, trying to be realistic with myself. Could I give an honest answer, as close to objective as any parent could be? I realized I could, because deep down, even with all my fears, I knew what I thought to be true about Schuyler.

"I don't think she's retarded," I said. "There's got to be a better way to say that, but no, I don't. I don't know that she's necessarily brilliant, any more than I'm brilliant, but I think she's capable of a lot more than the school gives her credit for. I think she's waiting for the right door to be opened, and then she's going to walk right through it. Do you want to know what I really believe?"

"What's that?"

"I think she's so badly delayed in large part because we've failed her, all of us," I said. "That's why I'm so excited about AAC technology. I think it might be the thing that could open that door for her."

"Well, I think you're on the right track here. But I'm going to be really honest with you about the Springboard. It's a good device for very young kids or kids who have some pretty significant cognitive issues, and it's good for someone who's just starting out in the augmentative communication process, as Schuyler would be. But the

Springboard is limited. It uses digitized speech, meaning the words are recorded, not produced by the computer, and it has a vocabulary roughly equivalent to that of a three-year-old. You said Schuyler's already five, correct? Even if she does have some level of cognitive disability, she'd still be using a device that would very likely be limiting for her within just a few months."

I thought back to the advanced DynaVox I'd seen, the one Margaret had insisted would be too difficult for Schuyler to use. "There was a DynaVox machine at the IEP meeting that seemed really advanced. The school's technology advisor sort of shooed us away from it, but I'm not convinced Schuyler wouldn't take to something like that and really flourish."

She smiled. "I didn't want to look like I was trying to upsell you, but that's what I was thinking, too. We have an equivalent device called the Vantage Plus. It uses a much more advanced language system and utilizes synthesized speech, not recorded speech, so it's much more flexible and can have vocabulary added to it very easily."

"So wait," I said. "This uses the computer voice, right? Would she sound like Stephen Hawking? I have to say, that idea creeps me out a little bit."

She unloaded another device from her bag. It was similar in size to the Springboard but was blue, and when she powered it up, the display showed a lot more keys than the Springboard.

"Here, listen for yourself," she said. "This is the voice most of the kids use." She punched up a settings page and selected a voice, then went to another page and hit a button that called up a pre-set sentence. The voice that came out was computerized but recognizably childlike, and had surprisingly human inflections.

"I use this language communication device to help me speak."

"Oh, that's not bad," I said.

"No, and most users eventually make adjustments to the pitch and tone, so everyone sounds unique. You know, when I get phone calls from different clients, I can usually recognize them before they introduce themselves, simply by the pitch of their voice settings."

She walked me through the Vantage Plus, showed me how the dynamic language worked and how it guided the user through sentence construction in a way that seemed very intuitive to me. She also demonstrated the language system, called Unity 84, and showed me how the device was set to operate at different levels, from a very simple, one-touch beginner's level to one that met the needs of fully cognitive adults.

I was blown away, not just by the device's capabilities but also by the possibilities for Schuyler. This was all so far beyond what the school had shown us, and while I was aware that I was looking at it through dad eyes, I also had a feeling Schuyler would take to this.

"Why would the school want us to use the Springboard if this device is so open-ended? Why not give her all the tools and see what she does with them?"

Tracy Custer hesitated. I could tell she was being diplomatic.

"Well, first of all, I've never met Schuyler, so I can't say they're wrong. The other thing is, I've never met anyone from the Manor Independent School District. In all my years at PRC, they've never contacted me for information or training or anything. So I can't say one way or the other."

She paused. "But one thing to consider is the price of the devices. The Springboard costs them about two thousand dollars. The Vantage Plus is about seventy-five hundred dollars, and that's before you include service agreements. The school is required by law to provide whatever is deemed necessary for the student, but very few doctors are going to specifically recommend a particular device, and so that determination is left up to the school. If Manor doesn't have a huge budget, I'm not surprised they'd take a conservative approach to this."

I was still floored by the numbers. "Seven grand, that's a lot of money."

"There are some other paths to funding, such as your insurance company, Social Security, etc. But generally, it's the schools that fund these devices."

That wasn't good news.

I spoke with Margaret the next day when I picked Schuyler up from school. She showed me the device she had Schuyler working with, a large plastic box with maybe a dozen buttons and a place for laminated overlays to slide into place. After looking at the DynaVox and Prentke-Romich devices, it looked like something from the 1950s.

"You know, Julie and I have been talking about this," I said. "We think Schuyler could really go somewhere with one of the more advanced models, like the ones PRC and DynaVox make. I'm not sure we're really exploring the possibilities here."

"I know, those are really amazing devices," she said. "But I don't know that Schuyler's really ready for something like that. I'm just afraid if we demand too much from her, she'll become frustrated and won't want to do anything at all."

"Really? You think? I don't know, I've always known Schuyler to be sort of a stubborn problem-solver. I don't see her turning away from a challenge."

"Well," she said with a rigid smile, "maybe she's different at home with you. I'm just not convinced she would do well with a device like that."

I felt it then, the thing I'd felt when we received the PDD-NOS diagnosis that didn't feel right two years before. I felt the condescension of the Expert toward the Parent, the kind smile parked in front of academic certainty.

The last time we'd felt that, we were right not to trust it. We didn't trust it this time, either.

"I guess we'll find out," I said. "We're going to try some of these devices out. I met with the representative from Prentke-Romich yesterday, and she's going to arrange for Schuyler to try out the

Vantage Plus for a while and see if it's right for her. I'm going to contact DynaVox and try to set up a meeting with them, too."

"Really?" Margaret stopped adjusting the insert for the Gab-O-Tron or whatever it was called. "You met with PRC? By yourself?"

"Yeah. We wanted to see what the more advanced models would do, and she was nice enough to bring one by to look at. She explained a lot about how it works and what it can do. It was a really productive meeting." I was working as hard as I could to keep any trace of smugness out of my voice. I was probably about 70 percent successful.

Maybe 65. Sixty, absolute minimum.

"Well, that's great," she said, her big smile still firmly in place. "I hope in the future you'll let me know about meetings like that so we can all be on the same page. I'd like to know more about their product line. I've heard the Springboard and the Vantage are a lot harder to use than the DynaVox. I hope you'll give me a call next time."

I grabbed Schuyler's bag and took her by the hand. "We'll sure do that. This came up pretty quick, and we wanted to move on it."

"Oh, I understand. I just want to make sure we're not rushing into anything here."

"Schuyler's been waiting a long time for something like this," I said as we walked to the door. "If I were you, I'd be prepared for things to move pretty fast."

That evening, we received a call from Tracy Custer. "Okay," she told Julie, "I've been with PRC for sixteen years and I've never even heard of the Manor School District. So perhaps you can explain why I just received a call from a tech coordinator named Margaret who suddenly wants to meet and talk about our product line. She didn't mention Schuyler at all, other than to say she had students who she'd decided would benefit from AAC technology and wanted to get together and explore some options."

"I'm pretty sure Rob talked to her," Julie said. "I think she got upset that we might make a decision without her. She probably needs this whole thing to be her idea. Isn't that her job?"

Tracy Custer laughed. "I'm not going to comment on that. I'm just glad the door's finally opening."

I called my friend Tracy in Dallas and told her what was happening. I was disheartened by another call I'd placed to our insurance carrier regarding an AAC device. They still had no idea what I was talking about and kept asking for a code that would explain exactly what we were asking for. Once I got that code from Tracy Custer, it was much easier getting an answer from our insurance carrier. That answer, of course, was no. We could file an appeal, of course. That would probably take about six months.

"I talked to our PRC rep," I told Tracy. "She said there was a case pending right now where an insurance carrier discontinued coverage for a little girl's *wheelchair*. How cold is that? *'Out of the chair, babe. We'll get you a sled so you can get dragged around.'*"

"What are the other options?" Tracy asked.

"The school clearly doesn't want to pay for this, and they don't have to, not when they can recommend the lower end device," I said. "We apparently make too much money in our snazzy retail jobs to qualify for Social Security assistance, and even if we did, it wouldn't cover this, not by a long shot."

"Do you remember how quickly your blog readers helped you get to Chicago to see Dr. Dobyns? You didn't even get a chance to ask for help."

"I was thinking about that," I said.

"Well, stop thinking about it and do something about it. Start writing up a Web page explaining what this thing is and what it will do for her. I'll help you put it all together. We can set a target goal and make a graphic that will visually represent how much money has come in. I'll make some graphics for you that people can put on their own pages, and that's what's going to bring people to you.

That's what's going to make it happen. Word of mouth. Remember the woman who got the Internet to pay off her credit card debt in like five months?"

"Yeah," I said. "Save Karin, right?"

"That's the one," Tracy said. "Or Kaycee Nicole? The cancer girl everyone sent money to, and she turned out to be a fake? You could raise the money for this, Rob. People love Schuyler. Even people who don't like you very much would contribute to help her."

"Well, Schuyler does have the advantage of being debt free and a real little girl with an actual disorder."

Schuyler's Fund was born that night. The page was up within a week.

Julie and I met Margaret at a big, shiny facility for special needs education in the Austin area. We saw her outside the building and exchanged all our pleasantries before going inside to meet with a representative of the DynaVox company.

Holly was young and pleasant, and she was very excited about her product. We saw how the DynaVox worked, and I have to say, initially I was very impressed. The DynaVox system seemed to be designed around the construction of pages that would organize small pieces of conversation into readily accessible buttons. It was fast and easy to use. Holly did an outstanding job of presenting her wares, particularly the top model, similar in price and capability to PRC's Vantage Plus.

As I began asking questions and exploring the device, however, I began to see why the Vantage was still likely to be a better long-term fit. Simply put, the DynaVox would allow Schuyler to easily say things and communicate her needs, but the Vantage would teach her to communicate. The PRC device seemed to have a much more robust language system, one that required the user to learn how to construct sentences and organize thoughts, not build pages. It would be riskier for Schuyler to use the Vantage, requiring her to learn a more difficult system, but I still felt as if in the end, she'd have more to gain by mastering not just the device, but the language as well.

Margaret asked a lot of questions and was positive and constructive in her comments. Even though she made it clear she wanted to recommend the low-end DynaVox device (something called the MiniMo, which she made a somewhat hesitant Holly bring out and demonstrate, even though it was clear none of us was very excited to see it), she nevertheless seemed genuinely curious about the more advanced model. When we were leaving, she even promised to attend the meeting I'd set up between Julie and Tracy Custer the next week. I left the meeting feeling as if perhaps I'd misjudged her. Margaret might have had a prejudicial attitude about the low-end DynaVox (which in addition to being cheaper was also the devil she knew), but she was open to our wishes as well, I thought as we left the parking lot.

That feeling lasted all the way until the following morning.

Margaret called and spoke to Julie. She informed her that the school district had rejected the higher end device by either company, just as we feared they might. The school's position was that there was no point in getting a higher end device for Schuyler, since there was no indication that she would ever be able to use it.

"How would they know that?" asked Julie. "She hasn't even had a chance to try either of them out yet."

"Well, they've had time to observe her with the other devices we've provided for her, and they came to the conclusion that the more advanced devices would be beyond her capabilities."

"They?" asked Julie. "You mean you, right? You're the one who makes that determination."

"I wasn't the only one who's been observing her," Margaret responded quietly. "This was a team decision." She hesitated. "So I wanted to let you know I've decided Schuyler should be using the DynaVox MiniMo, and I've submitted a request to the school district to purchase one. It's sort of a complicated procedure, getting the funding in place, but I'd say in about two weeks, we should be able to provide the device to Schuyler."

"Wait a minute," Julie said, trying to process what she'd just been told. "You've already made that decision? We haven't even had a meeting with PRC yet. You didn't consult with us before making this decision, Margaret. Don't we get a say?"

"Well, of course you do, Mrs. Hudson. But the final decision is going to come down to the school district, since they're the ones purchasing the device. And I don't think——"

"Rob has started looking for third party funding so we can get a device for Schuyler," Julie interrupted. "If that works out, we won't need the school to buy her anything, especially something we don't want her using."

"But it's very important for the school to make that purchase for her," said Margaret. "The school is legally responsible for providing a device for Schuyler. I think it would be a mistake for you to make that kind of investment without the support of the school."

Julie became quiet for a moment. "Are you saying that if we got her a more advanced device, you wouldn't support its use in her class?"

"Oh, no, of course not," Margaret said hastily. "You're Schuyler's parents, we're going to do whatever you ask us to, as long as it fits within the guidelines of her most recent IEP. But the school is recommending the DynaVox MiniMo, and she'll be able to start using it soon."

"If she uses a device purchased by the school, it's still the school's, right? And you could take it back whenever you wanted, true?"

"We'd never take it away from her as long as she was a student in Manor," Margaret said.

"What about the one you brought to the last IEP? Who was supposed to be using that one?"

Margaret stopped cold. "Well, that was for a few hours, I'll admit.

The student was an older child and he was totally understanding about my need to show it to you. He's very enthusiastic about it and I'm sure he was thrilled to give it up for a short time to help another student."

"Right," said Julie. "Listen, I need to talk to Rob, and I'm still going to meet with the PRC representative next week. I'm going to call him right now, but I don't think he's going to be very happy. He's pretty insistent about he and I being the ones who make this final determination."

"Well, of course you are," Margaret said.

Julie hung up and called me at work, and as she predicted, I was pretty pissed off. After everything we'd been through over the years, we weren't at all comfortable turning over the decision-making process to anyone else. Schuyler's special ed teacher, Michelle, was wonderful, and she supported Schuyler completely. But she had no experience whatsoever with AAC technology and had expressed a number of times how nervous she was about having to help Schuyler with a complicated device. Now an administrator was making choices without our input, choices which at least on the surface seemed to be based in part on budgetary concerns.

Margaret could endorse the device we thought was appropriate for Schuyler, but she also appeared to be embarrassed at the thought of us rejecting the school's recommendation in favor of us finding a way to make the purchase ourselves. To us, it seemed that her solution was to simply make the call without us and hope we didn't put up a fight.

"What's her phone number?" I asked Julie tersely.

That's when a funny thing happened. Before I got a chance to call Margaret, I received a work-related call from the Barnes & Noble head office in New York. Just as I was hanging up from that call, Julie called me back.

"What the hell did you say to her?" she asked. "Margaret just called me and she was really upset. Dude, I think you made her cry."

"I never got a chance to call her," I said. "If she cried, that was all you, friend."

Apparently my sweet wife had sufficiently impressed Margaret with our displeasure that she had called back twenty minutes later and had become very emotional with Julie. She hadn't intended to anger or offend us, and she was going to try to get one of the high-end DynaVox devices for Schuyler to evaluate.

"You know," she said to Julie, "I'm just trying to do what's best for Schuyler."

I have no doubt that Margaret was telling the absolute truth. I think she was trying to do the very best she could for Schuyler. But disregarding our wishes and opinions simply because we're the dumb old parents was the wrong approach to take. Did she really believe we were just going to say, "Okie dokie, whatever you say!" Or did the school actually turn down our request for the high-end device and Margaret decided to go for the MiniMo so she could still be the hands-on person in charge of the process? To this day, I have no idea why she attempted her end run.

I was also aware, quietly but painfully aware, that it was very possible that Margaret was right about Schuyler. Just because we'd become comfortable fighting with experts didn't mean we weren't aware of our limitations and our lack of objectivity. Schuyler might very well have lacked the capability to use the more advanced device. It could have been a waste of time; she might not ever get far enough on it to justify the expense. It could turn out to be a waste of money, and if the school paid for it, money that wasn't even ours to waste.

In the end, however, I would have felt, and appropriately so, like the worst father on the planet if I'd agreed to the purchase of a device with the vocabulary of a three-year-old for my five-year-old daughter, based on the opinion of a school administrator who believed that Schuyler was incapable of doing more.

A therapist from the same school district had declared Schuyler's physical development to be below that of 99 percent of children everywhere because Schuyler was being a pain during the evaluation. Another balked at including sign language in Schuyler's curriculum because she didn't know it herself. Now the technology advisor had decided that she couldn't justify a high-end learning/communication tool for Schuyler, and that Schuyler's parents perhaps didn't recognize her own expertise in this area.

Special needs parents are fools, every one of us. We tilt at windmills and charge into battle with the monster, rubber swords drawn.

Schuyler's monster has many faces. Sometimes it's a broken brain on an MRI film, and other times it's the smiling, condescending face of a bureaucrat selling our daughter short.

But the face of the monster that we are all the most reluctant to recognize is the one that looks remarkably like our own, irrationally railing against a system making what are perhaps reasonable decisions based not on love or hope or desperation, but logic and reality.

If we have the strength, we can see this face of the monster, and we'll recognize how pathetic it might look to some, the way we fight for something we may never win, not just for a device that might give a child a voice, but also for a future where that child might be okay, somehow and in some way. Not perfect, not even exceptional, but just okay. And happy.

I knew it then. I was probably unreasonable. I knew I was very likely wrong about what Schuyler was capable of. But the thing is, I might not have been wrong. In my heart, in my big stupid heart that broke for Schuyler every day, I didn't think I was wrong. And so once again I believed and I fought, because it was still the only way I knew how.

Things moved quickly after that. Julie and Margaret met with Tracy Custer, and according to Julie, Margaret was polite but not very engaged. I felt like this situation and her decision had become something of a point of pride to her. Only the week before, she'd made up her mind to get the DynaVox machine without ever having seen the products from Prentke-Romich Company. I thought it was only fair that she might at least pretend to be interested in learning about the PRC device before pretending to make a decision that we never even pretended was hers to pretend to make.

Julie reported that Margaret was sullen and argumentative, and there were some sparks between her and Tracy Custer, including one exchange that revealed to us that while Tracy Custer had worked with these devices for sixteen years and was also a speech pathologist, Margaret wasn't a speech pathologist at all, contrary to our assumption, but rather an occupational therapist. The whole meeting was apparently a huge contrast to the one we'd had with DynaVox, in which Margaret was in her comfort zone and dreamily asked the kinds of questions that would lead to happy answers.

The thing that irritated Julie the most was the feeling she was being handled. After the meeting with PRC, she was handed off to some technology representatives from the school district who became very stiff and defensive on behalf of the tech advisor. They informed her that the school district now wanted to do a speech evaluation of Schuyler to officially determine what kind of device to recommend for her.

Another test. This irritated Julie and me both; Schuyler was just about the most evaluated little girl in the world. We had a big blue binder full of evaluations. And we felt pretty certain that since the school had already stated that they wouldn't pay for the device with a vocabulary set equivalent to Schuyler's age group, this evaluation would likely be one more written documentation of *What Schuyler Can't Do*.

We didn't have even the slightest interest in hearing that again, and we saw absolutely no reason for another evaluation of the one thing about Schuyler—her non-speech—that we were all painfully and intimately familiar with. We certainly weren't going to wait for this Brand-New And Very Important Evaluation to move forward with acquiring a speech device.

The most interesting thing the district representatives told Julie was this:

1. They wanted us to do our evaluations of these devices through the school system, not on our own. We needed to use devices provided by the school district, not by the companies directly.

2. That said, the school district didn't actually have the devices to loan us. Maybe in a few weeks, for the DynaVox. They didn't have any PRC devices at all.

I wonder if they truly believed that was how it was going to happen.

Apparently not, because a week later, they found a PRC device for Schuyler to take home and evaluate. It wasn't the Vantage Plus, but a slightly older model. It still gave us a pretty good idea of what we could expect from the Vantage Plus, even without the better voice module and the more robust language center. This was sort of the driver's ed version.

The first day we got it, a funny thing happened. We'd waited for this device, we'd fought for it, and now we had our hands on one. I'd thought of little else in the weeks leading up to this, and now it was here. When I went to pick Schuyler up at school and her teacher handed the device to me, I sat down at the little table in her classroom and looked at it. Schuyler sat beside me, and I think we shared the same daunted look on our faces. The device looked up at us, challenging us to make good on all our tough talk.

We walked out to the car, where I put the device in the trunk. I drove Schuyler to Austin's Zilker Park. We flew kites and never took the speech device out of the trunk. Later, we went home and watched some *Sesame Street* for a while, showing off our number skills and laughing like the Count. We grew bored with that and switched

over to more exciting television, yelling at the screen as Indiana
Jones narrowly avoided getting squished by a giant rock.

"Oh, mo!" said Schuyler, gasping dramatically.

We sat and compared our feet (hers are surprisingly big and Fred
Flintstonesque, like mine) and watched more inappropriate television and laughed mockingly at each other, bonking each other in
the face with Julie's froofy little couch pillows.

Schuyler went to the bathroom by herself (a development that
had sort of snuck up on us during all the AAC device excitement),
and I followed her excited beckoning and stood in front of the toilet,
nodding approvingly at that which she had created. Like so many
other advances in her life, Schuyler had simply decided it was time
to be toilet trained, and that was that. Every time she went successfully, there was a celebration. You've never seen a tiny turd floating
in the toilet receive such applause. It must have felt like a little
brown Sir Laurence Olivier.

The loaner speech device sat on the table, untouched. After all
we'd done to get it, we were done with the monster, if only for an
evening.

It had been five weeks since we had set up the fund-raising page. It
was five weeks almost to the day that we shut it down.

We shut it down because our goal of ten thousand dollars had
been met.

Not by the school or the government or, with a few exceptions,
by any one person making huge contributions. It had been met by
ordinary people with lives like ours, people who had read about
Schuyler and who wanted to give her a chance to communicate and
live a real life, one with a voice. It was quite simply the most touching and astonishing example of human kindness I'd ever experienced. It remains so to this day.

Anytime I hear someone make fun of the now clichéd idea that it
takes a village to raise a child, I tell them about Schuyler's Fund. I tell

how in five weeks, hundreds of total strangers from all walks of life and from wildly different parts of the political and social spectrum came together to help a little girl whom most of them would never meet. I let the doubters see how other bloggers linked to my page to share it with people who didn't know my writing or the first thing about Schuyler, and how those people felt compelled to help.

You can believe God moved people to action, or you can believe people got tired of waiting for God and took care of it themselves. But believe something. Believe in the power of regular people to change the world. It may not seem like much, helping one little girl in the whole big world, but from where I stood, it seemed enormous.

It might just be the most amazing thing I've ever seen.

19

A Big Box of Words

On my days off from work, I'm usually not fit for polite society until about eleven A.M. It's not merely that I am a lazy man, although let me be absolutely clear: I am indeed a lazy man. I also stay up late, whether it's writing, goofing around on the Internet, or watching my favorite television shows—the ones Julie refuses to watch. Julie has not only made peace with going to bed without me. She's actually come to prefer it, because if I go to bed at the same time she does, I keep her up with my inane chatter until she finally mutters, "Why don't you go watch *Battlestar Galactica* or something?" from under the covers.

One morning in spring 2005, on a day I had taken off from work, I got up early and showered, shaved, and dressed before eight A.M. I then sat nervously in the apartment, waiting for the knock on the door. When it came, I actually looked in the mirror before opening the door.

It was the FedEx guy. And he had a box, covered with warning stickers about the delicate electronics inside. I signed for the box and hurriedly shut the door.

I didn't wake early and clean up for the FedEx guy, swell though he may very well have been. I can't really explain it, but I wanted to be ready for the box.

Schuyler's Big Box of Words.

The weeks leading up to that morning felt like a roller-coaster ride, with high peaks of promise with Schuyler and low moments of frustration with the school. Once we'd established that we had the funds to purchase the device of our choice, we made it clear to Margaret and the school that they could order the MiniMo if they wanted it for another student, but Schuyler was never going to use it. We were now committed to a high-end device, largely on the basis of what we'd seen from Schuyler and the PRC loaner.

From the beginning, we were concerned about how well Schuyler would cope with the subdirectories on the device. It was a hard concept, after all; I had problems with it at first, and I was theoretically an adult. Schuyler took to it almost immediately, however. She took a few hours to just explore it with us, seeing what all the buttons did and where it all took her, and she quite simply blew us away.

By the end of the first few days with the loaner device, she'd already figured out the basics.

"What color is Nemo?" Julie asked her, referring to the title character from the Pixar film. Schuyler searched for a moment on the screen, then hit a button with a rainbow on it. The screen changed and showed a palette of colors. She hit a button and then touched a long, horizontal area of the screen near the top where the words she'd selected were organized into sentences, and where the device would, when touched, speak whatever words had been entered.

"Orange." The voice on this older device wasn't as human as the one on the Vantage Plus, but it was still clear and only slightly creepy.

"Are you hungry?" I asked her the next day after school. She started to sign "yes" but then changed her mind, instead punching it up on the device. "What would you like?"

She thought for a moment, then hit the button for "eat." The screen changed to a menu showing different food choices. She hit the button for fruits, and when the screen changed, she made her choice and spoke.

"Eat banana."

"That's awesome," I said to her. "You're kicking butt with that thing already."

Schuyler didn't want praise, however. She wanted food. She touched the screen again. And again. And again.

"Eat banana. Eat banana. Eat banana. Eat banana."

I gave the kid a banana. When she made the connection between what she was saying on the device and the reaction she was getting, she squealed and clapped her hands. For a moment I felt a little guilty, as if we were using the device to train her to make food choices, but then it occurred to me that she was the one using the electronic device and I was the one fetching bananas. I was clearly the trained monkey in this scenario. She was thrilled to see how it worked.

Her enthusiasm was perhaps the most significant development, perhaps more important than whether or not she intuitively "got it." She did, but even better, she was fascinated by the device. She used it for everything at first, even simple things like "yes" and "no" and, well, "banana," words for which she had sufficient sign language in place. We knew that if a speech prosthesis was going to work for her, it was going to be because she took the initiative to make it happen, the same way she came to embrace sign language and, conversely, the way she completely rejected the picture identification system that every single one of her schools had tried to get her to use, going all the way back to New Haven.

My pity went out to the person who tried to make Schuyler do something she didn't want to do, or who tried to keep her from doing something she liked.

It wasn't long before I managed to get Schuyler in trouble with the Big Box of Words, as I was now calling it in my blog. In my efforts to keep Schuyler interested in the device, I tied it into one of her other dear interests, dinosaurs. I gave her a monster button, and unleashed her on an unsuspecting world.

The three of us were at dinner and were playing around with the PRC loaner, letting Schuyler attempt to tell us what she wanted for dinner. (She did pretty well, aside from her refusal to stop hitting the "ice cream" button.) When I'd called Tracy Custer to tell her we had the loaner in our possession and were starting to introduce it into Schuyler's routine, she emphasized that we should keep things fun for her at this stage, rather than trying to force her to embrace something so new.

I was playing with the greetings page, looking for a graphic that would adequately represent Swiper the Fox (from one of her television shows, *Dora the Explorer*) saying the phrase "Swiper, no swiping!" which on the show is chanted by the viewers to stop this twitchy, kleptomaniacal fox from stealing everyone's stuff. I wasn't having much luck with Swiper, but I did stumble across a mighty fine dinosaur button instead.

I needed to figure out how to record actual phrases, which the device would allow in special cases where you didn't want to go with the creepy little robot girl voice. I made a dinosaur button and recorded myself saying, in my scariest prehistoric monster voice, the word "Rire!" It wasn't terribly scary, but Schuyler lost her little mind with joy. Soon, she was using it to accentuate all the other little phrases she'd been figuring out at an astonishing rate over the past few days.

"I want eat ice cream. Rire!"

"I want drink milk. Rire!"

"I feel happy. Rire!"

All the way home, from the backseat of Julie's car, Schuyler would press different keys on the device, telling us the colors of her toys or the lights in the signs going by, and every statement closed with a monster roar, at the sound of which we'd feign terror. Every time the box said "Rire!" she would burst into laughter. We had a great deal of fun and she was completely fired up about the device. All positives, in my mind.

The next day, when I picked Schuyler up from school, Michelle praised her for her use of the device, even as she bemoaned once again her own unfamiliarity with it and her fear that she wasn't going to be adequately trained in its use. As we got ready to leave, she gave a little smile and said, "Yes, the entire class certainly enjoyed Schuyler's new dinosaur button." Michelle's tone made it clear that by "entire class," she was not actually including herself.

Schuyler had been using the device, particularly the monster button I had given her, to disrupt her class, in a way that had never been available to her before. Apparently the class would be quietly engaged in some regular school activity, and when the room became completely silent, Schuyler would hit the button.

"Rire!"

Every head popped up, every kid began growling, and suddenly Schuyler's pre-kindergarten special education Life Skills class turned into Jurassic Park. The teacher would calm everyone down and then, when peace was restored, Schuyler would do it again, with the same result. The teacher knew better than to take the device away from Schuyler, but she didn't know enough about how it worked to turn off the button.

Schuyler learned something important, a lesson her own father probably learned at roughly the same age. She discovered the chaotic power of being the class cutup.

I was immeasurably happy for her.

After another week or so with the PRC device, the school sent home another loaner, this time the high-end device from DynaVox. Schuyler was annoyed at the change but was also curious enough to dig into the new box to see what she could make it do. We kept it for a week, but after only a day or two, we felt pretty certain it wasn't the right choice for Schuyler.

It didn't seem to use dynamic linking nearly as well as the PRC device, for example. On the PRC, when you hit the "eat" button, the screen changed and the top row gave you menu choices (Italian, Mexican, lunch, dessert, and so on). Pick your item and it would then take you back to the main page, guiding you through your language choices in a way that would eventually foster and encourage patterns that corresponded with regular grammatical speech structure.

The DynaVox, while excellent for creating large pallets of speech samples for common phrases and questions, did not seem to lead you from one screen and part of speech to the next in the same manner. Hit "eat," and you'd then have to select a tab for "food" to take you to the choices screen, and you'd have to close that tab to get back to the main screen as well. It felt like a very big, very complicated picture identification system that actually spoke the words and concepts you had chosen, but without the benefit of a robust language engine. Also, as Schuyler's teacher noted as well, it was slow, enough so that Schuyler became bored waiting for the next window to open and moved on to something, anything, else.

It was clear to us that the PRC device was going to work best for Schuyler. Her extreme irritation at being forced to use the DynaVox made the final decision easy. In the end, Schuyler made the choice.

As soon as we told the school we were ordering the PRC Vantage Plus, we scheduled another IEP meeting for a week or two down the road, after Schuyler was to get her own device. Margaret was very quiet when we told her. I suspected that this IEP wasn't going to be one where she and I decided to be Very Best Friends Forever.

Tracy Custer invited us to attend a training session for the Vantage Plus, which was at that moment being assembled somewhere in Ohio and prepared to ship to us. I referred to the session as Speak N Spell Class because in my heart, I'm twelve, but it actually proved to be very informative. It didn't give us any additional insight into running the device itself, really; that part was pretty intuitive. (I had already managed to create tools for Schuyler to destroy her classroom learning environment, after all.) The class gave us a quick and dirty introduction to Unity 84, the language program that ran the Vantage Plus. More important, it allowed us to talk to other people who found themselves in the same situation as ourselves, which had really not happened before.

Most important of all, the PRC class also opened our eyes to the reality of Schuyler's school situation. Or perhaps it would be more accurate to say that it opened them wider, although by this time our eyes should have been as wide as Lulu's, our fly-faced pug. You see, every parent at the session had at least one representative from the school district's special education team, and in some cases several representatives.

Everyone, that is, except us.

It was a little embarrassing, particularly since we'd given Margaret and Michelle all the information as soon as we found out about the session. Margaret assured us that she'd be there. I felt like the kid whose parents don't show up for Parent/Teacher Night. It did give us the opportunity, however, to observe how the team members from these other school districts behaved. One district in particular, the Round Rock School District, seemed especially well represented and interested in the class.

After the class, we spoke with Tracy Custer as she was getting ready to leave, and mentioned the lack of representation from Manor.

"I noticed that," she said. "I was very careful to invite them, too. I'm frustrated because I know I'll get a call from them as soon as Schuyler's Vantage gets here, asking me to set up a training session for them. Most of what they need to know was covered today."

"Round Rock had their ducks in a row," Julie said. "They had four people here, all for one kid."

"They've got a good program, we work with them very closely and have for a long time." She lowered her voice slightly. "Tell me, do you guys own a house in the Manor School District?"

"No," I said. "We rent an apartment."

"Interesting," she said, then looked us both in the eye for a moment. "Well, that's something you might think about, then."

OPENING SCREEN: "MAY 17, 2005"

Schuyler standing beside table

ME: Hello!

SCHUYLER: *(waving)* Hi!

ME: Okay, can you come show me your words now?

Schuyler sits down in front of her Prentke-Romich Vantage Plus

ME: I'm going to ask you some questions now. What is your name?

SCHUYLER: *(touches screen a few times to get to the preprogrammed greetings page)* **My name is Schuyler.**

ME: And how old are you?

SCHUYLER: **I am five years old.**

ME: Now, who am I?

SCHUYLER: *(points at me and smiles)* Oo! ("You.") **Daddy.** *(points again)* Oo!

ME: Thank you! *(places a purple rubber duck on table)* What color is this?

SCHUYLER: *(navigates to colors page)* **Color pink.** *(hits backspace, corrects herself)* **Color purple.**

ME: All right, very good! *(Schuyler picks up duck and makes it hop away as I speak.)* Where do you live?

SCHUYLER: *(navigates back to greetings page)* **I live in Austin.**

ME: Are you hungry, Schuyler?

SCHUYLER: Yeah! *(navigates to main page)* **Eat.**

ME: What do you want to eat?

SCHUYLER: **Pizza.**

ME: Say the whole thing, please. Show me the whole thing.

SCHUYLER: **I want eat pizza.**

ME: Very good! *(Schuyler laughs and claps.)* Are you thirsty?

SCHUYLER: **Drink water.**

ME: You want water? Can you say the whole thing?

SCHUYLER: **I want drink water.**

ME: Okay, good, we'll do that in just a minute. Do you have a doggy?

SCHUYLER: *(nodding head)* Yeah. *(navigates back to preprogrammed greetings page)* **I have a dog named Lulu.**

ME: Schuyler, can you tell me what this is? What does it do?

SCHUYLER: **I use this language communication device to help me speak.**

ME: Schuyler? What does a monster say?

SCHUYLER: *(giggles and navigates to main page, hits button twice by mistake)* **Rire! Rire!** *(claps happily)*

ME: Okay, Schuyler, we're all done, can you say goodbye?

SCHUYLER: **Goodbye.** *(waves to camera)* Aye, ah-ee! Aye, ah-ee! ("Bye, Daddy")

The lights came up and the members of Schuyler's IEP team began murmuring among themselves. Margaret sat quietly, her face unreadable. Tammy looked over at me and smiled.

"So that's what she's doing at home," I said, closing my laptop, on which I'd been showing the brief movie they'd just watched. "I shot this two nights ago. She had the loaner device for two weeks, and she had just been using her own Vantage for two days. You can see that even now, she's able to answer questions using preprogrammed answers, and she's able to find and identify colors. She's using multiple levels to find food menu selections, and she's putting her choices into very simple sentences. And she's enthusiastic about it, she uses it now to answer questions that she's perfectly capable of signing. She's just barely getting started on this."

Tammy nodded. "Mr. Hudson, this is great, I'm so glad you brought this in. I've been reading Margaret's report, and I have to admit, I was concerned."

"We just read that this morning," Julie said. "I don't understand what's different at home from what happens when she's here."

I knew exactly what she was talking about.

Static one-hit voice output devices can be utilized successfully if supported in the specific setting. Preprogramming and setup would be necessary to ensure that Schuyler could have powerful and successful communication when she activates the button. The high tech dynamic devices have not been more successful, nor provided clearer communication than her other communication modes. Due to her need to have more opportunity [sic] learning the system, learning the language, and recognizing the power of a voice output, all modes should be used for communication.

Inconsistent willingness to use the devices has also hindered progress. However, Schuyler has great potential to use a dynamic voice output system in the future. Thus, even though the dynamic voice output is not educationally necessary at this point, she would greatly benefit from early intervention and training on the dynamic voice output systems for her future communication.

"I didn't know what Margaret's report said before I videotaped Schuyler on her device," I said, "but I'm glad I did it now. I'm concerned about this 'inconsistent willingness' to use the device. If there's a difference between what's happening at home and what's happening here, I'd like to bridge that so she's experiencing roughly the same thing in both places. She's thrilled to use it at home. I'd like her to feel that same excitement when she's here."

The meeting went our way, I'm happy to say. The movie had spoken for itself, and while Margaret was still a bit of a pill for the rest of the meeting, she didn't have any serious objections to embracing the device as part of Schuyler's curriculum. Indeed, she'd already said as much, if grudgingly, at the conclusion of her report.

"There's one last issue to work out," said Tammy. "I know you want Schuyler to attend summer school classes this summer, and that was up in the air. The issue is this: Will a child regress beyond what we consider to be typical during the summer, to such an extent that she will fall significantly behind her peers in the fall? The irony for Schuyler is that she has done so well on her device and in her general schoolwork that it would be hard to justify her inclusion in summer school.

"However," she continued, "Michelle has suggested that since Schuyler is so new to her device, we should make a request to the board that she be included in the summer program in order to continue her training. I'll let you know in the next day or two whether that's going to happen."

And just like that, the most productive IEP we'd ever had was over. We shook everyone's hand and accepted congratulations. Before people could leave, I stood up.

"The only other thing I want to mention is that when this report says that Schuyler's device is not 'educationally necessary,' I hope you all understand that we believe otherwise. It is our position that this is the most promising development yet for her, and we'd like for everyone to be on the same page."

It was a snotty way to end things, and perhaps had a touch of "How do you like her NOW?" but we had fought so hard to get Schuyler that device, and if I hadn't had a big fancy Web site with generous readers, we would have lost that fight. When we stepped back and looked at the whole story of the Big Box of Words, from the earliest discussions to the moment Schuyler's little fingers touched the screen, one thing was consistently true and was now being proven by her own success.

They were wrong about her, and we were right.

To celebrate the success of the meeting, we took Schuyler out and let her pick out some toys. After wandering the toy store for the better part of the evening, Schuyler chose some very fancy (and extremely noisy) dinosaurs, picking different ones for herself and for me. I assure you, there is no love in the world as sweet and tender as that of a little girl for her dinosaurs. We played with them nonstop for days. Schuyler chose the brontosaurus while I opted for the tyrannosaur. It seemed to make for a good balance.

We battled each other for a while but then united our roaring dinosaurs, with their snapping jaws and stomping feet, to defeat the forces of My Little Ponies and rubber bath ducks. Ponies and ducks, as any educated person knows, were historically the natural foes of the dinosaurs, after all. Our dinosaurs eventually moved into Dora the Explorer's house, where they showed excellent table manners when they weren't devouring the previous occupants.

It didn't take long for Schuyler to integrate her device into her play. We sat at the table together, me on my laptop and Schuyler with her T-Rex and her brontosaurus talking to each other, the PRC device between them. She jabbered quietly in her mysterious language, and then I watched the brontosaurus lean in toward the T-Rex as Schuyler hit a few buttons on the device.

"I love you."

It was a moving scene, although honestly, I didn't think it was going to work out between the carnivore and the herbivore, not in the long run. It was just a summer thing.

A few days later, we received the call from Tammy. Schuyler had been approved for summer school. At the time, we thought it was good news.

In the long run, I suppose it was, in a way which we could never in a thousand years have anticipated.

20

Speechless

As Schuyler's school year drew to a close, we gradually worked the device into her daily routine. It used a great deal of power through the day, enough so it needed to be charged every night. When we plugged it in after Schuyler went to bed, we would often find it set not to the main page, but rather to the spelling page, not an easy one to get to. This page simply had the alphabet laid out, allowing you to manually spell whatever you wanted and then allow the device to speak your word to the best of its ability.

We'd noticed that Schuyler frequently spent time on this page. It fascinated her, this ability to take letters that she'd been taught but which never made much sense and suddenly be able to do something with them, to put them together in ways that produced words. She spent a lot of time just futzing around on the spelling screen, usually creating words along the lines of "ahjfcgvnmsj." Lately, however, I kept finding something else waiting in the spelling field, left over from the day's experimentation.

"scuylher"

"scuhler"

"schuyler"

A few days later, we were sitting in the café at my store, waiting for Julie to arrive. I was reading a magazine and Schuyler was munching on a chocolate chip cookie and playing around with the box. She was spelling very slowly, so it wasn't until she was almost done that it occurred to me what she was doing.

"s . . . c . . . u . . ." (an irritated "grrr" and the sound of a deletion) "h . . . u . . . y . . . l . . ."

I looked up suddenly, watching her look of concentration as she finished.

"e . . . r . . . schuyler. Schuyler. Schuyler."

She repeated it a few times and then looked at me with a chocolate-coated smile.

"Holy crap, Schuyler," I said. "Who taught you that?" She shrugged and went back to her cookie, the device pushed away for the time being.

She'd been shown her name all her life, and we knew she could recognize it. But no one had been trying to teach her to spell it, not that I was aware of. As time went on, we watched her spell other words on her device, words that she hadn't been taught but which she picked up from whatever reading material was sitting in front of her. The device was teaching her to spell, it was giving her the instant gratification of hearing her successes and failures.

There are many quiet moments that I'll remember until the very end of my life, long after I've forgotten most everything else. I do believe that the day I watched Schuyler spell and then speak her name for the first time will be one of those forever moments. God, I certainly hope so.

About a week into Schuyler's summer school session, the school held an open house for parents. We were looking forward to it with a kind of nervous anticipation. The summer program had put Schuyler in a mainstream kindergarten class for most of the day, and none of the teachers had ever worked with her before. After a year under Michelle's care, we were nervous to see how she did with new teachers. We were also curious as to how her device use was going. That is, if you understand "curious" to mean "consumed."

We went into the open house with anticipation and hope. We left with . . .

Well, they gave us free doughnuts, I will give them that much.

It wasn't long after we sat down with our fancy free doughnuts and our coffee and orange juice that Schuyler's special ed teacher for the summer found us. I'm not sure if Evelyn was usually a special education specialist, although with the small staff of summer teachers and the few special ed students present, I doubted it. She was friendly enough, however, and she seemed to have genuine affection for Schuyler.

"Hi, it's so great to meet you," Evelyn said. "Everyone just loves Schuyler, she's such a joy to work with."

"Thank you," said Julie. "Yeah, we think she's pretty awesome."

"She's doing just wonderfully in class, she gets along great with everyone. She just opens up to everyone she meets, it's so much fun to work with her."

"Yeah," I said, "I don't think she ever had much use for a shy phase."

"Well, she's doing very well with her device, she even uses it in some of her class time. She used it this morning when one of the new teachers came in, she had it say 'Hello, my name is Schuyler,' and—"

"Wait," Julie said suddenly, reacting to something that I honestly missed when I heard it. "You said she's using it in *some* of her classes?"

"Yes, well, she doesn't take it to the gym because we don't want it to get damaged while the kids are playing, and Mrs. Barber doesn't want her to use it in the kindergarten class, but everywhere else . . ."

"I don't understand," Julie said, her voice starting to acquire an edge. I sat forward in my undersized kiddie chair.

Evelyn suddenly seemed nervous, as if the reality of what she was telling us had just sunk in. "Well, Mrs. Barber says that the box is a distraction in her class and so we leave it in the Life Skills room. She says that the box distracts the other kids and they all want to come look at it and watch Schuyler use it. Also, she says it's too loud."

"It's too loud?" Julie said. "You can adjust the volume. We can show you how to do that."

"Well, Mrs. Malison came by, and we talked about it with her as well. It was her idea to leave it in the Life Skills classroom."

Mrs. Malison. That was a familiar name to us. She was the speech therapist, the one who didn't want to include sign language in Schuyler's curriculum because she didn't want to have to learn it herself. Along with Margaret, she was the other strong advocate for getting the low-end device for Schuyler. I wasn't encouraged to find that she was part of this new issue.

"Okay, I've got to say, we're not at all comfortable with her not being able to have her device in the classroom with her," I said. "Are the other kids in the class allowed to speak?"

"Well, of course," Evelyn said. "Most of them speak Spanish, so it's a bilingual classroom."

"So that means they've got the option to speak out of turn in the classroom? They can disrupt the class like any little kid?"

"Well, yes, of course . . ."

"Does Mrs. Barber put tape over their mouths if they speak out of turn?" I could feel the anger start to creep into my voice.

"Of course not, that's—"

"That device is Schuyler's voice," interrupted Julie. "It's going to be for the rest of her life. Everyone needs to get used to that idea. If the other kids are being distracted by it, they just need to get used to it, too. She's going to use that in every class she's ever going to take."

"If Schuyler uses it inappropriately, then she's got to be taught when she can and can't speak up with it," I said. "She's still figuring this out, just like the rest of it. But she needs to be treated like any other five-year-old kid. If she speaks out of turn with her device, then sure, address that. But we don't want to hear that she's not being allowed to use it in the classroom. That's the whole reason she's in summer school in the first place. Mrs. Malison should know better."

Evelyn had a look in her eyes that suggested that she was out of her element. "Um, I'm going to go get Mrs. Barber so we can discuss this with her."

"Yeah, that's probably a good idea," said Julie. She was calm, but I could see her hand shaking slightly. She was royally and powerfully pissed off.

"Hi, we're the Rummel-Hudsons. Nice to meet you. Don't mess with our cyborg daughter."

The meeting with Mrs. Barber didn't go badly, not on the surface. She seemed to understand what we needed to have happen with Schuyler on her box and said simply that if the volume could be turned down on the device, she'd be fine. She certainly didn't seem happy about it, but then, I'm not sure we left the door open for much dissent. By now, Julie and I were a practiced, precision team when it came to laying down the law on expectations from Schuyler's teachers. We were like the Blue Angels of pushy parents.

We thought things had been settled, until the next day when I was driving Schuyler home and asked her what she wanted for dinner. She pulled out her device and started hitting buttons, and then sighed unhappily and crossed her arms.

"What's wrong?" I asked. "Just tell me what you want, we can have anything you like." I glanced in the mirror and watched her hit buttons again and then sigh in irritation and rudely push the device off her lap, onto the seat beside her. I pulled the car into the next parking lot and reached back for the device. I punched a few buttons, and the words appeared in the dialogue field, but when I touched the field, nothing happened. I had to go into the tools function, via a button at the top of the device of which Schuyler was unaware and which was hidden down a few menus, in order to see what was wrong.

Someone had gone into the tools function and turned off the speech function. My daughter had a mute button, and someone had found it.

"Did someone turn this off?" I asked her. She shrugged. "Is it like this every day?" She hesitated and then nodded. I realized they must have been doing this every day, but this time they'd forgotten to turn it back on at the end of class.

I switched it on and handed it back to Schuyler, but she was unhappy and refused to use it anymore. We drove on in silence.

When I called the director of the summer program, she insisted that no one at the school would have done such a thing. She said that it must have happened by accident while the teacher was cleaning the keypad. Which was great, of course, except that the toolbox button isn't accessible from the keypad.

Two days later, in the notes she sent home every day, the hapless special ed teacher mentioned once again having to have someone show her how to turn the speech function back on. Someone must have shown the rest of the staff how to turn the speech on and off, and it sounded even more likely that someone was turning it off during Mrs. Barber's class.

We sent a note to school the next day.

In addition to the instance you mentioned in your note about her speech module being turned off, it had also been turned off when she got home about a week ago. Turning off the speech module on her device is no different from denying her the use of the device at all. Not only is it against our expressed wishes, but I believe that you will find that it is also against the law, specifically Title II of the Americans with Disabilities Act, Section 504 of the Rehabilitation Act of 1973 (which covers any entity that receives federal financial assistance), and finally the IDEA, which is the law that governs her IEP. Whoever is turning it off needs to stop immediately. If you haven't already, please review Schuyler's IEP for a detailed explanation of her goals and expectations.

(Here's a tip for parents of special needs children that you might not get from actual nice people. Learn the Americans with Disabilities Act and the Individuals with Disabilities Education Improvement Act of 2004, or IDEA. Learn it well enough that you can threaten the evildoers and supervillains of your child's life, because businesses and schools are terrified of ADA lawsuits. I guess there must have been a lot of them; the ADA and IDEA have apparently spawned something of a little lawsuit cottage industry. I hate frivolous litigation as much as the next person, but broken kids don't get many fair shakes. This might be one of the few you can enjoy, at least until they are old enough to drive you to the mall and use the disabled parking places. By that time, you'll be old and decrepit enough to qualify for those parking spots on your own.)

Either the letter rectified the situation, or Mrs. Barber made sure to turn the speech module back on at the end of class from then on. By then, there was only another week and a half of class. It wasn't until then that I realized that really, we'd lost.

We checked her bag the evening after we sent the note home, but there was no response. Schuyler went to bed, Julie and I both got a beer from the kitchen and just sat in the silence of our apartment. It was the kind of silence that comes when people are done talking about a thing. The thing is still there, of course. It stands in the room, perhaps in the corner, over in that dark area that the lamplight doesn't quite reach. It's the monster, and stands in the shadow but nevertheless dominates the room. It breathes all the good air and replaces it with something flat and stale. Its very presence in the room deadens the sound of conversation, like heavy snow in New England where the silence is almost oppressive. You talk about anything but the monster, but in the end you stop talking altogether, because it's the only thing in the world to talk about, and after a while you just can't anymore.

We'd lost. We could write letters to the administrators of the school district, we could get the keystrokes from the device's data log and get teachers in trouble, we could be a pain in the ass about the whole thing, but in the end, they got away with treating Schuyler like a broken, disposable child, and there was no way to get that back.

The worst part was that Schuyler noticed. For the first time in her life, I believe she felt like a freak. Ever since we discovered it had been turned off, she had been subdued and oddly self-conscious about using the Vantage. She was made to see for the very first time that she was the only one using a device, and she learned that a little girl with a talking box isn't like the other kids.

What did you learn in summer school, Schuyler?

"I learned that I'm weird."

She would come home on the bus and watch Oswald, the big blue octopus on television who's also weird but who never judges anyone (and has a cool dog named Weenie), and she played with Lulu and her new dinosaurs and her father, who liked the dinosaurs as much as she did. She lived as much of a life as we could make for her where she wasn't so weird after all.

We could teach her a lot, but sometimes the best we could do was simply construct a place for her where she wasn't "Schuyler the Cyborg Girl Who Gets Treated Like a Martian," but was instead just a little girl.

That night, she was in bed and we were left with the silence. There was a lot not being said, about our fears for Schuyler's school and the fact that it might not be enough to move down the road to Round Rock, where we'd seen enthusiasm but would still be dealing with the same unfamiliarity with Schuyler's problems and specific concerns. We weren't ready to say that Austin might have been an idea born from our post-diagnosis panic. Most of all, we hadn't continued the conversation about Chicago because we weren't quite ready to start talking about that again. Not that night.

And the monster just watched us in our sad silence. He could wait, after all. He wasn't going anywhere.

21

Box Class

O kay, so I've got something I've wanted to tell you for a while, ever since you first told me how much trouble you were having with Schuyler's school," my friend Tracy, now living the fancy North Dallas life, wrote in an e-mail. We were discussing Schuyler's disastrous summer school experience and a phone call I'd placed to the Round Rock school district's special education department, in which I found out that while yes, they were actively learning as much as they could about AAC technology, they didn't actually have a program in place for its integration into their curriculum. It had been a rough week; we'd had high hopes for Round Rock.

"I don't want to come across as self-serving or trying to influence you guys just because I'd like to have you and Julie and Schuyler living nearby," Tracy continued. "But I thought you should know that the Plano Independent School District has an actual Assistive Technology Team, and it looks like they support speech devices like Schuyler's."

I followed the link she sent, and there it was. It was a simple Web page, with a short description of what Assistive Technology was all about, and it listed the team members and their credentials. There were six of them, devoted to nothing but high-tech solutions for their students with communications disorders like Schuyler's. Two were speech/language pathologists with specialization in Alternative and Augmentative Communication, two were audiologists, one was a special educator with a specialization in special education software and access, and one was an occupational therapist.

I read through the materials carefully, including a page dealing with nothing but AAC devices. I tried to keep my feelings in check, because there was a flood of them, all at once.

Here was a school district that understood and supported AAC learning. They put real money and resources into it, not lip service and not good intentions. They got it.

And they were in Plano, Texas.

I can remember back in my high school days when our football team made it into play-offs and the fans from Plano came out to Odessa to watch the game. The local newspaper made a huge, grand production out of how the Odessa Permian High School football boosters sent charter buses to the airport to pick up the Plano fans, almost all of whom flew (rather than making the six-hour drive) and many of whom came in their private planes. The Odessans took the Plano fans to a big barbecue dinner and then out to the stadium. After Permian beat the crap out of Plano High, the boosters put the Plano fans back on the buses and drove them back to the airport with a cheerful "Bye, y'all!"

The stories were meant to show how gracious the Permian fans were and what great country mouse hosts they were to the big city mouse fans from Plano, and I agree, it was a swell thing to do. (One can't help but wonder, however, given the legendary rabidity with which Odessans worshiped their football in the 1980s, if the Plano fans would have gotten a ride back to the airport if they'd actually won the game.) I always felt, however, that the amount of local news coverage granted to this act of homestyle generosity made us look like rubes and yokels. It was clear to me that, even after winning the game, we all went back to being Odessans, and they went back to being rich.

Plano, Texas, is our setting. Located twenty miles north of Dallas, Plano is a suburb, but a big one. Almost a quarter of a million people lived there in 2005, with a median household income of over $78,000. Collin County, where Plano is located, is the wealthiest county in the state of Texas. As of 2005, Plano served as the U.S. corporate headquarters for a number of huge companies, including JCPenney, Cadbury Schweppes (not just of the clucking bunny in the television commercial, but also formerly Dr Pepper), Frito-Lay, Cinemark Theatres, and Ericsson. The town fathers would probably like you to know that in 2001, the *Ladies' Home Journal* selected Plano as one of America's Best Cities for Women, and in 2004, *CNN Money* rated Plano as its top city of over 100,000 citizens in which to live in the western United States. Plano, it would seem, was swell.

When I thought of the possibility of living in Plano, however, my thoughts went in a different direction. In 1983, shortly before I entered high school in Odessa, Plano achieved notoriety after nine students committed suicide; a major contributing factor was found to be a persistent heroin problem in the schools. The problem received national attention again in the late 1990s, when Plano once again became known for a string of heroin-related deaths among its affluent teen student population, with someone overdosing at the rate of one per month in 1997. The youngest was a seventh grader.

Politically, it's probably not a surprise to discover that Plano was an overwhelmingly conservative town, with 71 percent of Collin County voting for George Bush in 2004. A 2005 study by the Bay Area Center for Voting Research rated Plano as the fifth most conservative city in America. (Austin, in contrast, was only the ninety-third most liberal.) This didn't make Plano a bad town. It just seemed to make it, you know, not exactly *my* town.

And, it is also worth mentioning, the city took its name from the Spanish word for "flat."

The thing I kept coming back to, however, was the city's reputation for good schools, heroin problems notwithstanding. I was surprised to see a school district with an Assistive Technology team, but not that such a thing would exist, if anywhere, in Plano.

Julie had a lot of questions about Plano, almost none of which I could answer. We talked about it at length and decided to write to the head of the AT team, Sherry Haeusler. She answered my e-mail quickly and was extremely enthusiastic about the AAC program in Plano. We exchanged a number of e-mails, and she found my blog fairly quickly and became familiar with Schuyler in a hurry. She invited us to bring Schuyler to visit and see for ourselves.

"What do you think?" I asked Julie about a week later as we contemplated a visit to Plano. "You ready to move again?"

"I don't know," she said. "I feel like we're chasing something we're never going to catch."

I spoke to Mairead at work and told her what we were thinking about. She was sad to hear we were considering moving, but she placed a phone call to the Barnes & Noble district manager in the Dallas area and discovered there was a store in the area that was looking for a music manager. Julie and I made an appointment to meet Sherry and the AT team, and I set up an interview at the store for the same day. We found an apartment complex in Plano owned by the same company as our current apartment, so we could simply transfer our lease if we decided to move.

Despite all our meetings and the apparent ease with which housing and employment were falling into place, moving was still very much an "if." I loved Austin, we both did. I had friends there, people I genuinely cared about, and I loved my job. I ran the music department in the largest store in Austin, and I had a staff of young hipsters who made me look both smart and cool. Austin was funky and original in ways that reminded us of both Kalamazoo and New Haven.

We didn't want to leave, certainly not for a giant Dallas suburb full of soccer moms and fast food restaurants.

Yet, Schuyler's teachers had taken away her speech device, one they had never entirely gotten behind as an educational tool in the first place. It was hard to imagine Plano's Assistive Technology team doing that.

Our first two meetings, with my potential employer and with the apartment complex, went smoothly. Perhaps a little too smoothly, in fact; after meeting with the store manager for about an hour, he offered me the job, flat out. I got the sense he was having a hard time filling the position, and as it turned out, I was right. The store, which was the oldest Barnes & Noble location in Texas, was slated to close in slightly over a year. But he seemed like a nice enough person, and the company was good about taking care of its own, so I wasn't worried about being out of a job when the store closed. He said that with Julie's history with the company, she would have no problem transferring to another store, either.

The apartment complex was much nicer than we expected. As we pulled into the parking lot, we saw a huge, beautiful duck pond on the grounds. Schuyler was immediately charmed.

When we'd told Sherry where the apartment was located, she'd set up a meeting with the principal and the special education head at the nearest school, in addition to herself and Linda Conerly, another member of the AT team. When we arrived for the meeting, we said hello to everyone and were led to a conference room. As we sat and talked to the principal and the teachers, Schuyler sat at the far end of the long table with Sherry and Linda, playing with some toys they provided and looking at picture books. They watched her intently as she played and asked her a lot of questions. She answered using her device, the volume turned down low so as not to disturb the rest of us.

The principal was impossibly young and pretty, considering the school principals I'd grown up with. She knew everything about her program, down to the smallest details, and had a pretty good idea of Schuyler's capabilities before the meeting even started. She spoke at length about the amount of funding and support that special education received in Plano. The school had recently built a new sensory room for its special needs kids, in which physical therapy using different tactile devices and surfaces could be administered. It was a technique that was particularly useful in reaching autistic children. I'd read about it before and knew how expensive the equipment was. The idea that they decided to buy it all at once was impressive.

As she spoke, and as the special education coordinator chimed in, I kept glancing down at Sherry and Linda. They weren't paying any attention at all, instead focusing on Schuyler. I realized they were taking notes.

"So," said the principal, "I feel like I've just been talking your ears off. Want to go take a quick tour of the school?"

We all stood to leave, but as Schuyler joined Julie for the tour and we all began to file out with the principal, Sherry touched my shoulder.

"If you don't mind," she told the principal, "Linda and I would like to talk to Dad for just a few minutes. We'll catch up with you, if that's okay?"

Julie looked at me with *"WTF?"* eyes, but I simply shrugged. "We'll be right behind you," I said. After they'd all left and it was just the three of us, Sherry closed the door and sighed.

"Okay, we really hate to spring this on you like this," Sherry said. "But we couldn't mention this before because we needed to evaluate Schuyler to determine if she would be a good candidate, and we didn't want to get your hopes up just to have them get crushed if she didn't work out."

"Candidate?" I asked. "I'm not sure I understand."

"There's a class we think Schuyler would be perfect for, especially now that we've seen her and how well she uses her AAC device."

"She hasn't had it very long," I said, "and she's gotten almost no help at her school."

"Well," Linda said, "she's already doing very well, from what we could see. She's very intuitive with it."

"The class we're talking about is a charter program we'll be starting in the fall. It's something we've wanted to do for a few years, and we've been developing the curriculum and the structure of the program for a while. We're really excited about it. There aren't very many programs to model it after, so there's been a lot of innovative thinking going into this. There are only three other classes like this in the country, as far as we can tell. There's one in Baltimore, one in Seattle, and one in San Francisco, I think."

"What's the class?"

"It's exclusively for users of AAC devices. We're structuring it for half a dozen students, all of them using devices similar to Schuyler's. In fact, the school will be providing all the devices, I believe, and they're all Prentke-Romich models, so there'll be consistency across the board.

"The idea of the class is to spend the next two or three years giving the students instruction in this special class on how to communicate with their AAC devices for part of the day, and sending them for part of the day to a mainstream class. Their AAC class will give them practical instruction in the use and the language of their devices, and then their regular class time will acclimate them to the concepts of communicating with neurotypical kids in a normal classroom environment."

I was stunned. "So wait a minute. You're talking about a classroom with nothing but kids just like Schuyler, all using AAC devices with each other."

Sherry smiled. "Yes, all of them learning to talk to each other, in an environment where it will seem like the most natural thing in the world to do. The idea isn't to isolate them from the rest of the student population, but to integrate them as completely as we can, so they'll be able to graduate from high school successfully and in the same time frame as their peers."

"High school," I repeated. "That's the first time a teacher has even realistically floated graduation as a possibility."

"A possibility?" said Linda. "We consider it the logical conclusion to the program, not just a possibility. There are AAC users out there in graduate programs in college. There's nothing that should stop Schuyler from doing whatever she wants to do, as soon as she's given the tools to do it."

I moved slowly to the table and sat in silence for a few moments. I was trying to imagine this class, with a herd of little Schuylers all talking to each other in their little robot voices, without so much as a whiff of weirdness. I had never even seen another kid use an AAC device before. Obviously I understood there were more of them out there, but I'd come to accept that Schuyler would always be the odd little girl with the talking box.

"Wow," I said. "The idea of something like this never occurred to us, not in our wildest dreams. We just came up here because the schools were good and you had an AT team. This class, I never thought . . ." I trailed off, my words catching in my throat.

Sherry smiled and leaned forward. "We'd hoped you'd appreciate the possibilities. We have one more open spot in the class, and we'd like to invite Schuyler to join us."

I sat back and sighed deeply. "You know," I said at last. "Julie's going to cry when we tell her about this."

We caught up with the rest of the group and continued the tour, but I wasn't paying much attention. I couldn't stop imagining this class full of kids, all using their little speech boxes as if it was the most natural thing in the world, like little cyborgs. Schuyler could get her shot at attending regular classes one day. She could be on track to becoming a regular kid. Pinocchio, with a happy ending.

I whispered to Julie at the first opportunity that as soon as we were done, we needed to talk outside. We concluded the tour and said goodbye to the principal and the special ed teacher. Linda and Sherry had slipped away earlier, and were waiting outside in the parking lot.

"What's going on?" Julie said. "What's all the secrecy?"

"Sherry and Linda wanted to wait until we were out of there to talk about this, since it takes place at another campus. They've got something to show us."

As we got in our car and followed them to the other school, I told Julie about the charter AAC class and the invitation to Schuyler to join.

I was right. She cried. I might have, too. Maybe just a little.

The classroom was like any other kindergarten class at first glance. It wasn't until we looked closely at the materials on the walls that we recognized the buttons from the Big Box of Words, blown up and laminated. I felt as if we had entered some bizarre Opposite World, where kids spoke on little computerized devices and learned to read and spell and perform math by way of key sequences.

It occurred to me that the one thing I'd never felt with Schuyler was that I could trust someone enough to hand her over to them to educate without having to guide and instruct and even bully them into doing it appropriately for her. Such a thing might actually be possible here. We'd always felt the conflict with her teachers, the idea that we were the idiot parents and they knew what was going to work best for Schuyler.

I have always been an advocate for public schools. I'm a product of one myself, after all, and I have always believed that a civilization that can't educate its own citizens regardless of their station is about a week away from being overrun by Visigoths. I am familiar enough with the reality of public schools, however, to be cautious. I also remember, from my own days of teaching, the disdain that many public school teachers feel toward parents who get deeply involved in their kids' education.

Those teachers were clear in their belief that they know what's best for their students. They're the ones who went to college, after all. They took classes. They filed lesson plans. They went to the Teacher Supply Store and purchased the life-sized cardboard Abraham Lincoln wall decorations with the hinged elbows and knees, for God's sake. The last thing they needed were know-it-all parents telling them what their kids were capable of.

The thing is, they're probably right much of the time. (*"I don't want no school teachin' little Bocephus that he evolved from some damned monkey!"*) I wanted to trust teachers. Any special needs parent or advocate knows, however, that even when the teacher has the very best interests of a special needs child in mind, and I believe Schuyler's teachers in Manor did, it is nevertheless true that the parent has experienced this disability with their child. Parents know what their kids need, even if they have no idea how to give it to them.

As we sat in the AAC class on tiny chairs and listened to the AT team describe this program, I felt something like relief, as if a heavy piece of luggage had suddenly been lifted from my shoulder. These teachers understood. Schuyler wasn't an alien to them. They'd known her for an hour and already grasped her disabilities, and more important her abilities, more clearly than any teacher ever had done before.

Julie and I hadn't had a chance to discuss this development privately, aside from a few minutes in the car on the way to the school as I told her about the bombshell from Sherry and Linda. I could feel how neither of us wanted to leave this place, as if stepping out of the classroom might make it all pop like a soap bubble, and yet we were dying to talk about it. When we finally said our goodbyes and promised to call them with an answer soon, we walked out to the car in silence.

Julie strapped Schuyler into the backseat and then sat down behind the wheel. She stared ahead for a few moments and then turned to look at me.

"Yes," she said simply.

"Yes," I replied.

Our last night in Austin was spent in an empty apartment. Everything was packed in a rented truck except for two mattresses and one big suitcase. We'd been in bed for a few hours when I woke to hear the door to Schuyler's room open. A few seconds later she was in our room, standing over our mattress. She did this sometimes, waking up and deciding to come sleep with us, perhaps after a bad dream. It was hard to know why, exactly. Her skills on her device were still inadequate for describing something as ethereal as a nightmare.

"Do you need to go to the potty?" I asked her.

"Mo," she replied grumpily.

"Are you sure, Schuyler? Do you want to go potty?"

"Mo."

"Schuyler, let's try to go potty first."

"Mo!"

Three o'clock in the morning wasn't exactly the moment I wanted to have this argument, so I gave in and let her climb into bed with us. Sure enough, about twenty minutes later, Julie awoke to find that Schuyler had wet the bed.

While Julie pulled sheets off the bed and cleaned things up as best as she could, I stripped Schuyler and made her go to the toilet. I knew that at that point, it was a purely procedural move; it was pretty clear from looking at the bed that Schuyler was empty. The routine of potty training was still only a few months old and needed reinforcement, however, and so Schuyler sat on the toilet, miserable and naked, not doing the thing she'd just done in our bed.

Finally I told her she could get off the potty, and I dressed her in fresh pajamas while Julie improvised a new bed situation. There was dry room enough on our mattress for one of us to sleep, so I took a sad and embarrassed Schuyler's little hand and led her back to her room and her bed, through the unfamiliarity of a dark and empty apartment. The room echoed strangely from the lack of sound-absorbing furniture.

We climbed into her bed, and she whimpered and cried miserably until I leaned over to the window and opened the blinds slightly. Instantly, the ever-present light of an urban apartment complex streamed in, and despite her sadness, Schuyler leaned over to look out.

"Wow," she whispered softly, as if she'd never seen such a thing.

We lay there, whispering about the lights and the trees and the birds she insisted were sleeping in them, and things weren't so bad. In fact, lying there with her talking about trees and the nighttime world outside her window, I think it was the finest evening I'd had in a long, long time. We fell asleep like that, our foreheads touching and her little hand in mine. About an hour later, she awoke long enough to ask me to shut the blinds, and then went back to sleep.

The following morning, we left. I took my heartbreak at leaving everything I loved in Austin and buried it as deeply as I could.

22

Howl

So, how are you liking Plano?"

A year after we moved, it was still a question I heard often. I was visiting Austin frequently, having turned my longtime photography hobby into a part-time freelance wedding gig, and while I was in town, I'd occasionally stop by the old store or hook up with my former staff. Everyone knew that I was pretty liberal, even by smelly hippy Austin standards, and the idea of me trying to survive in the reddest town in the reddest state in America was just as amusing to them a year after we'd left as it had been to me before we moved, armed as I was with my pocketful of preconceived notions.

My answer surprised them. My answer surprised me.

"You know what? It's not bad at all."

My initial impressions of Plano hadn't been completely favorable. Moreover, they'd actually proven to either be true or containing a good solid nugget of truth. The town was indeed largely wealthy, and most of the cookie cutter McMansions were largely hidden behind imposing "go away" fences. A great many cars driving around town sported bumper stickers for George W. Bush. Plano was indeed home to a large number of churches, and more than its fair share of what I heard referred to as "megachurches," including the 25,000 member (note to editors: that's not a typo) Prestonwood Baptist Church, known locally as the "Goditorium," which dwarfed anything I'd ever seen erected on the Lord's behalf in my life. Even before I'd broken up with God over Schuyler's condition, I hadn't had much use for Christianity, but I was still impressed at the high esteem with which Mr. Jesus Howard Christ was held in the Plano community. If he does indeed rise again one day, the King of Kings isn't going to get stuck in a smelly old manger if he blows through Plano.

Schuyler made her own adjustments almost as soon as we arrived. She was by now a beautiful little girl. It was already clear to me that in a few short years, I was going to be busy chasing off boys, and at an age when I would probably be too slow to actually catch them. I could only hope that old age would provide me with the requisite trickery to compensate for their youth.

Schuyler made friends quickly, as she always did, but she also sized up the other kids in a hurry, and promptly set out to remake herself in an image that contrasted sharply with the girls around her. We had always let her pick her own clothes, but now her tastes shifted. She still loved pink, but now she was likely to pick a pair of pink camouflage pants or pink leopard-spotted tights. Her Converse hi-tops became even more omnipresent, and at a cheap jewelry accessory store at the mall, she begged us for a bracelet with a tiny pink skull-and-crossbones dangling from its colorful mirrored beads.

After a scary moment in a store when she wandered away from us for a few minutes, we considered once again the unusual and terrifying implications of having a child who couldn't speak. She had her speech device, but there was no guarantee that she would keep it with her if she got lost, and her device usage was still not second nature for her. We went online and found a company that made medical alert jewelry. We let Schuyler pick one that would carry her message for her, along with her name and phone number, when we were out in public:

"I cannot speak, but I can understand you. I use an electronic speech device to communicate."

She looked past all the cute, girly jewelry and didn't light up until she came to the big, tough-looking dog tags. Within a few weeks, she was wearing her own tag with pride, and when she met new people, she would proudly hold it out from her neck and let them read it. Or insist that they read it, really.

One day, after watching her favorite shows on television, two of which featured girls with brightly colored hair, she brought her device over to me. She'd already programmed in what she wanted to say.

"I want purple hair," she announced. As soon as she pressed the screen to make the box speak, she folded her arms and waited. Her expression was dead serious.

"You want purple hair?" I asked. "Really? Purple?"

By now, it won't surprise you to learn that by the end of the week, Schuyler had purple hair. The color wasn't permanent and only lasted about two months, at which time she was ready for shockingly red hair. As in, Raggedy Ann red hair. I did it, with surprising skill and over only the mildest of protestations from Julie, for two simple reasons. Schuyler had correctly and enthusiastically asked for it with her device, and I secretly liked the idea of upsetting the conservative teachers and parents of Plano, Texas.

But here's the thing. No one was upset. In the months that Schuyler worked through her colorful hair stage, I can remember only one person who ever said anything negative about her hair, and that was an old man in a Taco Bell. Schuyler's teachers loved her punky clothes and her crazy hair, and her classmates treated her like some kind of minor celebrity, just as they had done since she was a toddler. When we picked her up from school, every kid in the place seemed to want to say goodbye to her, and when they saw her out in public, they reacted as if they were seeing their favorite television star inexplicably walking around at the mall. It was as if they never even noticed that she couldn't speak, or that she drooled when she grew excited. Against my every expectation, Schuyler was finding acceptance among people who I had just assumed would push her away.

Schuyler was winning Plano over with ease and on her own terms. I had to admit that Plano was beginning to do the same with me.

Once I got past my own snotty, liberal, heathen assumptions about Plano, I discovered, much to my surprise, that it was actually a rather nice place. The city was dotted with lots of parks and waterways; once I discovered that one near our apartment was populated with nutrias—strange, beaver-like creatures with bright orange teeth, as if they subsisted on Cheetos instead of tree bark. The streets were clean, with trash bins at every major street corner.

During the holidays, the fancier neighborhoods in Plano transformed into epilepsy-inducing orgies of light. Residents rented cherry pickers to hang their lights and broadcast music from tiny little FM transponders, synchronizing their light shows to music. Some of the houses even sported signs warning of high voltage. It was both ridiculous and enchanting. It also blew Schuyler's little mind.

The most important and perhaps surprising thing I learned about Plano was that if you were to try to come to some conclusions about the town and its people simply by observing the suburban sprawl and the look-alike houses and the zeppelin-hangar churches, you might just get it wrong. You might look at the big-haired soccer moms in their SUVs the size of monster trucks (made no less menacing by the cheerleading bumper stickers with names like Ashleigh and Madison in the window) and not realize that they are some of the nicest people in the world. You might also miss why many of them lived in Plano in the first place.

Simply put, the schools were amazing.

The first time I met Kathy Williams, I have to admit I was skeptical, for reasons that are no doubt deeply cynical. She was nice, she was friendly, and she was warm toward her students. In the past, I had always associated that kind of teacher as well meaning, which was perhaps the biggest left-handed compliment we had for teachers.

"Oh yes, she means well." I had no idea if she was qualified to teach the kids in the AAC class.

I was a moron. In addition to having an impressive educational background far beyond what you might expect from an elementary school teacher, Kathy Williams did something no other teacher had ever really done, the thing that had caused us to roll the dice and gamble on a move to Plano. She reached Schuyler.

Kathy was so loving and doting on her that it wasn't immediately apparent how hard she made Schuyler work. She didn't accept anything less than Schuyler's best. If Schuyler tried to communicate using incomplete sentences, Kathy would make her slow down and build sentences that made sense. If Schuyler became wild, Kathy could calm her down and get her to refocus, but she also appreciated how spirited Schuyler could be, and she encouraged it. When Schuyler would step outside the curriculum and begin exploring her device on her own, Kathy didn't force her back into the groove. She'd usually e-mail us and excitedly share the moment. She got Schuyler, and she opened up her world.

The first time I saw Schuyler in her classroom setting, the thing I was struck by was how normal it all felt. Six little kids, all reading books and raising their hands to answer questions, talking excitedly to each other in their own strange way, and sneakily farting around when they thought no one was looking. It wasn't like any class I'd ever seen Schuyler in before. She wasn't watching profoundly autistic kids spin through their pain and confusion, and she wasn't sitting forgotten in the corner while neurotypical kids went through their lessons. Every parent who has ever looked at a classroom full of kids and watched their own child participating just like everyone else knows the feeling. I never had, not until now.

There were half a dozen kids in what we had come to call her Box Class, and while of course none of them shared Schuyler's particular affliction, it was a veritable petting zoo of similar monsters. Schuyler was one of the more ambulatory kids, but she was by no means the only one. A few used braces or crutches, and one little boy was confined to a wheelchair, manipulating his device with the use of a head switch. They suffered from a variety of afflictions, cerebral palsy probably being the most common, and many had yet to be successfully diagnosed; their parents were in that uncertain place where we'd spent so many years, and my heart ached for them.

Schuyler loved every one of her classmates, excitedly pulling up their photos on her device at the end of the day. It was clear that she understood that they were all different from the kids she saw when she went to her mainstream class, but now the difference wasn't freakish.

They weren't weird. They were a village. A family.

It was in her class that Schuyler found a friend, a best friend in fact, and one who spoke the same way she did. Kathy sent us an excited e-mail one afternoon. She'd looked up from the lesson she was teaching to see that Schuyler and Samantha had sneaked away from the group and were sitting together by themselves, hunched over one device with the volume lowered and talking to each other with it, giggling the whole time. Kathy quickly grabbed her digital camera and snapped a photo, which was attached to the e-mail. It's still one of my favorites, a moment in time between Schuyler and the friend who wasn't a visitor to her world but who actually lived there as well. No one else could go there with them at that moment, not even Julie or me. They were there alone, giggling and engaging in secret girl talk, cyborg style. Samantha was Schuyler's little girl crush, and together they were heartbreakers, both for what they couldn't do but also for what they could. They were also going to be boy killers one day, it was already clear.

A few weeks before Schuyler's own seventh birthday, Samantha's parents threw their daughter a birthday party. When we walked in the door, Schuyler and Samantha squealed with delight when they saw each other and crashed into each other in a high-speed, full-contact hug. And that was it. They found each other and they stuck with each other, playing together the whole time and snubbing the other kids at the party, most of whom were neurotypical girls from Samantha's Brownie troop.

There were two things that touched me about the moment. First of all, there was something endearing to me about two broken little girls behaving like snobs to the other, nondisabled kids. If you don't talk with a box, you're not cool enough to run with them. Sorry, but that's just how they roll. Go play with your Bratz dolls and deal with it.

More touching was the manner in which Schuyler and Samantha spoke to each other. They didn't use their devices much, but rather spoke in their little Martian languages (which sounded remarkably similar to each other) coupled with a sign language that they apparently developed together out of ASL and made all their own.

Schuyler had neurotypical friends, but those friendships never seemed fair. It always made me crazy, watching good-natured little Schuyler end up as some talking kid's plaything because of her speech difficulty, but it seemed to happen every time and had the feeling of inevitability. Two years earlier, it would have felt unthinkable that Schuyler would find a friend, let alone several friends, who lived in her world.

The Box Class gave Schuyler a true peer group, and even considering all the good things that came her way from the move and her involvement with the AAC class, that may be the thing I valued the most about Plano.

Two days before Christmas 2006, over a year after we moved to Plano, I took Schuyler to the mall to see her very first mall Santa, or the first that she actually wanted to see, anyway. In years past she'd vetoed Santa, but her classmates in Plano had apparently talked up the experience enough to spark her interest. Julie was at work; being a cog in the retail machine, there was no way she was getting the day off. Appreciating the importance of the event, we had scoped out the various mall Santas during the preceding weeks, so we felt confident that we found a good one.

Schuyler took her audience with The Man seriously. She spent the morning practicing what she was going to say, programming the box over and over. We waited in line for over an hour, and she spent the whole time anxiously straining to see Santa. When it was finally her turn, she hesitated uncharacteristically for just a moment before jumping into his lap.

"Merry Christmas!" he said in a very Santa-like voice. We'd picked a good one. "What's your name, sweetheart?"

Schuyler looked at me and I quickly handed her the device. She hit buttons quickly.

"My name is Schuyler."

If he was surprised or put off, Santa didn't show it. He looked at her awestruck face for a moment and then smiled warmly. "And do you know what you'd like for Santa to bring you this Christmas?"

She typed quickly. **"I want earrings and necklace and bracelet and ring."**

"What a pretty little girl!" he said. "You'll look like a princess!"

The assistant asked if we wanted a picture. As the very non-elflike assistant set up for the photo, it occurred to me that at a glance, this scene looked very much like any other kid visiting Santa.

I could tell it was different for him, though. While the previous kids had been rushed through pretty quickly, Santa took his time with Schuyler. He asked her questions, which she answered on the device, and he spoke to her, so softly that only she could hear what he said. She listened intently and nodded solemnly every so often, very aware of the importance of this conversation. Her eyes shone and she watched his face with reverence. It was often hard to know for sure what was going through Schuyler's mind, but one thing was very clear. Schuyler believed.

The photo was taken. Santa gave Schuyler a long hug, and I saw

his eyes close for just a moment. Schuyler hopped down and looked
back at him one last time before bouncing off. I saw Santa push up
his glasses and quickly wipe his eyes with his white gloved hand before turning and motioning to the next child in line. As we walked
away, I saw him turn and look at her, watching her thoughtfully.

Schuyler made Santa believe in her. I knew just how he felt.

We walked the short distance to the mall play area to wait for Julie,
who was getting off work and meeting us, apparently not having
suffered enough retail magic for one day. The play area was one of
those giant "things to crawl all over" themes that you see in malls
these days, with huge structures made from slightly squishy materials. In this case, it was oversized food, with a giant steak and a fried
egg as large as a helipad.

Julie arrived, and we sat down and relaxed at last while Schuyler
ran around, jumping off of giant bacon and climbing on a muffin the
size of my Volkswagen. There were clearly more kids playing than
parents watching. Despite the posted rules and a little rare gem
called common sense, a large number of parents were dropping
their kids off while they shopped.

As she played, Schuyler suddenly found herself confronted by a
little girl whom Julie and I had been observing closely. She was probably two years older than Schuyler and much heavier. We'd been
watching her play a little game she might call "I'm Standing Here
Now, So You Go Somewhere Else." Her goal was apparently not to
occupy the space so much as to drive the other kids away.

"This is going to be bad news if she does that to Schuyler," Julie
said.

Sure enough, she did.

The girl was calling other kids names and shoving them, but
either Schuyler didn't notice or she simply didn't care. When
Schuyler tried to stand on the giant grapefruit topped with a cherry
the size of a basketball, the mean girl was there waiting.

Schuyler tried to ignore her, but that only seemed to make the girl angry. Julie and I both tensed, ready to intervene. Then Julie sat back and sighed, closing her eyes.

"I'm not going to get involved, I'm not going to get involved, I'm not going to get involved," she muttered, like a mantra.

"Am I allowed to smack a ten-year-old?" I asked. "Can I toss someone else's kid if she clearly deserves it?"

"I don't think so, no," Julie said. "Schuyler goes to school all day with God knows what kinds of punk-ass kids. I want to see how she handles this." Exhaling once more, she opened her eyes. She didn't pick the best moment to do so. She opened them just in time to watch the girl hit Schuyler on both shoulders, hard enough to make her fall back a few steps.

We both sprang to our feet, or at least I thought we did. It felt like we were up in a flash, and yet we hadn't taken a step when, in the blink of time it took her to get her footing and wind up, Schuyler quite simply hit the girl with a closed fist, right in the middle of her face. We heard the sound from where we sat, maybe twenty feet away, like something from a cheap television crime show.

We stopped, shocked into stillness. The girl stopped, too. Despite the directness of the hit and the "smuck" sound it made, the girl seemed more surprised than anything else. Schuyler stood her ground, not moving but with a serene look on her face. The girl screwed up her face in anger.

"You can't talk!" she screamed in Schuyler's face, bending down slightly. "You're a crazy retard! You're *stupid*!"

Schuyler looked up at her, weighing her options. She didn't have many, particularly with her device sitting next to us on the bench. Her hand moved up to her tag as if to hold it out to the girl, but after a moment's hesitation she thought better of it. Instead, she leaned forward into the girl's face, her fists balled at her side.

Schuyler opened her mouth, closed her eyes and howled like an animal. It was a guttural sound, louder than I think I'd ever heard.

from her, full of all the frustration and stubbornness that got her through every day of her life. It wasn't pretty and it wasn't refined, but in that *Lord of the Flies* world of the playground that we as parents like to pretend we don't remember, it was what she had, and so she unloaded it. The girl was so surprised that she just walked away. The whole thing was over before we got there.

I wished it was different for Schuyler. I wished that the world, *her* world, was some other way than this, that God had accepted my offer that night in front of the darkened church and taken her monster from her to give to me instead. But Schuyler had no time for sentimentality. She was a sweet kid and the most loving human being I'd ever known, in a world where, frankly, love was almost always suspect.

But when she had to be, Schuyler was also the best pragmatist I knew. Sometimes, she taught me, all you get is a howl. I saw that sad fact and I raged against the injustice. Schuyler saw it, and she howled with all the air in her lungs and all the fight in her body, without hesitation, because a howl was what she had.

Against all the rules of civilized parenting, I was proud of her.

We left the play area and found the mall's food court. Schuyler had appeared unflustered by the girl at the time, but now I could tell she was brooding over the fight. As Julie went to get food for us, I found a table and sat with Schuyler. She was silent and still, but every thirty seconds or so she would look around her, clearly searching for the girl and perhaps spoiling for a rematch.

"What's wrong, Schuyler?" I asked finally.

She refused to answer at first, until I slid her device across the table to her. She looked at it for a moment, then punched up a quick answer, not looking at it as she made it speak.

"Schuyler mad."

"Why are you mad?"

She paused, and then instead of using the device, she simply signed the word "girl" (a slightly threatening sign on its own, with the tip of the thumb drawn across the jawline like a scar from a knife fight) and then hit herself on the chest. She looked around again, and then refused to speak any further about it.

Julie returned with our food and we ate in silence. After about half an hour, I slowly pulled Schuyler's device over to my side of the table. This took a certain amount of finesse; Schuyler had been taught in her Box Class not to share her device with anyone, and while she made exceptions with Julie and me, she did so grudgingly. I punched up the free spelling page and typed up a message, then turned the box around and slid it across to Schuyler. As soon as she looked up, I touched the screen and the Vantage spoke.

"Schuyler eats boogers."

She looked at it for a moment before a tiny smile crept across her lips. She hit a few buttons.

"No."

She then put down her burger and started punching up a longer reply. I could see from the smirk on her face that she was cracking herself up. Finally she turned it around so I could see as she touched the screen. The voice spoke clearly and seriously, as it always sounded to me.

"Daddy eats bugs."

"Good lord, you two," Julie said. "That's as good as a paternity test."

I winked at Schuyler and she laughed. She turned back to her lunch and, as far as I could tell, didn't give the girl on the playground a further thought.

I had spent the past seven years worrying about Schuyler. I worried about her before she was born, and I worried for her when she was a tiny baby and then a stumbling toddler. When her speech delay became apparent, my worry increased, and when she was diagnosed with bilateral perisylvian polymicrogyria, that worry became my own monster.

We'd gone through so much with Schuyler, and for Schuyler.

We'd moved so many times, chasing the idea of a perfect community in which to raise her, and found that the one where we fit the least was the one that might finally save her. We'd stepped to the brink of divorce only to learn that come what may, neither of us wanted to raise her alone, and neither would accept the idea of another person trying to take on a parental role in her life. We learned that infidelity wasn't strong enough to break us, that we might not be very good at being a traditional married couple but we were the only people who were going to raise Schuyler, so that was that.

We'd experienced sorrow and worry, and we'd experienced hope. We'd seen our worst fears surpassed, and our greatest expectations exceeded. Until Schuyler entered my life, I'd never known how much I could hurt for another human being, or how proud I could be of one. And through it all, Julie and I had wavered and fumbled and gotten it right and gotten it wrong, but Schuyler had never changed or given up hope or behaved as if she believed she was anything other than exactly who she wanted to be. While we tripped and panicked and fretted, Schuyler quietly persevered.

It was clear now that all my anxiety and all my sadness was mine alone. Schuyler was in a good school, with a support staff and a means to communicate and a future that was unreadable but no longer presumed to be a sad one. All of our worry and all of our work to try to create a future for her had gotten us to this place and this reality, and it wasn't perfect but it was better than we'd dreamed possible that day in Dr. Simon's office three years before. Schuyler's monster had a leash now.

And none of it mattered. In the end, stripped of her device and her support and even her basic sign language, standing alone against a mean girl or a hard world and armed with nothing more than her will, her sense of justice and her animal howl, Schuyler nevertheless knew that monster or no, she still had a right to move through the world on her own terms.

She was going to be okay. She was always going to be okay.

Epilogue

All parents have a narrative for their children. Some are blatant and perhaps a little horrible, like the ones on a television show that Julie and I have recently become addicted to, about the parents of kids who play sports and who live out their own past failures or glory days through their own children. The rest of us watch them and say, "How awful!" and "My little girl is going to chart her own course, she'll decide what her future's going to be all about, not me." But in our secret hearts, we whisper, *"I hope she plays the trombone. . . ."* (No, I really do. I suspect Julie's secret heart and mine are whispering different things.)

The hardest thing about being Schuyler's father has been releasing myself from my secret narrative for her. I say releasing myself, not her, because it was never hers and wouldn't have been even if she'd been born with a healthy, typical brain. With Schuyler, there's no such thing as typical, and there's no narrative. The only thing I can say about her future, with her Big Box of Words and her fiery heart, is that it will defy expectations. When Schuyler was just a developing baby, not even born, I wrote that I thought she was destined for something extraordinary. Now, in the late winter of her seventh year, I know I was right. I've been wrong about so much, but somehow I was right about Schuyler.

We're celebrating today. Sherry and Linda pulled us aside at the last parents' meeting to tell us how they think Schuyler is ready to move up to the most advanced level on her speech device, moving from a screen with forty-five available buttons to one utilizing eighty-four. This is the setting that adults use. It was less than two years ago that we were told that she would most likely not be capable of using the device at all. She'll have to make a slow transition to this new level, which uses an entirely different and much more complex structure. Even now, however, she keeps it set on the new layout, exploring the new possibilities and only grudgingly switching back to forty-five keys when she has to say something. For Schuyler, the world moves too slowly.

The future for Schuyler is uncertain. Our most dreaded fear, the seizures that statistically seem almost certain to come, have yet to manifest. It hangs over us like the sword of Damocles, but sometimes I forget that those head storms might be waiting to ambush her at all. Then I remember and the fear settles back in. That black lump reappears in my chest when I imagine her having *grand mal* seizures. When I can step away from my fear, however, I also know that even if they do come, she'll endure and adapt and keep going, powered by an unstoppable will that she possesses and I do not.

Years ago, almost a decade, in fact, Julie was visiting during my last days in Texas before my move to Kalamazoo. My best friend, Joe, who would later introduce me to the concept of "the pleasurable irritation of the new" and would stand beside me as my best man at our wedding, took Julie and me out to Deep Ellum, a hipster area of Dallas where much of the city's live music scene was flourishing. I think we both knew it was goodbye, not just for us but for Dallas, too. Joe would move to California a few years later, and while we stayed close and remain so to this day, our common geography was slipping away from us both even back then.

We ended up in a club where Paul Slavens, one of Joe's favorite local musicians, was singing and playing acoustic guitar. The music was beautiful, with quirky harmonies and complexities of sound that kept my ear guessing. During a break, Joe slipped away from us and went to speak to him. When he started his next set, Slavens announced that he'd had a request from Joe to dedicate the next song to his friends Rob and Julie, who had endured a great deal of hardship in order to be together and were about to begin their lives with one another.

I don't remember much about the song, other than how it was sweet and sad, but when I think back on that night, I'm not struck by any sense of irony. It would be easy to feel as if we were prematurely celebrating an end to adversity when our real battles actually still lay several years in the future. But when I think back on that evening and on that song for young, unbroken lovers seemingly on the far side of adversity, I can't help but feel as though everything that lay ahead of us already existed.

Perhaps linear time is an illusion. Maybe, just maybe, the three of us all sensed that the world waiting in the future would be bigger than all of us, bigger and more uncertain and yet somehow more perfect than we could possibly anticipate. I wonder if somehow Joe sent us into that future with that last gift of a song, like a soldier being sent into an uncertain battle with a little extra ammo and a few extra meal rations. When I think back on it now, it seems impossible that Schuyler wasn't always a part of my life. She was real and her monster was real, only waiting for time to catch up to them and lead them into our lives.

As I write this, we're back in the giant food playground where Schuyler stood her ground at Christmastime only a few months before, fists clenched at her side and feet planted firmly on this world that has never seemed entirely hers. On this day, things couldn't be more different. She's made friends, two little girls just as pretty and rowdy as herself, and their brother, who gamely keeps up with their play despite a cast on his leg. They run around the playground, leaping over giant food and squealing happily. At this moment, they're all monsters, wild and free, untethered by words that they neither want nor need at the moment.

Eventually they calm down and assemble inside the giant coffee cup, as large as a Jacuzzi. Schuyler runs over and excitedly grabs her device. She runs back to the giant cup and climbs inside, and for the next twenty minutes, Schuyler and her Big Box of Words hold court. At first gathered with her three new friends, Schuyler soon finds herself surrounded by kids, at times almost a dozen, all watching her as she demonstrates her Vantage Plus. She introduces herself, asks everyone her usual introductory questions, such as when their birthdays are and how old they are, and even leads the group in a rousing, computerized version of *Old MacDonald Had a Farm*. (The box can sing, although it's not going to place on *American Idol* any time soon.) When one little girl attempts to take the device away and use it herself, Schuyler sternly refuses. "No," she says on the box, and points to the ground outside the cup until the girl glumly complies. The other kids are captivated by the device, but more than that, I think they are enchanted by Schuyler.

As I walk over to snap a few photos, I see the other parents watching the gathering warily. Perhaps it is the sight of all their kids, huddled together as if planning the Revolution of the Small. Maybe it's just the unusual spectacle of a child, seemingly disabled but somehow transformed by her monster into something unique and maybe even just a little bit wonderful. The photo I take will become one of my favorites. I've never seen her happier.

She doesn't have verbal words for the things that thrill her, or none that most people can understand, anyway. When she runs over to tell me about her new friends, too excited to find the words on her device, I smile and I miss out, my heart breaking just a little bit. One day, and maybe soon, she'll be able to make all those words come clearly and expressively through her device. For now, she largely remains an enigma, the most daunting one of my life. She is the source of my joy and my sorrow, and for all my resentment at him for giving her this burden, it is nevertheless when I am with Schuyler that I feel closest to God.

I think about God more than ever these days. He remains inexplicable to me, like Schuyler, but as I watch her burst through her life, unafraid of this grand rough world, I get the sense that it's going to work out. Whether it's God or Fate, she's being watched out for. I sit and watch her and I feel something like peace.

Lately, I've dreamed about God. In my dream, I'm in another park, watching Schuyler play in the sun, and when I turn, God is sitting beside me. He looks like Leonard Bernstein.

He smiles at me, perhaps a little sadly, and shrugs.

"I can't tell you why I created her monster or where it's going to take her," he tells me with a sigh. "I only know that she is exactly who she's supposed to be, and so are you. What happens next is a mystery to me, too."

Schuyler knows. But she's not telling.

ACKNOWLEDGMENTS

There are so many people to whom I owe so much, not just for help-ing to give Schuyler a shot at the life she deserves, but also for help-ing to bring her story to the world through this book.

Schuyler's Monster happened because two amazing professionals be-lieved in the possibilities that Schuyler's story held. I want to thank my tireless literary agent, Sarah Jane Freymann, who understood ex-actly what I was trying to say from the very beginning, even before I really knew myself. I also want to express my gratitude to Sheila Curry Oakes, executive editor at St. Martin's Press, for her unwaver-ing advocacy of this book, and also for her editorial magic, protecting me from looking like a complete idiot anywhere but in my e-mail. (That's no small task, I promise.) My thanks also to Alyse Diamond and Laura Lee Timko, the two hardest working people I know, and to everyone at St. Martin's Press for your outstanding work.

Two people above all others opened my eyes to the idea that my future could be waiting for me within the written word. Dr. Kenneth Roemer at The University of Texas at Arlington lit a fire that has flickered from time to time but has never gone out. My beloved cousin Shannon has believed in me since we were both earnest and confused teenagers living at opposite ends of Planet

Texas, exchanging long letters of quiet outsider desperation and, almost by accident, becoming writers in the process. You're next, Shannon.

Thank you to Dana Brenckle, Jim Haller, Tracy Edmondson, Erin Shea (who was also the first person to kick me in the butt to write this book), and all the others who were mentioned within, and who make up the tapestry of Schuyler's life. I also want to express my appreciation to all the people who have read my online writing over the years and who have followed Schuyler's life from the very beginning. I particularly want to thank everyone who contributed to the fund that led to her acquisition of her speech device. Your generosity defies logical expectation.

Dean Donald Gatzke and The University of Texas at Arlington have been extremely supportive and forgiving of all the work that goes into a book like this. The term "day job" doesn't really begin to describe my employment there, for which I am extremely grateful.

I want to express my gratitude to Monique van den Berg for her special contribution to the Reading Group Guide. My life goes so much more smoothly when I have friends who are smarter than I am.

I'd especially like to thank the members of our families for being a part of Schuyler's life. She loves you all with wild abandon.

Schuyler's success is a bit like that of an astronaut. It's her smiling face in all the pictures, but she couldn't have gotten where she is without a huge support team over the years. Our thanks go out to Dr. Simone Simon, Dr. Laura Ment, and all the medical professionals at the Yale School of Medicine, without whom we might never have known what afflicted Schuyler until it was too late to help her.

We are particularly grateful to Dr. William Dobyns at the University of Chicago for his wisdom and honesty where Schuyler is concerned, but also for the hard work that he has done to help identify and tame all the monsters that vex his patients all over the world.

To Tracy Custer and all the folks at the Prentke-Romich Company, I'd like to thank you for giving us the light at the end of the tunnel, and the sound that accompanied it.

When I began this book, I never expected it to have either heroes (aside from Schuyler, my all-time hero) or a happy ending, but then, we never dared hope that we would find a place like the Plano Independent School District. Our thanks go out to Sherry Haeusler, Linda Conerly, and the rest of the Plano ISD's Assistive Technology Team, and also to Schuyler's AAC classroom teacher, Kathy Williams, and Renee Rucker, principal at Plano's Gulledge Elementary School, known in Schuyler's world as the Land of Oz.

Most of all, I'd like to thank Julie for more than I could possibly express here. Together, we built a superninja princess.

One day, Schuyler will be able to tell you herself how wonderful you've all been. What a strange and wonderful day that will be.

Julie Rummel-Hudson

ABOUT THE AUTHOR

Robert Rummel-Hudson studied English and music at
The University of Texas at Arlington, where he is now
employed as "Minister of Propaganda" for the Dean of
the School of Architecture. He has been writing online
since 1995. He and his family live in Plano, Texas, where
Schuyler attends a special class for children who use
Alternative and Augmentative Communication devices. Most of her days are now spent in mainstream
classes with neurotypical children her age.

1. In the central metaphor of the book, the author refers to Schuyler's condition, polymicrogyria, as a "monster" to be fought. Why is this an appropriate metaphor? What other metaphors might the author have chosen? According to the author, Schuyler also has an affinity to choose monsters as her friends and allies. What does this tell you about Schuyler?

2. The author talks about language of special-needs parenting as being "sugar-coated terminology" that functions as a "distraction and a false comfort." He prefers to refer to Schuyler as "broken." Why does he use this term? Do you agree or disagree with his decision?

3. The story is split into three acts, each with an underlying stylistic difference. What are those differences, and what do you think is the rationale behind this structure?

4. Some have read *Schuyler's Monster* as a "prodigal son returns" exploration of faith, and others have read it as a progression through different degrees of skepticism. What do you think about the author's evolving relationship with God? What role do you think God plays in Schuyler's story?

5. The author talks about the role of the "Internet village" in Schuyler's story. If "it takes a village to raise a child," do you agree that this village can be virtual? How would you or could you participate in this village?

6. Schuyler's condition is unique, placing her in a middle ground between a mainstream classroom for neurotypical students and a classroom serving more severely disabled children. What approach do you think the public school system should take when it comes to Schuyler and other children like her?

7. Robert and Julie deal with infidelity on both sides of their marriage, and ultimately decide to stay together. What explanation does the author give for the infidelity, and what are the reasons for their ultimate decision? Do you agree or disagree with this outcome?

8. The author makes a case for maintaining an open mind when it comes to people with disabilities. What is your reaction upon seeing or interacting with a disabled person? Why do you think these types of interactions typically make people uncomfortable? Is this discomfort necessarily a bad thing?

For more reading group suggestions, visit
www.readinggroupgold.com.

A
Readi
Grou
Guid

St. Mar
Griffi